GLOBALIZATION

Theory, Culture & Society

Theory, Culture & Society caters for the resurgence of interest in culture within contemporary social science and the humanities. Building on the heritage of classical social theory, the book series examines ways in which this tradition has been reshaped by a new generation of theorists. It will also publish theoretically informed analyses of everyday life, popular culture, and new intellectual movements.

GLOBALIZATION
Social Theory and Global Culture

Roland Robertson

SAGE Publications
London • Newbury Park • New Delhi

SAGE Publications Ltd
6 Bonhill Street
London EC2A 4PU

SAGE Publications Inc
2455 Teller Road
Newbury Park, California 91320

SAGE Publications India Pvt Ltd
32, M-Block Market
Greater Kailash - I
New Delhi 110 048

British Library Cataloguing in Publication data

Robertson, Roland
  Globalization: Social Theory and Global
  Culture. – (Theory, Culture & Society
  Series)
  I. Title   II. Series
  306

  ISBN 0–8039–8186–4
  ISBN 0–8039–8187–2 pbk

Library of Congress catalog card number 92–50327

Typeset by Photoprint, Torquay, Devon
Printed in Great Britain by The Cromwell Press Ltd,
Broughton Gifford, Melksham, Wiltshire

To Kate

CONTENTS

ACKNOWLEDGMENTS

I can only indicate here a few of those who have, in various ways, helped me. I express my thanks to Bryan Turner, whose wide-ranging interests and publications have stimulated me for many years. To Mike Featherstone I am grateful for his encouragement, his skepticism about such notions as 'order' and 'religion,' and his informed interest in contemporary culture. I owe a lot to Frank Lechner, both for his work and observations on globalization as a graduate student in the early 1980s and for his more recent, insightful contributions to globalization analysis. To Ronald Miller I also owe much for his long-standing interest in globalization and as interlocutor in intense conversations about the making of the contemporary world. Bill Garrett has been a source of continuous encouragement, as well as in terms of his own work on human rights and the theory of religion. John Simpson recognized the significance of the global perspective in its various manifestations from an early stage and he also has been a source of thoughtful comment. Recently I have begun to collaborate with Tom Robbins on aspects of globalization and I am pleased to acknowledge that. Stephen Barr of Sage Publications has been enormously helpful in a number of respects.

There are others who have stimulated, challenged and prodded me, particularly various groups of graduate students at the University of Pittsburgh. Joe Roidt, of a recent cohort, has provided assistance and helpful comment. I hope that those I have not named individually here will understand. Some of them are in any case mentioned in the following chapters. The University of Pittsburgh, to which I initially came as a visitor in 1967, has provided a setting in which area, comparative and international studies have been encouraged. Secretaries in the Department of Sociology worked very hard for me in the last phase of putting this book together and I am very grateful for that.

My greatest debt is undoubtedly to my wife, Kathleen White. Her own work in planning and administering programs in international studies has been a source of inspiration, as has her independent eagerness to live in and talk almost incessantly about the multifaceted and politically charged, globalized world on a day-to-day basis.

None of the above, it should be said, is to be held responsible for what is said in this book.

Much of the following originated in presentations at conferences and/or was published in the first place in books or journals. However, it should be emphasized that none of the chapters is published here in its original form. Each of those which derives from a previous publication has, in varying degrees, been revised and in most cases considerably expanded.

Chapter 2 is a modified and expanded version of 'The sociological significance of culture: some general considerations,' which appeared in *Theory, Culture & Society*, 5 (1), 1988.

Chapter 3 is a revised and expanded version of 'Mapping the global condition: globalization as the central concept,' which appeared in *Theory, Culture & Society*, 7 (2–3), 1990.

Chapter 4 is mainly a combination of a revised version of 'Modernization, globalization and the problem of culture in world-systems theory,' which appeared in *Theory, Culture & Society*, 2 (3), 1985 and part of 'Globality, global culture and images of world order,' which appeared in Hans Haferkamp and Neil J. Smelser (eds), *Social Change and Modernity*, Berkeley: University of California Press, 1992. The former was originally written jointly with Frank Lechner, who has kindly agreed to its revised publication here. He is not, however, a party to the present version.

Chapter 5 is a revised and expanded version of 'Globalization and societal modernization: a note on Japan and Japanese religion,' which appeared in *Sociological Analysis*, 47 (S), 1987.

Chapter 6 is a revised and expanded version of 'Social theory, cultural relativity and the problem of globality,' which appeared in Anthony D. King (ed.), *Culture, Globalization and the World-System*, London: Macmillan; Binghamton: State University of New York, 1991.

Chapter 7 is a revised and expanded version of '"Civilization" and the civilizing process: Elias, globalization and analytic synthesis,' which appeared in *Theory, Culture & Society*, 9 (1), 1992.

Chapter 8 is an edited version of 'Globalization theory and civilization analysis,' which appeared in *Comparative Civilizations Review*, 17 (Fall), 1987.

Chapter 9 is a modified version of a review essay entitled 'Globality and modernity,' which appeared in *Theory, Culture & Society*, 9 (2), 1992.

Chapter 10 is a much revised version of 'After nostalgia? Wilful nostalgia and the phases of globalization,' which appeared in Bryan S. Turner (ed.), *Theories of Modernity and Postmodernity*, London: Sage, 1990.

PROLOGUE

My work on the general theme of globalization and its implications began in the mid-1960s. In a series of publications, initially with Peter Nettl, in the years 1965 to about 1972 I grappled with problems which were situated at the intersection of modernization theory and the discipline of international relations, with particular reference to the then popular problem of 'the modernization' of Third World societies. In that project my interests were basically 'secular.' The resulting papers did not for the most part raise issues of the kind that one found in the sociological discussion of religion, although I briefly considered substantive religion as a form of discontinuity in what some writers saw as a relatively simple world of converging societies. However, during those same years, from the mid-1960s through to the early 1970s, I became increasingly involved in debates within the sociology of religion, first in Britain and then in the USA. In a sense, at least as far as publications were concerned, I had by the mid-1970s arrived at a point where my most visible concern was indeed with religion. But from the beginning my interest in religion had been marked by specific orientations, which may explain why I have always had strong reservations about the sociology of religion as a relatively sequestered enterprise and why, on the other hand, my work in that area of inquiry led me increasingly to mix my interests in religion with my work on globality and globalization.

From the outset, undoubtedly under the influence of my own reading of the classical sociologists of the period 1880 to 1920, I was never able to regard 'religious' topics as intrinsically interesting. Indeed to this day I have not been able to muster much, if any, intellectual empathy with those who claim that they are studying religion directly. Rather, in my work on religion I have been primarily interested in 'religion' as a site of expression of issues, the issues of 'modernity,' in which the key social and sociological theorists of about a century ago were interested; but, it must be emphasized, in my case with reference to the relationship between the twentieth and the twenty-first centuries, rather than the period crossing the boundary between the nineteenth and twentieth centuries. To cut a long story short, my analyses of various topics and phenomena within the purview of the sociology of religion have almost invariably dealt with the relationships between religion and other aspects of human societies and between the study of religion and other disciplinary and subdisciplinary foci, as well as the underpinnings and ramifications of change in the sphere of religion. At the same time I have tended to treat religion comparatively and along lines raised in general debates among social theorists. Generally speaking, I have followed the implications of Durkheim's claim that religion has to do with 'the serious life.'

In part that brief description of my interest in religion indicates why my concerns with religion (in its broadest sense) and globalization should have met. However, I ought to be more specific about the circumstances of such convergence and why it was that most of my earliest *explicit* work on globalization, in the period 1980 to 1984, was situated within a sociology-of-religion framework, at the same time pointing to the inadequacy of that framework. Even though I have occasionally written about it, I have never been greatly interested in the theme which actually lies at the center of 'normal' sociology of religion, namely the debate about secularization. To a considerable extent the question of whether societies are becoming less or more secular has, when all is said and done, been pivotal in defining what the discipline and the profession of the sociology of religion are all about, at least in the influential UK–USA orbit. One of the reasons for my relative lack of interest has been precisely because I have tended to think that that question concerning secularization has been posed as a way of defining the 'vested' interests of the sociologist (of religion) as much as it has involved a focus upon puzzles about trends in 'the real world.' At the same time I have become increasingly conscious of the extent to which 'religion' became during the nineteenth century, but particularly in the first quarter of the twentieth century, a categorical mode for the 'ordering' of national societies and the relations between them. In that sense 'religion' was and is an aspect of international relations.

This is but one example of the ways in which, to a considerable degree, my interests in religion and globalization converged. Another, in fact an older interest, derives from the apparent simultaneity of 'fundamentalisms' and of church/state and religion/politics conflations and tensions across much of the globe in the late 1970s and early 1980s. This cluster of issues, just like the issue of the diffusion of religion as a category, appeared to require a definitely global focus, a focus on the world as a whole. Yet another consideration which facilitated convergence arose from what I have described as the double meaning of the ideas of 'world' and 'worldliness' in classical sociology, most notable in the writings of Max Weber. I will have occasion to consider the significance of this double meaning in the body of this book. Let me simply state here that in an explicit way Weber made the notion of images of the world central to his writings (not just his 'sociology of religion'), in the sense of the world as the sphere(s) of mundane activity. At the same time, Weber had quite definite views of increasingly worldwide international relations or 'world politics,' views which are best placed in the category of *realism* and which constitute a neo-Darwinian conception of international relations. My thinking about globalization (as well as religion) has been affected by this consideration of Weber's dominant view of 'world' as it is manifest in his explicit work on religion in relation to his less explicit view of 'world' as the arena of international struggle, a consideration which is relevant to contemporary questions about modernity and the idea of postmodernity. That observation also has a great bearing upon what Bryan Turner (forthcoming) has called, in response to some of my work, soteriological issues of a global nature and also upon what we might now mean, in a heavily globalized world, by sociology, or any other intellectual endeavor, as *a vocation*, or calling. Ernst Troeltsch, Karl Jaspers, Max Scheler and Karl Mannheim were among the German or Germany-based philosophers and sociologists who attempted to move the debates about 'soteriology' and, more directly, vocation, away from its Weberian base.

Yet another intellectual encounter was significant in my recognizing more fully the connection between my interest in religion, on the one hand, and what I came to call globalization, on the other – in connecting more systematically my preoccupations with the 'soft' and the 'hard' aspects of life (as seen from a 'Western' perspective). That encounter was occasioned by meetings with Benjamin Nelson, on the one hand, and Vytautas Kavolis, on the other, in the mid-1970s within the context of a shared interest in the comparative study of civilizations. Those meetings served to consolidate my general but underdeveloped commitment to 'bringing civilizations back in.' I had ventured in that direction in my work on international systems and modernization with Nettl, but exposure to the nuanced study of civilizations and their encounters – the quotidian, as opposed to the explicitly 'real,' relations between civilizations and between societies, as well as 'sub-societies' – helped greatly in deepening my understanding of globality in all its richness. My encounter with 'the civilizationalists' has, upon occasion, been held against me. Those people, or at least the most prominent members of the group concerned in the 1970s with what Vytautas Kavolis has called 'civilization analysis,' have in various ways been marginalized, particularly in the USA, by 'tough-minded' social scientists. Nelson, for example, has frequently been characterized as 'unsystematic,' or (in its polite form) as 'a maverick.' But it is important to acknowledge that 'the civilizationists' played an important role (along with a less central member of that group, Talcott Parsons) in my ongoing attempt to make analytic and interpretive sense of what may generally be described as the global field. On the other hand, it must be said that my own attempts to 'order' the latter is at odds with the views of 'the civilizationists' I have named (Parsons excepted).

Perhaps the two most salient points of departure from 'the comparative civilizationalists' in my work have consisted of my greater appreciation of 'mainstream' social and cultural theory, on the one hand, and, even more significantly in the present context, *Realpolitik*, on the other. My deep concern with the latter requires some adumbration, not least because the subtitle and thus the contents of this book indicate 'a cultural focus.' Until very recently only a few pioneering sociologists – such as Raymond Aron, Peter Heintz, Johan Galtung, Gustavo Lagos and Amitai Etzioni – had, in the 1960s, ventured into the field of international relations *per se*. My work on international relations and modernization with Nettl in the mid-1960s attempted to build upon, add to and revise the work of such people in an even more definitely sociological direction. Nowadays it is a little, but only a little, more common for sociologists themselves to address 'world politics' as a relatively autonomous domain of action and interaction (and that acknowledgment of autonomy is, for understandable reasons, now being 'taken back' to some extent by those interested in the issue of gender and international relations). However, in the present climate of attempts at 'interdisciplinarity' and increasing recognition of the one-sidedness of conventional disciplinary conceptions of the world, such acknowledgment becomes increasingly necessary, even when taking the feminist critique of the discipline of international relations very seriously. In an autobiographical sense my own perspective on this matter is undoubtedly to this day colored by the fact that one of my earliest, serious intellectual choices revolved around the question of whether I should study sociology or international relations as an undergraduate. To some extent such phrases as 'a cultural focus' and 'cultural sociology' reflect a kind of compromise between an interest in globalization (much more narrowly, international relations) on the one hand, and religion on the other. Much more importantly, however, I believe that it is directly necessary to adopt a cultural focus to what is often called world politics.

We have come increasingly to recognize that while economic matters are of tremendous importance in relations between societies and in various forms of transnational relations, those matters are considerably subject to cultural contingencies and cultural coding. Even more relevant in the present context, it is becoming more and more apparent that no matter how much the issue of 'naked' national self-interest may enter into the interactions of nations there are still crucial issues of a basically cultural nature which structure and shape most relations, from the hostile to the friendly, between nationally organized societies. In any case, polyethnicity and multiculturality have become increasingly significant internal and external constraints on foreign policy formation. In fact it is not too much to say that contemporary world politics, like such politics at various phases in the history of 'international society,' is empirically intertwined with central themes in debates about modernity (and postmodernity). For example – and this issue will receive attention in some of the chapters that follow – it is not easy to grasp the central issues in the debates about modernity-and-postmodernity without taking definitely into account the variety of ways in which societies have, as it were, entered modernity, not to speak of the fact that a number of societies have attempted as an aspect of their political (as well as military and economic) policies and actions to deal directly with the cultural themes and problems which have been attendant upon the spread of modernity. Japan, to take a major example, has been periodically engaged since the early part of the Meiji period in an attempt to 'transcend the modern,' while the discourse of postmodernity has become intertwined in Latin America with political issues concerning modernity, 'indigenization' and democratization.

At the same time successive generations of international relations specialists and sociologists have greatly contributed to an unfortunate division of intellectual labor. This has resulted, at least until very recently, in the neglect of national cultures, identities and traditions, as well as civilizational religiocultures, as direct and explicit subjects of interest on the international relations side, and in an inattention to 'extra-societal' issues on the sociological as well as the anthropological and political-science sides. To some extent the discipline which currently goes by the name of cultural studies has helped in the breaking down of this barrier. And indeed certain aspects of cultural studies are brought into play in some of the following chapters. So it is of the greatest importance from my point of view for it to be understood that the vagaries of 'tough' world politics and international relations are crucial to my general approach to globalization and global complexity. But I also believe that cultural factors enter into the domain of *Realpolitik* much more than has been conceded by many, but certainly not all, of those specializing in the study of international relations and related matters. It might be said that, again in varying degrees, all of international politics is cultural – that we are (but one must not certainly exaggerate the novelty of this) in a period of globewide *cultural* politics (and also, of course, in a period when culture has become more explicitly politicized, which has to do with the politics of culture.)

Some of the immediately preceding considerations are closely connected to the by now quite widespread observation that the 'official' line between domestic and foreign affairs is rapidly crumbling. Much of what is said in this book is a response to, as well as a manifestation of, that circumstance, which really has two aspects. With the rapid growth of various supra-national and transnational organizations, movements and institutions (such as global capitalism and the global media system) the boundaries between societies have become more porous because they are much more subject to 'interference and constraint' from outside. On the other hand, internal-societal affairs are themselves increasingly complicated and oriented to the outside by a variety of factors, including greater consciousness (which may well be grossly misinformed) of other societies, allegiances to groups within other societies (much but certainly not all of that occasioned by diasporation), economic penetration and the 'internationalization' of national economies. This overall trend, however, should *not* lead us to think of the demise, or even the significant attenuation, of the reality of the nationally constituted society. The tensions between the first trend and the second is a dominating theme of the present book. To put it in a nutshell, we need to develop images of the global *whole* which allow for the continuation of the pattern of globalization under greatly changed conditions. We also need, *inter alia*, to see where individuals and constructions of the individual, as well as humankind, fit into the picture.

Some of my ideas on globalization were developed within, but never limited to, a sociology-of-religion perspective. (A number of relevant papers, plus others, are to be published in book form separately.) It may be worth saying here that among the issues raised in that context were those of the relativization of societal and other standpoints and the attendant problems of identity, particularly collective identity. I have struggled both within that perspective and beyond it to make sense of the contemporary concern with identity in conditions of accelerated globalization, defined in very simple, introductory terms as the compression of the world into 'a single place,' attempting to decide the extent to which that empirical concern should be regarded as an *aspect* of globalization or a form of resistance to it. As will be seen, I lean strongly in the former direction, while allowing for the latter; that view being closely related to my ongoing attempt to develop a model of globality that in principle covers the primary features of the global-human condition as a whole, not simply the 'macro' aspects thereof.

In the mid-1980s some people got the impression that the move in the direction of what I now tend to call global unicity entails some kind of utopian view of global unity. Whereas the first term is, in my usage, neutral with respect to the risks, costs, benefits and dangers of rapidly increasing interdependence, interpenetration, global consciousness and so on, 'unity' and closely related terms imply – even when placed in quotation marks – social integration in quite a strong sense. I may thus have partly deserved this misinterpretation through my choice of words on some occasions, which, particularly within a focus on religion, led some people to enthusiasm for what they perceived to be a religiously and/or morally integrated world. Indeed this misleading view of globalization as constituting a definite move to 'world peace' and integration is still to be found (and, of course, actively promoted by certain sociocultural movements). All I want to say at this stage is that I have all along been indicating the problems occasioned by globalization and the dangers inherent in attempts by particular societies, movements or other entities to impose their own 'definition' of the global circumstance. Globalization is, at least empirically, not in and of itself a 'nice thing,' in spite of certain indications of 'world progress.'[1]

Finally, while I have on occasion said that my primary interest has been in globalization as a relatively recent phenomenon, that is certainly *not* the same as saying that globalization in its most comprehensive sense is relatively recent. Perhaps my dominant interest, at least up to now, has been in trying to isolate the period during which contemporary globalization reached a point when it was so well established that a particular pattern, or form, prevailed. I may well have slipped from time to time into giving the name 'globalization' only to the terms in which the world has moved very rapidly towards wholeness since about 1870 (notwithstanding the presentation of alternative paths, as well as counter-trends). But my intent all along has been to argue that overall processes of globalization (and sometimes deglobalization) are at least as old as the rise of the so-called world religions two thousand and more years ago. They have been deeply intertwined with in-group/out-group relations and this is one of the reasons for the growing debate about the relationships between modernity, globalization and the idea of postmodernity.

Note

1. To some extent the problems raised here are related to the issues that have arisen in connection with the distinction between system integration and social integration. In that sense system integration has to do with interdependence on a global scale, while social integration concerns normatively binding relationships among people across the world. Clearly there is more of the former than the latter. The system/social distinction does not, however, capture a number of crucial cultural matters which are dealt with in this book.

1

GLOBALIZATION AS A PROBLEM

The Crystallization of a Concept and a Problem

Globalization as a concept refers both to the compression of the world and the intensification of consciousness of the world as a whole. The processes and actions to which the concept of globalization now refers have been proceeding, with some interruptions, for many centuries, but the main focus of the discussion of globalization is on relatively recent times. In so far as that discussion is closely linked to the contours and nature of modernity, globalization refers quite clearly to recent developments. In the present book globalization is conceived in much broader terms than that, but its main empirical focus is in line with the increasing acceleration in both concrete global interdependence and consciousness of the global whole in the twentieth century. But it is necessary to emphasize that globalization is not equated with or seen as a direct consequence of an amorphously conceived modernity.

Use of the noun 'globalization' has developed quite recently. Certainly in academic circles it was not recognized as a significant concept, in spite of diffuse and intermittent usage prior to that, until the early, or even middle, 1980s. During the second half of the 1980s its use increased enormously, so much so that it is virtually impossible to trace the patterns of its contemporary diffusion across a large number of areas of contemporary life in different parts of the world. By now, even though the term is often used very loosely and, indeed, in contradictory ways, it has *itself* become part of 'global consciousness,' an aspect of the remarkable proliferation of terms centered upon 'global.' Although the latter adjective has been in use for a long time (meaning, strongly, worldwide; or, more loosely, 'the whole'), it is indicative of our contemporary concern with globalization that the *Oxford Dictionary of New Words* (1991: 133) actually includes 'global' as a *new* word, focusing specifically, but misleadingly, on its use in 'environmental jargon.' That same *Dictionary* also defines 'global consciousness' as 'receptiveness to (and understanding) of cultures other than one's own, often as part of an appreciation of world socio-economic and ecological issues.' It maintains that such a use has been much influenced by Marshall McLuhan's idea of 'the global village,' introduced in his book *Explorations in Communication* (1960). The notion of compression, or 'shrinking,' is indeed present in that influential book about the shared simultaneity of media, particularly televisual, experience in our time. There can be little doubt that McLuhan both reflected and shaped media trends, so much so that in time we have come to witness (self-serving) media attempts to consolidate the idea of the global *community*. On the other hand the media fully acknowledge the 'nationality' of particular media systems, and report at length on the tough realities of international relations, wars and so on. Such realities are far from the communal connotations which some have read into McLuhan's imagery. In the same period when McLuhan's notion of the global village was becoming influential there occurred the 'expressive revolution' of the 1960s (Parsons, 1978: 300–24). That was, to put it very simply, a 'revolution' in consciousness among the young in numerous parts of the world, centered upon such themes as liberation and love, in both individual and collective terms. In fact the *Oxford Dictionary of New Words* maintains that the current term 'global consciousness . . . draws on the fashion for *consciousness-raising* in the sixties' (1991: 133).

Undoubtedly the 1960s 'revolution' in consciousness had an important effect in many parts of the world, in its sharpening of the sense of what was supposedly common to all in an increasingly tight-knit world. Yet, as we will see more fully, this sense of global interdependence has rapidly become recognized in numerous other, relatively independent, domains and fora. World wars, particularly World War II with its 'humanity-shaking' events and its aftermath, the rise of what became known as the Third World, the proliferation of international, transnational and supra-national institutions and the attempts to coordinate what has become known as the global economy have played crucial parts in the twofold process of 'objective' and 'subjective' 'globalization.' And surely McLuhan's own Catholic-tinged observations concerning the media-centered 'global village' were partly shaped by such developments (Miller, 1973).

Some of these considerations will be further explored in subsequent chapters. I have tried both to bring these and other considerations into some overall shape and to connect them to my primary discipline of sociology. At the same time, I have some ambivalence about whether what I am doing is 'sociology,' an expanded or revised version of sociology, or much more than can be captured by such a designation. In the current, but increasingly contested and complex, climate of 'interdisciplinarity' it may not really matter. But on the whole I feel that present discussions of globalization constitute an extension and refocusing of sociological work, work which enables sociology and more generally social theory to transcend the limitation of the conditions of its own maturation in the so-called classical period of the discipline. Although there are various 'global openings' in the work of the classical sociologists, sociology's 'official' role has been to address societal, or comparative-societal, issues. In any case, discussion of globalization touches just about every aspect of the academic disciplines, including their moral foundations and implications. The position I adopt with respect to these moral issues is that matters concerning the global complexity induced by globalization must be confronted on their own terms, that 'critical' and moral concerns must to some extent depend on an appreciative understanding of what is 'going on' in the world as a whole. At the same time I fully recognize that sociologists and others who are seeking to analyze and comprehend contemporary global complexity are participants in projects of globalization, reglobalization and, even, deglobalization.

Mention of the idea of deglobalization – loosely speaking, attempts to undo the compression of the world – should remind us again that what we currently call globalization has been a very long, uneven and complicated process. In the immediate context we should be aware that movements, institutions and individuals have not merely been implicated in actions that have propelled the overall globalization process but that quite frequently there has been resistance to this. In the contemporary world the use of the term 'globalism' as a *negative* comment on what has with equal pejorativeness been described in ideological terms as 'one-worldism' or 'cosmopolitanism' is not uncommon in political and other campaigns; and of course there is a quite long genealogy of such terms. But we have to be very conscious of the fact that negative gestures, gestures of opposition, are typically expressed in contemporary terms and in reference to contemporary circumstances. I will try to show that just as ostensibly anti-modern gestures are inevitably in a sense modern, so are anti-global gestures encapsulated within the discourse of globality. In *that* particular sense there can be no foreseeable retreat from globalization and globality.

Leaving on one side for the moment the quite important question of anticipations of the study of the global 'system,' it can be said that the contemporary sociological analysis of 'the world' in its relatively mundane sense began explicitly in the 1960s. At that time a number of attempts were made to discuss the topic of the modernization of Third World societies – that is, the manner in and the degree to which nationally organized societies achieve 'maturity' – within the context of the overall pattern of *relations* among all nations conceived as a system of *international stratification* (Lagos, 1963). Applying models which had previously been applied only to *intra*-societal structures to relations between societies was a novel idea in the early 1960s (even though in its French origin the idea of the Third World already implied stratification, in the sense of the 'third estate'). Some of this work was connected to 'peace studies,' particularly in the writings of Johan Galtung (1966), while another connection was pursued in terms of the ways in which orientations to the processes of modernization were positively or negatively established on the part of political elites in a fluidly conceived international system (Nettl and Robertson, 1966; Nettl and Robertson, 1968; Robertson and Tudor, 1968). Other ideas concerning the increasing necessity for a 'global sociology' (Moore, 1966), the study of 'war and peace' in broadly sociological terms (Aron, 1966; Robertson, 1968), and the non-power dimensions of relations between national societies (Etzioni, 1965), and so on, flowered in the same decade. Needless to say, some specialists in international relations and other fields were moving in roughly the same direction.

To the extent that the discussion of the currently popular theme of modernity arose in those developments of the 1960s it was largely in terms of the conventional sociological analysis of the move from *Gemeinschaft* ('community') to *Gesellschaft* ('society'). While that and related stage-images of the 'old' and the 'new' had originally been developed in the context of primarily European debates about the diffusely conceived pros and cons of modern life in late nineteenth- and early twentieth-century Europe and, to a lesser extent, North America, its translation to the poor and underprivileged societies of the Third World involved in the main thrust of modernization theory (or at least in terms of the stereotypes of the latter with which we now, for the most part, operate) a considerable truncation of the original question. In much of societal modernization theory and the individual modernization theory (Inkeles and Smith, 1974) which followed in its trail, 'modernization' referred most frequently to objectively measurable attributes – such as education, occupation, literacy, income and wealth. There was little attention to subjective, interpretive aspects of modernization. In so far as culture was invoked it was largely in terms of the functional significance of 'the Protestant ethic' in having supposedly stimulated a disciplined orientation to work, political participation, and so on.

At the same time there developed an interest arising out of modernization theory which had little to do, on the face of it, with a 'world system.' I speak of the debate about convergence and divergence. Put simply, advocates of the convergence position argued that all, or nearly all, societies were, at different speeds, moving towards the same point, mainly as the result of the overriding emergence of 'industrial man' (Kerr et al., 1960), while adherents to the divergence stance emphasized the idea of there being different paths to and forms of 'modernity' (rather narrowly conceived) and that in that sense there was not convergence but divergence. Needless to say this debate has been revived in the light of the collapse of communism in much of the world by the early 1990s and the wave of societal democratization that swept across the continents in the late 1980s and the early 1990s (notwithstanding resistance in China, parts of the territory of the old Soviet Union, the Middle East, and elsewhere). Aspects of the convergence–divergence debate pointed, in a few cases strongly (Inkeles, 1981), to crystallization of what was at least implied in the convergence framework as a homogenized 'world system.' In discussing and assessing the convergence–divergence debate, Baum (1974, 1980) was to add an important concept to those of convergence and divergence: invariance. Baum claimed that societies are converging in some respects (mainly economic and technological), diverging in others (mainly social relational) *and*, in a special sense, staying the same in yet others. In other words, Baum firmly injected the issue of *societal* continuity into the debate. Unfortunately few have taken up this important question, centered on matters concerning the links between identity and authority (although see Lechner, 1990b). Baum did not in any case locate his argument within a conception of the 'global system.' Questions of the degree to which globalization encourages or involves homogenization, as opposed to heterogenization, and universalization, as opposed to particularization, are crucial, as well as complex.

It should be noted that in the course of debate about modernization in the late 1950s and the first half of the 1960s the issue of postmodernity, or postmodernization, was diffusely raised. That, in turn, was to feed into the developing debate about post-industrial society, which has become part of the modernity-and-postmodernity debate of recent years. However, we need note here only that the question of postmodernity arose in the debate about modernization (in its narrow sense) primarily in terms of the relatively simple notion that there must be 'something after' modernity (as it was conceived in the rather narrow terms previously indicated). In my work with Nettl (Nettl and Robertson, 1966, 1968) we attempted, *inter alia*, to transcend this simplistic perspective by emphasizing that 'modernization' (or 'progress' in the version taken over from the West by some communist regimes) was much more fluid and 'subjective,' as well as cultural, than the 'objective' approach of many mainstream modernization theorists. This in large part arose because of what we regarded as the essentially reflexive character of modernization. Using the examples of Meiji Japan and the Russia of Peter the Great, we tried to show that 'latecomers' to the project of modernization (conceived somewhat more broadly than in mainstream modernization theory) were particularly prone to various dilemmas as to which images of modernity should guide them and from where, in relation to the important issue of national identity, they should select the pieces of such images. We could equally well have spoken of many other societies confronting such predicaments, in other parts of Asia or in Latin America, for example. Our extended discussion of what we called 'the inheritance situation' in newly independent societies of the Third World was closely linked to this general emphasis on reflexive modernization (Nettl and Robertson, 1968: 63–128). We argued that not merely latecomers but all societies implicated in projects of modernization are also involved in processes of interactive comparison with other societies. In that perspective 'modernization' has been an ongoing problem for virtually *all* societies. While the explicit focus of our work was upon the 'macro' problem of politically structured relations between societies in the international system, that work was greatly informed by a comparative-international approach inspired by symbolic interactionism (and, less explicitly, pragmatism). The reflexive nature of contemporary modernization is well illustrated by the way in which Japan is currently attempting to impose 'higher' standards of 'society' on the USA, to which the latter must in some way respond.

In the early 1970s a strong, effective and quickly very influential challenge to narrowly conceived modernization theory arose, one which had some of its roots in basically Marxist ideas about the impossibility of 'socialism in one country.' The historically detailed world-systems theory of Immanuel Wallerstein (initially stated at length in Wallerstein, 1974b) grew out of his own dissatisfaction with narrowly conceived modernization theory, which considered societies only *comparatively*, with Western societies as the major reference points, as opposed to seeing them as parts of a *systematic pattern of relations* among societies. It is to the question of the crystallization and expansion of that system that Wallerstein and his numerous followers have devoted their attention since the early 1970s, the primary emphasis being upon the expanding 'world' conceived as a capitalist system of exchange. Wallerstein's very important, but I believe one-sided, work on the world-system has overlapped, sometimes in contentious ways, with other forms of 'world-system' theory and 'world history' which have emphasized economic factors and processes in the making of the modern global circumstance. It is important to note that some of the issues that led to Wallerstein's critique of modernization theory paralleled those which Nettl and I advanced in the second half of the 1960s, in spite of obvious differences. On both sides there was a firm intention to bring the countries of the Third World firmly into the overall picture (Simpson, 1991). Rather than seeing those countries as merely problematic newcomers to or laggards within the world or international system, both positions involved the view that much more had to be said about the *formation* of the present world as a whole, the ways in which different societies had been, so to say, inserted into that system. In both cases there was, then, a definite commitment to seeing, in one way or another, the world as exhibiting systemic properties. The differences should be equally apparent. I have continued to develop the theme of societal reflexiveness and do not consider the world to be exhausted by its systemic characteristics, whereas what is usually called world-systems theory continues to pursue the theme of systemicity, looking to a world-socialist *future* for the time when men and women can make history 'voluntarily.' Yet there is a tendency to share the view that the old *Gemeinschaft*-to-*Gesellschaft* problematic, which plagued old-style modernization theory, much of sociological theory and research before and after the latter, and which now underlies much of 'the theory of modernity,' has been misconceived.

The strong view advanced by Wallerstein is that the *Gemeinschaft* problem was largely produced by an increasingly worldwide, capitalist *Gesellschaft* and that obsession with the basically internal-societal problem of the transition from *Gemeinschaft* to *Gesellschaft* set the social sciences off on an entirely wrong foot (Wallerstein, 1991a). I have some sympathy with that view, although on different grounds and not quite to the same degree. The general basis of my agreement may be indicated via Wallerstein's orientation to the theme of what he has called 'timespace realities' (1991a: 135–48). Whereas it is my view and Wallerstein's that the matter of negotiated and contested categories of time and space has been intimately bound up over many centuries with the asymmetrical 'creation' of the world (in a secular sense), Giddens tends to think of 'time-space distantiation' as a product of relatively free-floating and ahistorical 'structuration' (Urry, 1991). (Giddens has in some of his most recent writing attempted to join the idea of the disembedding of action from 'local' contexts, as an aspect of the move into 'modernity' and then 'high' modernity, to the interpretation and analysis of globalization. This will be discussed in Chapter 9.) Nonetheless, my own approach differs substantially from that of Wallerstein. I do not, for example, assume that one can or should, so to say, wipe out the significance of the *Gemeinschaft*-to-*Gesellschaft* problematic by sheer analytical reasoning. That problematic and its contemporary expression in terms of ideas such as the project of modernity has not simply been an analytical issue. For better or for worse, it has in one way or another greatly informed the reality of the world we study and the theories we form about it. I think something like a middle ground should be established between those who emphasize world systemicity and those who tend to think of current trends towards world unicity as having issued from a particular set of societies, as an outgrowth of the shift from 'the traditional' to the 'modern' and the theorization thereof.

It is in reference to the first issue, that of world systemicity, that the debate about globalization has the most continuity. While the particular debate about globality and modernity in its broad sense, as well as about postmodernity, is certainly of importance, the fact remains that the explicit attempt to 'map' the world as a whole is older. One must make a rough, certainly not a hard and fast, distinction between those attempts – which have been greatly caricatured by Giddens (1990) – and the way in which 'globalization' has been theorized within recent and relatively mainstream debates in general social theory. Another complication must be added. Wallerstein and the numerous other system-theorists are by no means of one mind in their analysis of global formation (Chase-Dunn, 1989). At least in the present context, the most interesting general pattern of variation within the overall world-systems group concerns the issue of the terms in which the contemporary world-system has actually been formed. In part this is a question of historical length as well as depth. Indeed one of the points of disagreement and contestation, not only within Wallerstein-ian world-systems theory but also, perhaps even more importantly, in rival schools of basically economic explanations of the origins of the world system, concerns the age of the world-system, or systems. The latter use of the plural is necessary because, strictly speaking, the term 'world' does not necessarily, in world-systems theory, apply to the *entire* world. Needless to say, the latter is the main focus of the present book. Thus Wallerstein himself has been concerned almost exclusively with the making of the modern world since the fifteenth century (in the sense of the current worldwide system). Nevertheless there are disputes over the extent to which the making of this *capitalist* world system was framed and/or preceded by previous developments, as well as over applications of the work of Wallerstein to 'pre-modern,' i.e. pre-sixteenth century, circumstances. In world-systems theory the whole question of what is normally understood by the idea of modernity is relativized and diminished by the claims of increasingly worldwide *system* formation. In Wallerstein's perspective capitalism becomes stronger as the system develops; and societies increasingly come to play roles in the worldwide system as a consequence of their positions in the world-systemic division of labor. Political and military relations flow along the lines indicated by these more basic economic relations, while culture, including religion, is largely epiphenomenal. Culture is not, however, unimportant in Wallerstein's own work, for it serves, often in subtle ways, to support and sustain the increasingly worldwide system.

As I have said, I regard this scheme as one-sided. That objection has been made by various other critics of world-systems theory. However, those critics have not, for the most part, presented an alternative conception of what Wallerstein calls, I think misleadingly, the contemporary world-system. The way in which I speak of globalization *is*, on the other hand, centered on such a conception, which involves the attempt to take the notion of globality very seriously. While it may be convenient for certain purposes to speak of a world or global *system*, much of the thrust of my own thinking centers on my attempt to depict the main general contours of the world as a whole. Thus the concept of globalization as used in this book is specific, yet much more wide-ranging, open and fluid than Wallerstein's conception of the world-system. Even though they have a few important things in common, globalization analysis and world-systems analysis are rival perspectives.

Sociology and the Problem of Globalization

Nineteenth-century social theorists and sociologists, such as Comte, Saint-Simon and Marx, made what many now call globalization central to their analytical (as well as their political) work. During the later period of so-called classical sociology the situation became particularly complex on the sociological front, mainly because of the hardening and expansion of the apparatus of the nation state and the strengthening of nationalism. So the classical sociologists were faced with the Janus-faced problem of the simultaneity of 'nationalization' and 'globalization.' In a sense, modern sociology was born from this dilemma; it may in fact be regarded as partly a victim of the dilemma. Let us then inspect briefly the history of sociology in this light. In doing so we will find that in the most crucial founding stages of sociology there were both openings to the theorization of globalization and closures which have constituted impediments to such theorization.

Although there is much in the writings of Emile Durkheim, Max Weber, Georg Simmel and their contemporaries that suggests a definite interest in globalization and its ramifications, for the most part they (although Simmel is a 'peculiar' case) concentrated on the problems of 'societality,' at least as far as their contemporary times were concerned. In that regard the large issue of what we now, more explicitly, call modernity received much attention, most clearly in the writings of Weber. Working within the parameters of classical sociology has misleadingly involved concentration on the basically internal affairs of 'modern societies,' a perspective which was, to a large extent, consolidated by the rise, during the period of 'high' classical sociology, of the discipline of international relations (the new 'dismal science'). Thus sociology (as well as anthropology) came to deal, often *comparatively*, with societies; while international relations (and portions of political science) dealt with them *interactively*, with relations between nations. Certain aspects and consequences of this division are dealt with in the following chapters.

Slowly at first, in recent years more rapidly, the division between the internal and the external has been destabilized. Out of that destabilization has been born the present and growing interest in globalization, in which new academic areas such as communication and cultural studies have played significant roles. Interest in the phenomenon of globalization is multifaceted. A growing number of movements, organizations and interest groups have their own perspective on, as well as interests in, globalization; while 'analysts,' who certainly cannot be simplistically separated from 'participants,' have different interests in that issue. 'Globalization' has also become a significant ingredient of advertising. It has, as well, become a matter of great concern in considerations of the curriculum in many educational systems, along with an often competing interest in multicultural – indeed 'postmodern' – education.

Albrow (1990: 6–8) has argued that we can identify five stages in the history of sociology, considering the latter from within the current concern with globalization: *universalism*; *national sociologies*; *internationalism*; *indigenization*; and *globalization*. Although I have some reservations about this scheme it is, on the whole, a helpful way of considering the history of sociology in relation to the theme of globalization.

In referring to what he calls the stage of *universalism* Albrow (1990: 6) points to the aspiration of early sociology 'to provide a science of, and for, humanity based on timeless principles and verified laws.' The universalistic stage of sociology had roots in strands of the Enlightenment which stressed such ideas as humanity, fraternity and, indeed, universalism. It reached its strongest point in the philosophy and sociology of Saint-Simon and Comte, on the one hand, and Marx, on the other. It was, says Albrow, a sociology greatly inspired by the natural sciences; although it should be added that unlike the natural sciences there was in the minds of two of its most well-known practitioners, Saint-Simon and Comte, a strong practical component in that both sought, although in different ways, to expand the very empirical conditions to which their cognitive schemes could be applied. Thus the allegedly positive stage of scientific thought was not fully guaranteed even in 'rationalistic' West European societies, let alone the rest of the world, without additional practical effort. Paradoxically, a new kind of religion was thought to be necessary, not merely to provide a sense of order and commitment to 'real life' but also to sustain and expand the scientific commitment to a universal, foundational analysis of humanity. Saint-Simon drew up a program for the reorganization of European society 'which was in fact a forerunner, suited to its period, of future world government' (Merle, 1987: 7). His ideas were elaborated in a review which was called the *Globe*, whose reach can be demonstrated in the words of one of his disciples, who wrote that 'the era of universal politics which is opening up is that of contact with Africans and Asians, Christians and Moslems' (Merle, 1987: 7). Another disciple wrote that 'there is in fact only one great branch of knowledge, that of humanity, which includes everything and epitomizes everything' (Merle, 1987: 7). Moreover, Saint-Simon's followers were actually involved in large projects for 'world' organization, including the cutting of the Suez Canal and the colonization of Algeria.

As Turner (1990b: 344–8) has argued, Saint-Simon saw a close relationship between a new form of social science, or rather the establishment of the study of society on a scientific basis, on the one hand, and the coming of 'globalism,' on the other. Saint-Simon basically thought that a science of society was impossible without the unification of humanity and vice versa. This general thrust of Saint-Simon's thought was at the core of Comte's simultaneous advocacy of a *positivistic* science of society, which he called sociology, and a 'religion of humanity.' The programs of Saint-Simon and Comte were, from our point of view, marked by a mixture of scientism and utopianism; although Saint-Simon should be called a utopian only to the extent that, as Durkheim (1962: 222) put it, 'one would apply the same term to his industrialism.' For Saint-Simon believed that it was industrialism which promoted cosmopolitanism and internationalism. Marx's approach was, of course, different, although he was influenced by Saint-Simon. In general terms Marx agreed that the combination of labor and industry on a global scale would result in 'peace.' But his image of the path to this was much more sophisticated than that of Saint-Simon. Capitalism as a determining mode of production would provide the grounds for universalization on a global scale. The proletariat, as an exploited but potentially global class within expanding capitalism, would eventually develop and install a genuine global universalism.

In speaking of the stage of *national sociologies* Albrow (1990: 6) is concerned with 'the foundation of sociology on a professional basis in the academies of the Western world, especially in Germany, France, and the United States, but also in Italy, Britain, Spain and non-Western countries, such as Japan.' While he argues that the 'universal aspirations' were not given up, he maintains that 'the intellectual products . . . took on striking characteristics of the national culture' and professional contacts became largely confined by national boundaries. Thus the fusion of national sociologies with 'the residues of universalism' produced a quest for 'exclusive intellectual hegemony which was not so remote from the imperial territorial ambitions of the nation-states associated with the parent culture.' There is much to agree with in this characterization, but I think that Albrow exaggerates the difference between the first and second stages. The universalistic stage was undoubtedly concerned directly with humanity as a whole, *as if* it made no difference where 'the universalistic message' came from, but Saint-Simon and Comte did nonetheless project a distinctively French view of that whole. Within the stage of so-called national sociologies we see in Durkheim's work a continuation of a nineteenth-century tendency – to be found, for example, in the writings of John Stuart Mill and Karl Marx – to try to establish a 'universal' theory by weaving together central themes from what were perceived to be the 'higher' Western traditions. So Durkheim in his social epistemology sought to synthesize German idealism and British empiricism. But the result of the synthesis was in fact – and Durkheim openly proclaimed his epistemology in this way – a *French-rational* synthesis. Thus although Durkheim operated within the national frame of reference, he was concerned with the theme of 'universalism.' I will return to this later.

The stage which Albrow (1990: 6) calls *internationalism* started, he says, after World War II with the collapse of national sociologies and the general disaster of the two world wars. Internationalism in science 'was taken for granted.' However, it was basically divided in ways that roughly corresponded to Cold War divisions, between 'an all-embracing modernization thesis, especially in the American Parsons version' and the 'internationalism' propounded by Marxist proletarianism. Albrow provides no stage, however transitional, between the phase of national sociologies, the collapse of which he surely exaggerates, and the phase of internationalism – which would make the national-sociologies phase stretch all the way from the late nineteenth century to the post-1945 period. This is unconvincing, because it was during the 1920s and, even more so, the 1930s that the problem of *relativism* first became thoroughly thematized in sociology and anthropology. In sociology we find the attempts of Max Scheler and Karl Mannheim to deal directly with the issue of the relativism – or, which is not exactly the same, the relativity – of perspectives. To be sure, Simmel had made relativity a central ingredient of his interpretation of modernity, but he did not confront the problem of *global* relativism or relativity, as Scheler did (Stark, 1958). And while Mannheim's pragmatic sociology of knowledge was ostensibly directed at intra-societal relativism and relativity there can be little doubt that in a general sense his concern to overcome or resolve those problems was a manifestation of a more widespread and diffuse concern with the theme of commensurability. This was also the period of the rise of relativistic anthropological perspectives, contrasting with the evolutionism, historicism or diffusionism of previous anthropology. In sum the lack of ostensible 'internationalism' should not lead us to conclude that concern with *problems* arising from globalization were not present. The rising concern with relativism can thus be regarded as a manifestation of the problems raised by increased global compression, as well as by the crystallization of distinctive ideologies of world order. Those ideologies – such as German fascism, Japanese neo-fascism, communism and Woodrow Wilson's 'self-determinationism' – themselves arose in relationship to the great acceleration of the globalization process which had begun in the late nineteenth century. Again, this is a point which I will take up later.

Albrow does make an important point about the bifurcated internationalism of the post-1945 period. I would add only two, closely related, points. First, it is ironic that Albrow should single out Talcott Parsons as the representative of an extreme position with respect to 'the increasing worldwide penetration of Western rationality' expressed as 'an all-embracing modernization thesis.' In fact, Parsons spent his entire career striving to resist sociologies based upon instrumental rationality (which was in any case a distinctively Germanic *Problemstellung*). Second, tempted as he may have been by 'modernization theory' and in spite of having often been designated as a leading proponent of it, he always insisted that the Cold War would be ended by the democratization of communist countries and the generalization of their *internationalism* (Parsons, 1964). He also maintained that it was through *a convergence* of communism's collectivism and capitalism's individualism that we would reach beyond the Cold War. That this would be an asymmetrical convergence (in favor of the West) is not particularly relevant in the present context, nor are certain weaknesses in his projections. What is of relevance is that of the people to blame for promoting a one-sided view in a bifurcated field of 'internationalism' Albrow has not chosen a good candidate. However, the general idea that the thrust of modernization theory in the 1950s and 1960s constituted the prevalent form of Western 'internationalism' is accurate. I would add only two things. First, modernization theory has deeper roots than Albrow claims. Quite apart from its embeddedness in the *Gemeinschaft– Gesellschaft* problems, it had a more immediate grounding in the 'applied sociology' which was encouraged during World War II in the USA. Indeed sociology in the USA came of age through its mixture of professionalism and patriotism in the early 1940s (and Parsons played a significant role in that respect.) Specifically, the immediate origins of 1950s and early 1960s modernization theory lay in the Allied, but particularly the American, attempt to force democracy on (West) Germany and Japan. It was in the 1940s setting of World War II that we find, in a very interesting way, a context in which the idea of 'modernization' was nurtured. Second, the idea of the Third World had some of its highly problematic origins in American President Woodrow Wilson's model for a 'self-determined world,' presented in Paris at the conclusion of World War I. At the same time the Wilson Principles constituted one of the grounds of the fissures in twentieth-century 'world politics.' From another point of view, Wilson sought a universalistic entitlement to particularism.

The phase of *indigenization*, according to Albrow (1990: 7), was centered upon the crystallization of the Third World. Albrow rightly says that this phase has to be distinguished from the phase of national sociologies – but he does not provide entirely convincing accounts of its difference. In attempting to improve on his typification of this period, I would say that it was, and to a large extent still is, one in which practitioners of 'national sociologies' have attempted for the most part to *insert* their perceived 'traditional sociologies' into a worldwide sociology. It is obvious that such an attempt requires continuity with a 'universal language' (Archer, 1990). It makes no sense to produce an entirely idiosyncratic point of view, unless one simply wants to *retreat* from the world. Even then the terms in which the retreat takes place are likely to be constrained by contemporary discourse. However, much of the point of 'indigenization' in sociology is to enlarge and revise the prevailing discourse so as to make 'local' sociology definitely present on the global scene.

Albrow maintains that there are two leading characteristics of Third World indigenization as it developed in the 1970s: opposition to external, particularly Western, terminology and methods and a stress on the perceived national-cultural tradition, although there has been a strong tendency to lean on Marxist models. In any case, one can delineate the general indigenization movement into relatively distinct tendencies. One such tendency is to be found in Latin American contexts (which Albrow does not discuss), where it has not so much been the case that foreign theories, methods and substantive themes as such have been rejected, but rather that particular ways of 'Western' thinking – mainly Hegelian and Marxist, but recently postmodernist – have been invoked in order to account for 'dependency' and to produce a form of praxis with respect to the surmounting of deprivation. So the primary targets of such tendencies have been – at least until quite recently – theories of societal modernization which, according to their critics, propose that 'development' can occur only along a US trajectory, in terms of a definite pattern of differentiation, and on a society-by-society basis. The recent importation of and enthusiasm about ideas concerning postmodernity have enhanced this view, but this time as part of a worldwide 'cultural turn' in the social sciences. Specifically, the idea of postmodernity in Latin American societies seems to fit a relatively autochthonous genre of literary expression, namely magical realism, and, from a more distinctively sociological standpoint, provides a kind of solution to the question of whether Latin America is moving from premodernity to modernity. The idea of postmodernity confirms the view that the question of modernity can be transcended. Postmodernism is seen as legitimizing *mixtures* of the traditional and the modern. There is much to be said for the argument that Latin America is the importer of 'alien' ideas *par excellence* and that it does not seriously fall into the category of indigenization. But although the first part of that view may be persuasive, the second does not follow from the first. The point is that imported themes have been syncretized into unique constellations of ideas with certain elements of autochthony constraining receptivity to some ideas rather than others. The notion of indigenization is relevant because the syncretic bundles are for very 'domestic' purposes.[1]

In coming to what Albrow (1990: 7–8) calls the present, but not necessarily the last, phase, he speaks of the *globalization* of sociology. Globalization, he says, is directly the result of the interaction of 'nationalism' and internationalism, and indirectly of all the preceding stages. The principle of globalization 'results from the freedom individual sociologists have to work with other individuals anywhere on the globe and to appreciate the worldwide processes within which and on which they work' (Albrow, 1990: 7). 'A universal discourse has arisen with multiple interlocutors based on different regions and cultures,' says Albrow. And he goes on to remark that globalization does not only mean that sociologists can communicate openly but, first, that they are 'confronted with the full diversity . . . of sociological dialects and special visions' and, second, that they are constrained to focus on globalization as 'a process at a new level of social reality.' Albrow adds that that new reality is best described by the term 'global society.'

Albrow's outline of the history of sociology in relation to globalization becomes increasingly concerned with relations between sociologists on a worldwide basis, rather than with the issue of the analysis of the global circumstance as such. As he moves through the stages which he has identified in the history of sociology Albrow shifts his attention from sociological *ideas* to the scope of *relationships* among sociologists and he tends, with respect to the more recent stages, to conflate the two. The second issue is certainly not unimportant; it is indeed relevant to the consideration of globalization. But the globalization of sociology must not be confused with the sociology of globalization. The second is my concern. It is the theorization of the world which is my immediate interest. So let us turn directly to that theme.

Openings to Globalization in Mature Classical Sociology

In spite of my observations about the relative lack of attention on the part of sociologists of the period 1890 to 1920 to what we would now consider crucial aspects of a particularly acute period of globalization, we can see that in that period ideas were produced which have a strong bearing on that theme. For example, in the works of both Simmel and Durkheim we find definite concerns with the category of humanity, which in the scheme that I will articulate shortly relates to a particular aspect of the overall delineation of the global circumstance.[2]

Writing in reference to Kant's notion of basic human presuppositions and Nietzsche's advocacy of autonomous human action, as opposed to action heteronomously guided by cultural, societal or religious constraints, Simmel became interested in two closely connected aspects of the problem of humanity. On the one hand, he made the point, in revision of Nietzsche, that looking at human experience in the frame of 'humanity' was but one of four forms of apprehension or analysis, the other three being culture, society and individual. From Simmel's perspective, Nietzsche had chosen but one way of considering human experience. It was equally valid to consider experience in, for example, the frame of society. Simmel thus relativized Nietzsche's position. He argued that Nietzsche had somewhat arbitrarily selected one frame of analysis, claiming that it was the only appropriate one. On the other hand, Simmel maintained that Nietzsche's way of thinking was, in significant part, a refraction of empirical changes (Simmel, 1986). The latter point indicated Simmel's tendency to focus not merely on the analytical categories of human experience as such, but also on the empirical circumstances which led to the intellectual production of one-sided theories, a strategy he also employed in relation to Marx (Simmel, 1978).

Simmel argued that what he called the 'values of human existence' differ profoundly from social values, in that the latter rest primarily upon the effects of individuals, whereas human values involve the 'immediate existence of man.' Following Nietzsche, Simmel (1950: 63) insisted that it is the 'qualitative being of the personality which marks the stage that the development of mankind has reached.' It is thus not only in a quantitative sense that mankind is more than society.

> Mankind is not merely the sum of all societies: it is an entirely different synthesis of the same elements that in other syntheses result in societies. . . . Society requires the individual to differentiate himself from the humanly general, but forbids him to stand out from the socially general. . . . In recent historical periods [the] conflicts into which [the individual] falls with his political group, with his family . . . etc., have eventually become sublimated in the abstract need . . . for individual freedom. This is the general category that came to cover what was common in the various complaints . . . of the individual against society. (Simmel, 1950: 63–4)

Durkheim approached a similar problem, but from a very different angle. The primary difference pivots on Durkheim's insistence that the fully developed individual is a social being, in contrast to Simmel's view that the individual is increasingly an extra-societal entity. Durkheim claimed that we would soon as individuals have little in common but our humanity. In fact, Durkheim appeared to think that the diversification of individuals to the point where they had nothing much in common as members of specific groups would constitute a consummation of men and women's societality. In other words, for Durkheim the diversification of individuals occurred directly in terms of a general trend within modern societies (a view which clearly does not involve direct consideration of migration and the formation of what Balibar (1991), has usefully called 'world spaces'). The long-term result of processes of (social) individuation was a pluralistic assimilation by individuals of what might be called essential societality. Individuals become the bearers of 'deep societality.' Here, of course, is a remnant of Comte's thinking, in the sense that when

Comte tried to establish a program for the institutionalized celebration of society, he labeled that form of celebration the 'religion of humanity.' There seems to have been a tendency within the early French sociological tradition to equate that which is most basically social (or societal) with the notion of humanity. Striking confirmation of this is to be found in a comparison of maxims drawn respectively from Kant and Durkheim, and the use of Kantian ideas by Simmel in his discussion of the category of humanity. Kant argued that although a man is profane, the mankind in him is sacred; while Durkheim (1974: 34) maintained that if the individual is spiritual, 'society' is hyperspiritual. The fact that Simmel, as well as Durkheim, invoked Kant's original maxim in order to make somewhat different points is of considerable interest in relation to the issue in question.

On the other hand, we find that Durkheim (1961: 463–96) spoke of the transcendence of concrete, national societies in reference to what he called 'international life,' in such a way as to imply that there would arise in the twentieth century a category of concern, which by conventional sociological standards does not, strictly speaking, belong at the societal but at the civilizational or extra-national level (Durkheim and Mauss, 1971). Additional substance can be provided by pointing to Durkheim's claim that, in the modern world, categories of thought become increasingly released from their social or societal moorings and, as he put it, take on a life of their own. In this, and many other areas of Durkheim's *oeuvre*, we encounter a generalized interest in the relationship between particularism and universalism, one crucial aspect having to do with the relationship between what has sometimes been called Durkheim's moral relativism – morality as being societally specific and bound up with the social realities of each society – and his humanity-oriented moral universalism, which, in effect, relativized societal relativism.

In dealing with Max Weber the situation is much more complex. Weber was very skeptical about the modern concern with what has come to be called human rights. It would appear that he thought that in the modern world concern with matters which we now address in terms such as 'humanity' could in extreme form derive from a kind of charismatic fanaticism (Weber, 1978: 6). And yet there is a strand of Weber's work which indicates, according to Nelson (1969), a world-historical trend in the direction of 'universal otherhood.' That trend was, of course, in continuous rivalry with the counter-trend of 'tribal brotherhood.' In any case, there is little doubt that Weber knew well that there were trends in the modern world which raised acutely the problem of the degree to which one could sensibly assign the individual to the simple status of member-of-society. Nothing displays this trend in Weber's thought better than the two famous essays, 'Politics as a Vocation' and 'Science as a Vocation' (Gerth and Mills, 1948: 77–158). Particularly in the former, Weber raised what might be called the modern Lutheran problem concerning the link between the ultimate concerns of individuals and the functional operation of societies.

Notwithstanding the nature of Weber's own 'intra-societal' attitude toward that predicament, it is clear that he, as a social scientist, acknowledged the tension between the demands of purely societal membership and the demands of what Simmel, following Nietzsche, called the state of one's being.

One of Weber's leading interests was, of course, in the making of the 'iron cage' of modern life. The major challenge was how one should live in relation to it. Weber resisted all arguments and practices which involved or implied absolute rejection of the alleged iron cage. He was equally adamant in denying that the charismatic glorification of reason had helped to create definitely modern forms of economic and political individualism. Weber argued against Rousseauesque ideas concerning the social celebratory origins of modern ideas about democracy, emphasizing instead the contribution of Puritanical asceticism. However, as cogent as Weber's arguments in these respects may be, the fact remains that he left relatively unattended the consequences and implications of his image of a dualistic condition in which the 'non-societal' domain is constituted by a mass of discrete individual-personal values. In the perspective of his great concern with Germany's future and 'fate,' Weber found the kinds of ideas which I have identified in the writings of both Simmel and Durkheim distinctly uncongenial. For Weber the world as a whole was basically to be seen as an arena of struggle between nations. Of course, in so far as Weber saw that struggle as occurring in an increasingly singular world economy (Collins, 1986: 19–44) he can be said to have had a partial image of a compressed world, in fact a one-sided view of what is now called globalization. Moreover, in that he argued that struggles between nations were in part about the preservation and enrichment of societal values he certainly but, only in a negative sense, saw that culture is an important ingredient of the global field. In these ways Weber was almost certainly reacting to and attempting to reshape the global and the universal thrust in the writings of Kant, Hegel and Marx, by employing Nietzsche's ideas on the 'polytheism' of values to relationships between nations. While inheriting much of Hegel's conceptual apparatus in his work on religion, Weber was eager to promote what has sometimes been called a comparative-differential and concretely historical perspective on 'universal history,' rather than the abstract, 'spiritual' or 'utopian' views of his great German predecessors (Robertson, 1985e).

One might well say that Durkheim's and Simmel's views were, in their different ways, also one-sided. But in Durkheim's case there was more openness generally to what is now called globalization, in spite of his neglect of many of what we see to have been obvious concrete manifestations of globalization in his lifetime. In the case of Simmel we can see that his relative detachment from societal matters *per se* (although he clearly expressed his commitment to 'the European ideal') in the frame of his concern with forms of life in general led to the production of ideas which are relevant in theoretical terms to the concept of globalization.

Coming to Terms with the World as a Whole

In my initial attempt to develop a flexible model of the global whole, a paper by Dumont (1979) played a significant part. It is interesting to note that in his own effort to deal with the problem of totality (a notion which was also important in the formative years of Wallerstein's (1974b) world-systems theory), Dumont spoke as a philosophically minded social anthropologist – one who had sought to comprehend 'the West' by approaching it from *outside* (Dumont, 1977, 1983). Moreover, in tackling the problem of totality Dumont credited a central member of the Durkheimian school, Marcel Mauss, with having been a source of inspiration. Dumont argued that the discipline of anthropology was committed simultaneously to the rival ideas of the 'unity' of mankind and the uniqueness of individual societies. He attempted to resolve this contradiction by arguing that the world as a whole, the world in its totality, should be regarded as consisting in a set of globewide *relationships between societies*, on the one hand, and of *self-contained, 'windowless monads,'* on the other. Whatever the limitations of Dumont's attempt to deal with the epistemological problem of allowing for both uniqueness and discontinuity, and wholeness and continuity, his particular focus is important.

It has been the question of the relationship between the epistemological terms in which it is possible to think of the world and the primary 'objects' which appear to exist in the world that has formed a central part of my thinking about globalization. I have sought to lay bare the quintessential features of the terms in which it is possible to conceive of the world, taking into account the empirical constituents of the world of relatively recent times. My model of what, in the most flexible terms, may be called the global field is centered on the way(s) in which we think about globality in relation to the basic makeup of that field. My formulation is more multifaceted than that of Dumont, in that I think in terms of four major aspects, or reference points, rather than two. These are *national societies*; *individuals*, or more basically, *selves*; *relationships between national societies*, or *the world system of societies*; and, in the generic sense, *mankind*, which, to avoid misunderstanding, I frequently call *humankind*. To repeat, this model or image is based upon both epistemic and empirical observations. Sparked by 'Dumont's question,' the attempt to set out the basic features of the global field involves a mixture of intuition and historical investigation concerning the terms in which the world as a whole is conceived to be, in a special sense, *possible*. Much of Chapter 3 concerns elaboration of this perspective.

In the broadest sense I am concerned with the way(s) in which the world is ordered. Whereas I am setting out this model of order in what may appear to be formal terms, the intent which actually guides it is to inject *flexibility* into our considerations of 'totality.' In so far as we think about the world as a whole, we are inevitably involved in a certain kind of what is sometimes pejoratively called totalistic analysis.[3] But even though my scheme does involve a 'totalizing' tendency, it does so partly in order to comprehend *different* kinds of orientation to the global circumstance. It will be seen in Chapter 4 that movements, individuals and other actors perceive and construct the order (or disorder) of the world in a number of different ways. In *that* sense what my model does is to facilitate interpretation and analysis of such variation. So there is a crucial difference between imposing a model of the global field on all the present and potential actors in that field and setting out a model which facilitates comprehension of variation in that field. The latter is an important consideration. My interest is in how order is, so to speak, *done*; including order that is 'done' by those seeking explicitly to establish legal principles for the ordering of the world (Lechner, 1991). To put it yet another way, my model is conceived as an attempt to make analytical and interpretive sense of how quotidian actors, collective or individual, go about the business of conceiving of the world, including attempts to *deny* that the world is one.

Nevertheless, in spite of my acknowledgment of certain denials of global wholeness, I maintain that the trends towards the unicity of the world are, when all is said and done, inexorable. For example, the trends towards economic protectionism in the early 1990s (paralleled by a certain kind of 'fundamentalism' concerning identity and tradition) are in one sense negative reactions to increasing compression of the entire world, but they are also reactions that are, however tortuously, reflexively monitored (Giddens, 1987). Compared to the older protectionisms and autarkies of the eighteenth and the nineteenth centuries (Moravcsik, 1991) the new ones are more self-consciously situated within a globewide system of global rules and regulations concerning economic trade and a consciousness of the global economy as a whole. This certainly does not mean that protectionism will be overcome by such factors, but it does mean that relevant parties, including 'average citizens,' are increasingly constrained to think in terms, not necessarily favorable terms, of the world as a whole, more specifically the global economy.

It must also be emphasized that although in this chapter I set out what I call a flexible model of globality in *sychronic* terms, as a one-shot, basically contemporary image of what is involved in thinking about the 'theory-and-practice' of globality, the model is in fact applied *diachronically*. It is intended to take strongly into account changes in each of the four major components (societies, individuals, international relations, and human-kind) in tandem with shifts in the relations between them. Such considerations are dealt with intermittently in a number of the following chapters. Globalization as a process is closely bound up with this diachronic perspective. Yet it should be clear that my model of the global circumstance is both multidimensional and much more global than is usually meant by social-scientific and other connotations of that word. Hence the extended discussion of the problematics of the model in subsequent chapters. Multidimensionality refers in the present context to a mode of grasping the basics of what I sometimes call the global-human condition,

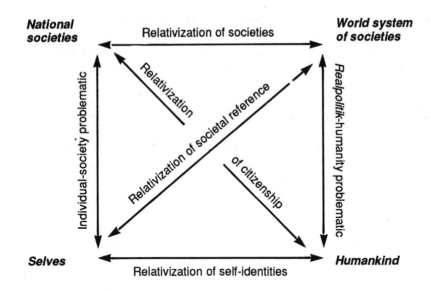

Figure 1   *The global field*

basics which at one and the same time take into account the most general features of *life* in relatively recent history and the growing concern with the connections between different conceptions thereof. We can again see that globalization involves *comparative interaction* of different forms of life.

Globalization refers in this particular sense to the coming into, often problematic, conjunction of different forms of life. This cannot be accurately captured in the simple proposition that globalization is 'a consequence of modernity' (Giddens, 1990), which I consider specifically towards the end of this volume. Present concern with globality and globalization cannot be comprehensively considered simply as an aspect of outcome of the Western 'project' of modernity or, except in very broad terms, enlightenment. In an increasingly globalized world there is a heightening of civilizational, societal, ethnic, regional and, indeed individual, self-consciousness. There are constraints on social entities to locate themselves within world history and the global future. Yet globalization in and of itself also involves the diffusion of the *expectation* of such identity declarations.

This model, which is presented diagrammatically in Figure 1, gives the basic outline of what I here call the global field but which for other purposes I call the global-human condition. The figure indicates the four major components, or reference points, of the conception of globality, the basic way in which we are able as empirically informed analysts to 'make sense' of globality, as well as the form in terms of which globalization has in the last few centuries actually proceeded. Discussion of different, or alternative, forms in terms of which globalization *might* have occurred or, indeed, did partially occur are discussed in later chapters, particularly in

Chapter 3. To provide an example at this stage, it is clear that Islam historically has had a general 'globalizing' thrust; but had that potential form of globalization succeeded we would now almost certainly comprehend contemporary 'globality' differently. There would be a need for a different kind of model.

The model is presented in primary reference to twentieth-century developments. In that it partly summarizes such developments it draws attention to increasing, interrelated thematizations of societies, individual selves, international relations and humankind. At the same time, it opens the way to the discussion and study of the ways in which the general pattern came historically to prevail. It also allows for different, indeed conflicting, empirical emphases within 'the field,' which are discussed in Chapter 4. Discussion of what I call the phases of the increasingly dominant form of globalization, occurs specifically in Chapter 3, and with respect to phases since the middle of the nineteenth century in later chapters. A number of other points should be stressed.

First, while I have emphasized that my perspective allows for empirical variation with respect to what later in this book I call images of world order and that my primary task in analyzing globalization is to lay bare and open up relatively neglected aspects of that theme, there are clearly moral and critical dimensions of my approach to globalization. I will only mention the most general here. There is certainly a sense in which I am trying to tackle directly the problem of *global complexity*, a point which will become even clearer towards the end of this book when I address the question of the shifting contents of the four major components of my model. It will, I hope, also become clear that I am arguing for the moral acceptance of that complexity. In other words, complexity becomes something like a moral issue in its own right (Robertson, 1989b). Specifically, the way in which I tackle the issues of globality and globalization suggests that in order for one to have a 'realistic' view of the world as a whole one must, at least in the contemporary circumstance, accept in principle the relative autonomy of each of the four main components and that, by the same token, one should acknowledge that each of the four is in one way or another constrained by the other three. In one sense, then, overemphasis on one to the expense of attention to the other three constitutes a form of 'fundamentalism.' Simply put, one cannot and should not wish away the reality of one or more aspects of the terms in which globalization has been proceeding. This certainly does not exhaust the issue of the extent to which my approach to globalization is moral and critical. But it must suffice for the moment.

Second, there is the issue of the processes which bring about globalization – the 'causal mechanisms' or the 'driving forces.' What happens here to arguments about the dynamics of capitalism and the forces of imperialism which have undoubtedly played a large part in bringing the world into an increasingly compressed condition? In arguing that mine is a cultural perspective on globalization I do not wish to convey the idea that I consider the matter of 'the forces' or 'the mechanisms' of globalization unimportant. However, I am well aware that that is well-trodden ground. The spread of Western capitalism and the part played by imperialism have been addressed at great length, as has the increasingly complex crystallization of the contemporary global economy. In contrast, the discussion of the disputed terms in which globalization has occurred and is occurring has been greatly neglected. It is that and directly related issues which form the main concern of this book, and it is hoped that such a cultural focus will place work in the more traditional vein in a new light. While the use of the term 'culture' here is certainly not as broad and all-embracing as is to be found in some tendencies within the relatively new field of cultural studies, it is employed much more fluidly and adventurously than in conventional sociological work. In particular, my approach is used to demonstrate discontinuities and differences, rather than the traditional sociological view of culture as integrating. It is also meant to indicate a particular way of doing sociology, rather than a sociology that concentrates on culture as such.

Third, in my representation of the global field I have emphasized a number of processes of *relativization*. That term is meant to indicate the ways in which, as globalization proceeds, challenges are increasingly presented to the stability of particular perspectives on, and collective and individual participation in, the overall globalization process. As I have said, this picture of the global field has been produced in primary reference to contemporary globality and globalization. It is an ideal-typical representation of what is meant here by global complexity. In one important respect it indicates overall processes of differentiation in so far as global complexity is concerned. Broadly speaking, application of the model involves the view that processes of differentiation of the main spheres of globality increase over time. Thus differentiation between the spheres was much lower in earlier phases of globalization; while the effects of such differentiation have been encountered unevenly and with different responses in different parts of the world. Clearly these processes of differentiation have definite, and problematic, implications for socialization in the contemporary world (Turner, forthcoming). An important aspect of this has to do with the ways in which school, college and university curricula are currently being revised in some societies along 'international' and/or 'multicultural' lines.

There are numerous ramifications of the adoption of a fully global approach to the world, ramifications which are not exhausted by a concentration on the recent and contemporary form of globalization as such. While exploration of the latter is a particular concern of this book, that is not its only concern. In concluding this introductory chapter I should like to consider briefly one of these larger issues: the theme of world history.[4] Books and essays about world history have proliferated in recent times, this development constituting something of a revival of a genre which was intellectually popular during what I call in Chapter 3 the take-off phase of modern globalization that peaked at the beginning of the twentieth century. This can be attributed to two closely related sets of circumstances. On the one hand, the fact and the consciousness of rapidly increasing interdependence across the world has sharpened the concern with an understandable trajectory of the whole of humanity. On the other hand, whereas earlier writing in that vein consisted, and to some extent still consists, in variations on one 'grand narrative' depicting the rise and the 'triumph' of the West, there has been an increasing tendency for world history to be written with respect to heretofore unheard 'voices.' Current controversies about the teaching canon are thus significant manifestations of globalization, not least because in the contemporary phase of globaliza- tion the concept of the homogeneous national society is breaking down, in spite of the reassertion of nationalism in certain parts of the world. At the same time those controversies themselves generate new conceptions of world history.

A good example of a fairly recent attempt to develop an alternative to the grand-narrative approach is that of Eric Wolf, who writes that his 'central assertion is that the world of humankind constitutes a manifold, a totality of interconnected processes, and inquiries that disassemble this totality into bits and then fail to reassemble it falsify reality' (Wolf, 1982: 3). Like Wallerstein, Wolf believes that the modern tendency to endow 'nations, societies, or cultures with the qualities of internally homogeneous and externally distinctive and bounded objects' leads to the creation of 'a model of the world as a global pool hall in which the entities spin off each other like so many hard and rounded billiard balls' (Wolf, 1982: 6). Also like Wallerstein, Wolf contends that this situation was largely produced by the intellectual division of labor among the nascent social sciences in the middle of the nineteenth century. While I have great sympathy for this general view, such an approach – which in Wolf's case leads to a fascinating empirical study of 'the connectedness of human aggregates' (Wolf, 1982: 387) across a vast portion of the world since 1400 – involves a diminution of the importance of studying the actual trajectory and form of contemporary globalization.

We need to recognize both Wolf's 'totality of interconnected processes' *and* the form of totality which has developed in recent centuries. That social science has both consolidated and refracted what from Wolf's standpoint are essentially denials of real, empirical 'totality' is a refreshing proposition. But even though normal social science may well have turned 'names into things' (Wolf, 1982: 6) and produced an image of a world of sharp boundaries between societies, it has not been entirely responsible for that situation. Social science, and here we are particularly concerned with sociology, developed *in the wake of* national-societal boundary setting. That it was unreflexive in that respect and *contributed to* the prevalent way of thinking in terms of discontinuities between the 'internal' and the 'external' is undoubtedly the case. But to go to the other extreme and deny the reality of 'things' is unwarranted. In this book I attempt to find a bridge between the view that Wolf seeks to sustain and the reality of the world in which we now live. This does involve me in an attempt to transcend the divisions of which Wolf speaks, but not by trying to wipe them out. Thus 'world history' is conceived on two levels. On the one hand, world history is to be done in terms of the formation of the world along the lines which I am indicating. On the other, it must be done in due recognition of the ways in which different, indeed an increasing number of, 'entities' in the contemporary world are making and remaking their histories in terms of the constraints of the current phase of globalization. 'Modernity' has undoubtedly enhanced this kind of reflexivity, which itself has *also* helped to produce a certain kind of wilful nostalgia. But 'modernity' should not, in my view, be employed as the essential *explanans*.

Of course, we are all in a certain way contestants in this 'postmodern game' of making histories and inventing traditions. The world as a whole is, in a sense, a world of reflexive interlocutors. One of the major tasks of the contemporary sociologist is to make sense of this vast array of interlocutions, in which he or she is at the same time one of the interlocutors.

Notes

1. For an excellent discussion of nostalgic interpretation on the part of Latin Americanists, see Merquior (1991).
2. A few of the remaining pages of this chapter rely a lot upon Robertson and Chirico (1985). An early version of the latter was presented at a conference of the International Society for the Comparative Study of Civilizations (US), Syracuse University, 1980. Over the years the model of what I now often call 'the global field' has been altered in significant ways, in a more emphatically global and processual direction. I am grateful to JoAnn Chirico for her contributions to my early thinking about the themes of humanity and humankind. The delay in the publication of this paper was due largely to the fact that it was scheduled to appear in a collection (edited by another academic) which came to naught. In its published form of 1985 it is centered empirically on the simultaneous occurrence of religious 'fundamentalisms' and church–state tensions in a variety of societies in the late 1970s and early 1980s (Robertson, 1981), but that was not a feature of the original 1980 paper. Revised versions of the formulation first stated in 1980 have informed much of my work on globalization since the early 1980s.
3. For a well-argued case against 'totalizing theory' see Poster (1990). Arguments opposing such theories are particularly popular among 'poststructuralists.' Fraser (1989: 13), while arguing against 'ahistorical philosophical "metanarratives",' expresses her approval of what she calls 'big empirical narratives.' By and large I agree with that distinction and, moreover, would claim that my form of globalization analysis approximates the latter.
4. A particularly good example of historical sociology in the broad tradition of world history is Mann (1986). For an acute discussion of the properties of Western societies which make them 'extensive,' as well as 'intensive,' see Meyer (1989).

2

THE CULTURAL TURN

Culture has become a very conspicuous concern of sociologists and social theorists, that development being reflected in and promoted by the many journals and organizations devoted to cultural and 'intercultural' matters which have been founded in recent years. Some of these have, indeed, been partly responsible for the developing interest in what in this book is called globalization. By now it must surely be clear to most sociologists that in contemporary sociology and social theory there is an awakening, some would say a reawakening, of interest in the social relevance as well as the intrinsic significance of culture and cultural change. For not merely is culture increasingly visible as a topic of specialized concern, it is evidently being taken more seriously as a relatively 'independent variable' by sociologists working in areas where it had previously been more or less neglected. Yet there also appears to be a widespread sense that those who are convinced of the significance of culture as a general sociological topic are limited by an absence of theoretical resources. In other words many of those attracted to the sociological study of culture apparently feel that theirs is a young and highly embryonic focus. In only a limited sense do I share that view. After all, modern anthropology has been focally concerned with culture since its crystallization in the 1880s; while the idea of culture has, in one way or another, been a prominent feature of the academy and of intellectual life generally for much longer than that. It is, I believe, both presumptuous and self-defeating to help spread the attitude that in spite of our conviction that culture is important we are only in the very early stages of dealing with it. In so far as we are confused, we would, I suggest, be advised to consider carefully the body of already produced materials on the history of, debates about and, above all, the circumstances which are currently encouraging interest in culture. Specifically, I suggest that even though the contemporary interest in culture is almost certainly a manifestation of an increase in sociological reflexivity we ought to be even more reflexive and consider the proposition that *the decline* in sociological interest in culture after the period of classical sociology (that is, after 1920 or thereabouts) needs as much attention as the recent increase in such interest; a major possibility in that connection being that mature modernity was unfavorable to concern with culture, whereas what is often diagnosed as postmodernity – or postmodernism – encourages it.

Some Basic Issues

The present discussion is part of a larger project, in which I am concerned with five main issues. First, I am trying to pinpoint the terms in which doubts about the viability or promise of culture as a sociological interest are currently being expressed. Second, I am considering the circumstances which are, in contrast, currently encouraging a strong interest in culture. Third, I am tracing the genealogies of the concept of culture in sociology *per se*, comparing those genealogies with previous and contemporaneous developments on other intellectual fronts. Fourth, I am endeavoring to explicate the lessons to be learned from those considerations, with particular reference to my own thesis that we do not need a specialized sociological concern with culture so much as we require a sociology which is thoroughly sensitized to and permeated by insistence upon the centrality of culture. Fifth, I am particularly concerned with the application of 'culture' to the global field, a theme to which I pay particular attention in later chapters. The present chapter is not specifically concerned with globalization and globality, but it is relevant to those themes and prepares the way for subsequent discussions.

I make little or no attempt in what follows to nail down a substantive definition of culture. There are quite a few reasons for this. Most basically, perhaps, the fact that culture as an idea has, particularly in the Western world, a very long history (or, better, societal and civilizational genealogies), commencing with the ancient Greek philosophers, suggests that we ought to entertain seriously Nietzsche's dictum that that which has a history cannot usefully be defined; even though for purposes less general than those which guide the present discussion we probably could not sustain the Nietzschean rule. The mere fact that there have been so many definitions of culture produced by social scientists and those working in the field of cultural studies in recent decades also suggests that there is a need to discuss 'the problem of culture' rather than culture 'itself.' Closely related to this is the fact that culture has had for a long time both analytical and critical usages. 'Analysts' have ostensibly been concerned with the concept of culture for explanatory and/or interpretive purposes; while 'critics' have explicitly shown interest in culture for diagnostic and/or praxiological reasons. There has been and still is considerable overlap between those two entrances to the study of culture, most obviously in critical theory and postmodernistic theory.

Another thorny parametric issue arises from the idea of the *differentiation* of culture – the degree to which there is variation across time and space in the degree to which culture is, or is perceived to be, a distinct realm, with relative autonomy *vis-à-vis* social structure and/or individuals. This issue parallels (at least in part) the problem encountered by economic sociology and anthropology with respect to the degree to which one can, for example, speak of a primal society having an economy which is analyzable directly by the methods developed with reference to modern economies. The 'formalists' have argued that one can and should directly address primitive economies; the 'substantivists' have said that this is not appropriate (Bloch, 1983: 164–72). This problem has also been addressed as a contrast between thinking of the economy as always 'disembedded,' as if it were at least analyzable as differentiated and relatively autonomous, on the one hand, and conceiving of it as, in varying degrees, 'embedded' in the sociocultural fabric, on the other (Granovetter, 1985). There is a similar problem in the discussion of culture, where many have attempted to establish a highly circumscribed definition of culture without due regard for the fact that culture's significance varies considerably in a society's or a civilization's history, as well as across societies and civilizations (Bellah, 1964). Again we find a reason for wariness about extensive *a priori* definition.

I will argue, along lines which have much in common with those of Sahlins (1985), that there is a need for more discussion of what I call *metaculture* as a way of addressing the varying links between culture and social structure and between culture and individual and collective action. I will maintain that one of the major lacunae in discussions of culture has been not merely the problem of the ways in which relationships between culture and social structure, and between culture and what is nowadays called agency, vary empirically but also the issue of variation in the manner in which individuals and collectivities are constrained by deep metacultural codes to connect (or try to keep separate) culture and social structure and culture and action. As it is, an enormous amount of intellectual energy is still being expended in the search for universal truth with respect to these problems. Much of social theory since Rousseau and even earlier philosophers has involved attempts to deal with culture–structure and culture–agency (not to speak of the most currently discussed structure–agency) linkages eternalistically – that is, by presenting empirically *indifferent* 'solutions' which often refract only the particular 'codes' of the societies which a particular theorist has internalized. So even though it is, I believe, unwise to work with a highly circumscribed and very substantive definition of culture, because the 'status' of the latter varies considerably across both large and small-scale sociocultural entities, as well as temporally, we do need a systematic conception of the terms in which that variation occurs.

Culture and Sociology

A 'fundamentalistic' interpretation of sociology confines the work of sociologists to the analysis of *social* structures and relationships. However, in spite of the fact that from time to time sociologists, as well as social anthropologists, have attempted to limit the scope of their analyses along such lines (including, interestingly enough, a major contributor to the analysis of culture: Simmel) and even though most sociologists would consider that the pivotal focus of their discipline is constituted by the *social* aspect of human life, there has been a more general tendency to concede that beliefs, values and symbols are intimately and significantly related to social interaction, the operation of organizations and movements, the functioning of societies, short- and long-run change and conflict, and, even, that sociological study is hampered if these are neglected. Since the crystallization of sociology as a discipline, notions such as ideology, doctrine, representation, *Weltanschauung*, 'spirit,' ethos, and culture itself, have been important, although heavily disputed, ingredients of the discipline.

This acknowledgment of the importance of cultural concepts and phenomena has, nevertheless, often been reluctant and it has not been until very recently that the issue of culture has reached the embryonic stage of general thematization in sociology (as opposed to social or cultural anthropology) in spite of – perhaps, even, because of – the strenuous efforts of Talcott Parsons and his followers. One of the best indicators of the underdevelopment of what is sometimes, I believe misleadingly, called 'cultural analysis' (Wuthnow et al., 1984) in sociology is the way in which culture has typically been treated in American and American-influenced sociology textbooks. The subject is often discussed in complete isolation from political ideology, religious doctrine and other ideational matters; and it is often cast in terms of American cultural *anthropology* of the 1930s (as in the required invocation of the material–ideal culture distinction), with some discussion of the Whorf–Sapir thesis on the linguistic construction of reality and 'the problem of ethnocentricism.' It is also often laced with comments on subcultures and countercultures and the theme of 'culture against man.' Generally, there is an emphasis on the idea that culture is *a product* of social interaction. Indeed the theme of 'the production of culture' is one of the few respects in which there has, at least until recently, been a visible, specialized cultivation of the topic of culture on the part of American sociologists. In recent years the sociobiological theory of human culture has been added as a major topic in textbook chapters on culture, further trivializing its treatment. The peripheral status of culture as a sociological theme, at least in American sociology, is not inadequately reflected in Wuthnow's recent assessment: 'While theories, methods, and research investigations in other areas of the social sciences have accumulated at an impressive pace over the past several decades, the study of culture appears to have made little headway' (Wuthnow, 1984: 1).

But there is much more to the story than that. For starters, just how accurate is Wuthnow's statement (which is part of an introduction to essays on Peter Berger, Mary Douglas, Foucault and Habermas)? One might well reply that a sociological survey of the more visible recent work in 'cultural analysis' ought to – or, at least, might – include systematic discussions of, among others, Parsons, Geertz, Sahlins, Swanson and Bourdieu. In invoking this short list all I am suggesting is that Wuthnow and his colleagues have seriously underestimated the degree to which the study of culture on the part of sociologists *has* made 'headway.' The problem is not so much that there has been a paucity of fruitful sociological discussion of culture but that relatively little of the vast amount of work on it has been shown to be clearly relevant to 'normal sociology.' Thus Archer (1982: 263) gets a little closer to the truth in saying that 'the conceptualization of culture is extraordinary in two respects. It has displayed the weakest analytical development of any key concept in sociology and it has played the most wildly vacillating role within sociological theory.'

One can roughly divide what, for the sake of convenience, we can continue here to call cultural analysis into two parts: that which is sociological and that which is 'non-sociological.' This distinction needs a lot of consideration. If we use the term 'sociological' to embrace not simply that which is to be found at the center of professional sociology but also analytical work on culture which takes as its point of departure the problem of connecting ideational and symbolic themes to social-structural and social-relational matters then there *is* a large and impressive body of materials of sociological relevance, most of which, however, has not been taken very seriously, at least until recently, by sociologists. One thinks, in particular, of the French sociological-anthropological tradition which effectively began with Durkheim and was immediately nourished by Mauss and Lévy-Bruhl and later by Dumézil and Lévi-Strauss, to mention but two of the earlier and two of the later important figures (Littlejohn, 1985). The more widely discussed works, at least among sociologists, of such people as Mary Douglas and Foucault stand in that tradition (notwithstanding the Nietzschean aspect of Foucault's endeavors and his turning to the relationship between knowledge and power). Quite a lot of British social anthropology has been deeply affected by this French tradition, even though it has been less explicitly theoretical in character. In sum, there has been a vital and continuous debate, with wide-ranging empirical embellishment, about culture from a sociological perspective, in the broader sense of the latter. But the most prominent, recent national form of 'normal sociology' – the American – has not taken it very seriously. (Nor, for that matter, has it been taken seriously – again, at least until quite recently – in many other national contexts.) This has arisen partly from the relatively non-sociological focus of American anthropology and the attendant division of labor between *cultural* anthropology and *social* sociology. In the USA the culture of modern societies has, for the most part, been studied by literary critics and historians, although that is now rapidly changing.

The observations of Wuthnow and Archer, as well as those of Swidler (1986), reflect, I believe, a mixture of mainstream sociological neglect of the centrality of debates about culture in anthropology and, even more disturbingly, the 'false consciousness' of sociology as a discipline which for long perpetuated an illusion in modern societies concerning their putative lack of symbolic foundations (Sahlins, 1976). It would not be too much to say that modern sociology as a 'scientific profession' has been, particularly but certainly not only in the USA, a culture-resistant discipline. But quite apart from the apparent resistance of mainstream sociology to the thematization of culture (in spite of a very lively tradition of sociological-anthropological concern with culture since the period of classical sociology), there remains the matter of what I have called 'non-sociological' treatments of cultural phenomena. Here I have particularly in mind bodies of work produced by students of myth, ritual, cosmology and cosmogony – for example, Mircea Eliade and Joseph Campbell. Surely these must count as contributions to 'cultural analysis' *per se*. But what, if any, is their relevance to sociology? The same question can, of course, be asked of some schools of literary-critical analysis of cultural phenomena, including deconstructionism and 'textism,' particularly in view of the growing salience of the academic field of cultural studies. Suffice it to contend here that the suggestion that they are *ir*relevant, that they should not be regarded seriously by the sociologist, is exceedingly rash. Dismissal prejudges the question of whether, and, if so, to what degree, sociocultural life is permeated by myth or constrained by primordial symbolic structures. Even more importantly, insistence on the marginality of the study of the structure and transformation of civilizational patterns of ideas and symbols hastens 'the retreat of sociologists into the present' (Elias, 1987) and assists in the diminution of culture to the mere status of a resource or what Swidler (1986) *approvingly* calls a 'tool kit.' For, as Archer (1988) in effect argues, the major sociological problems centered on culture cannot be adequately confronted without careful and sustained analytical recognition of the relationship of autonomy-within-interdependence between culture as objective thought *and* culture as an ingredient of action.

Given sociology's ostensibly pivotal concern with 'the social' – so adamantly propounded by Durkheim, who centralized the place of the social domain in human life and Simmel who, in contrast, apparently thought that the social should be isolated by bracketing cultural and psychological 'contents' – in what ways can or should culture make an 'appearance'? On the face of it, a strict devotion to the social domain would seem to allow culture (as frequently conceived as a realm of values, beliefs and symbols) into the analytical picture only as a way of *explaining* social phenomena or as *explainable by* them. In other words, culture as a field of inquiry is only needed by sociologists, so the argument has often appeared to go, if it can be shown that it is of fundamental importance in accounting for variation within the domain of social structure and social action (Swidler, 1986); while to the extent that cultural variation itself can be accounted for in strictly sociological terms then, while not essential for sociology, it triumphantly exhibits the power and scope of 'the sociological method.' Very generally speaking, I suggest that much of social and cultural anthropology has, largely because of its practitioners' greater exposure to global heterogeneity, tended to follow the first path; while sociology (in the circumscribed Giddensian sense of a discipline which studies aspects of *modern* societies) has followed the second path, largely because of its greater exposure to apparent homogeneity, in so far as it has taken culture seriously at all. Recent developments have, however, undermined these neat and simple orientations to culture. Before turning to some of those it is necessary to consider some major genealogical features of the concept of culture.

Genealogical Considerations

In the middle of the nineteenth century, primarily via Marx's critique of Hegel's idealism, there began to develop a general controversy, which persists to this day, about the status of cultural factors: the degree to which culture stands in a relatively autonomous, constraining relationship *vis-à-vis* social (and/or personal) life, and the degree to which culture is an epiphenomenon *vis-à-vis* the social domain, or even 'lower' aspects of life. In various ways that sociological problem stood at the center of the work of the major sociologists of the so-called classical period (1890–1920), even though it rarely, if ever, reflected accurately the ways in which Marx himself attempted to *overcome* the idealism–materialism dilemma (Dupre, 1983). (I cannot here begin to fathom the critical issue of the ways in which the idealism–materialism *Problemstellung* has been confused with the subjectivity–objectivity issue.)[1] Max Weber's vast body of writings on the making of the modern ethos (with special reference to the place of religion in that development), Simmel's attempts to treat that theme on a more limited historical scale but in greater depth with respect to the nuances of modern life and its ideational and psychic underpinnings, and Durkheim's extensive attempt to show the links between cultural phenomena and social structure are almost certainly the major examples.

It is clear that Weber worked partly in reference to the materialism–idealism cleavage which had developed so strongly with the rise of both Marxism and the Kantian revival (plus the hovering presence of Hegel). His promotion of such concepts as ethos, spirit, world images and ideal interests was central to his attempt to counteract the excesses of economic determinism (as in the works of Engels and Kautsky), as was his continuing interest in processes of rationalization, which is certainly not to say that Weber was in any meaningful sense a committed idealist. Durkheim was less directly affected by the Germanic materialism–idealism debate. In the clearest statement of his interest in the general issue, Durkheim (1961) declared that he was attempting to overcome the limitations of both German idealism–rationalism, which, according to him, emphasized the collective and *a priori* status of knowledge, and British empiricism, which, stressed the individual and experiential basis of cognition. His solution to the clash was to produce a 'French' synthesis of the collectivism of the German approach and the experiential empiricism of the British perspective, yielding a theory which emphasizes the constraining social-structural basis of the major forms of cognitive classification, morality and religion. There is a strong emphasis in Durkheim's thought which suggests that culture is determined by social structure. That view has been taken most seriously, in somewhat different ways, by Swanson and Douglas (Robert-son and Lechner, 1984). A more flexible perspective on this matter has been proposed by Alexander (1988).

Simmel's less influential and infrequently discussed contribution to the analysis of culture was – on the face of it, ironically – more explicit. He addressed the topic of culture in a sustained, direct manner, using the term often and very specifically, unlike Weber (who used it diffusely and connotatively) and Durkheim (who seldom spoke directly of 'culture'). The irony is substantially reduced if one fully appreciates that Simmel regarded what he called objective culture as a relatively autonomous phenomenon and that his cultural analysis was strategically separated from his very circumscribed conception of sociology. In Kantian mode, Simmel explored the major categories – or, in his terminology, *forms* – of culture in relation to cultural *content*. Yet his approach was somewhat Hegelian and loosely Marxian, in that he was substantively concerned with the relation-ship between subjectivity and objectivity – specifically, subjective culture and objective culture. His analysis was doubly critical: first, in explicating the form(s) of culture (that which makes culture *possible*); second, in addressing in the perspective of 'tragedy,' the conflicts (what we might now, more appropriately, call contradictions) in modern culture (Simmel, 1968).

While it is clear that the materialism–idealism issue, as well as the objectivity–subjectivity theme, was very significant to the classical socio-logists, there were other important matters of relevance to the concept of culture in the background, notably the German distinction between culture and civilization, which involved distinguishing between culture as the central member of a family of terms of approval (such as cultivated, cultivation and culturally unique) and *civilization* as a negative character-ization of the modern world.[2] In contrast the French tendency was to ignore the family of ideas revolving around culture and to analyze, in a much more positive and optimistic vein, the character and origins of modern civilization. 'Culture' resonated in Germany with a mixture of humanistic and historicist themes (Merquior, 1979: 39–61), the former being represented in the emphasis on self-cultivation and cultivation of the ideal, the latter in the stress on the cultural uniqueness of particular societies and civilizations. The historicist view had largely been shaped by Herder in his insistence on 'the specificity and irreplaceability of each culture or people' (Dumont, 1984: 106; Berlin, 1991). However, Fichte's less historicist and proto-Hegelian view that one particular culture 'embod-ies humanity at a particular time' (Dumont, 1984: 111) was (fatefully) also very influential. In any case, the fact that culture has a very particular history in the German context has to be kept carefully in mind, not least because of the fact that it was a historicist conception of culture that was diffused from the German to the American context in the early twentieth century, most specifically via the anthropological writings of Boas (Stock-ing, 1968; Sahlins, 1976; Bloch, 1983: 125–8). Whereas the reaction against nineteenth-century evolutionism in British anthropology increasingly took the form of a functionalist conception of primal communities (in Africa, Asia and Oceania) as each being fundamentally constituted by unique social structures, American anthropological reaction involved attention to unique *cultural* patterns of primal communities (in North America), the latter perhaps echoing the German distinction between cultural wholeness and 'civilizational' disintegration. The American anthropological focus gave rise to an even more concentrated interest in cultural configurations – on a very large scale in the work of Kroeber, in a more circumscribed form in the writings of Margaret Mead and Ruth Benedict. The study of modern 'civilization,' in its German sense, was largely left to sociology, although eventually the anthropological sense of cultural uniqueness was wedded, apparently for strategic-professional reasons, to an important segment of American sociology in the Kroeber–Parsons collaboration, centered on the problem of the formal, interdisciplinary definition of culture (Kroeber and Parsons, 1958).

Cutting the story very short, the characteristic conceptions of what we now tend to call culture to be found in the major national-societal settings of modern social science and social theory have been as follows. First, the German concern has been with the problem of 'true' culture in relation to the problem of the social *distortion* of 'knowledge' – hence the particular form taken by German sociology of knowledge (notably through the writings of Scheler and Karl Mannheim), the Frankfurtian critique of 'Enlightenment civilization,' and the Habermasian concern with communicative truth (as opposed to 'systematically distorted communication'). Second, the French preoccupation has been with the structure of human thought in relation to variation in social structure, the major constant during the twentieth century being the insistence that modes of thought are collectively sustained. There has also been a continuing interest, from Lévy-Bruhl to Foucault, in the phenomenon of large-scale *discontinuity* (as opposed to distortion) in cognitive structures, whether between civilizations or in the history of particular civilizations. Third, the British concern has been not so much with the relationship between socially shaped interests and knowledge (the German focus) or between social structure and modes of thought (the dominant French perspective) but with *the natural intimacy* of culture and social relationships and structures – culture as the *way of life* of a people (as in the work of, among others, F. R. Leavis, T.S. Eliot, E.P. Thompson and Raymond Williams, as well perhaps as Anthony Giddens and even Stuart Hall). Finally, the American conception of culture has, despite the Boasian influence, largely been *utilitarian* in its major tendency, with the view that unique cultural patterns are produced largely by individuals in specific social settings and circumstances. Culture is that which individuals, groups and societies produce and acquire in order to function effectively. They need 'tool kits' (Swidler, 1986). In extreme form that can suggest that culture is largely 'achieved,' as in the American conception of nationality. (It should be said, however, that American sociologists have become increasingly conscious of the extent to which national and ethnic cultures are matters of manipulation and, indeed, 'invention.')

These skeletal characterizations obviously indicate that there is something more profound than culture *per se* to which we must attend in culture-focused sociology, namely the factors which yield variation in conceptions of culture. That is where my concept of metaculture becomes even more relevant. Metacultures (or cultural codes) constrain conceptions of culture, mainly in terms of deep-rooted, implicit assumptions concerning relationships between parts and wholes, individuals and societies, in-groups and out-groups, and societies and the world as a whole (Robertson, 1978: 166–76; Holzner and Robertson, 1980: 33–9; Robertson, 1980). They also shape the different ways in which – and, indeed, the degree to which – substantive culture will be invoked and applied to 'practical action' (Sahlins, 1976, 1985). In other words, culture does not merely vary in status from society to society and from civilization to civilization. There is also extensive variation in the manner of its invocation, as well as in its very meaning.

The Amplification of Concern with Culture

In turning to consideration of some of the circumstances that are amplifying interest in culture, I begin with the realignment of the relationship between sociology and anthropology. The initial separation of anthropology from sociology is almost entirely attributable to a particular conjuncture in the long-term process of globalization. Anthropology constituted, in effect, the disciplinary announcement of the Third World, although this is not so clearly applicable to American and German as to French and British anthropologies. Founded in the most superficially 'successful' of the imperialist countries of the early modern era (France and Britain), modern anthropology thematized not merely cultural diversity (either as almost infinite variety or as, at least, a world of two or three basic cultural forms) but also, in a way which has yet to be fully explored, central problems of modernity and modernism (Ardener, 1985). During the last twenty years or so social and cultural anthropologists have increasingly included so-called modern societies in their purview (including the global field), while sociologists have become much more concerned with societies and civilizations beyond the modern West. In the process we have become more sensitive to the cultural factor. I believe that it is unfortunate that this has led to so much energy being devoted to the problem of relativism (Geertz, 1984). It would be much better for us to focus on *actual* intersocietal and intercivilizational encounters (Nelson, 1981) and long-term processes of cultural *syncretization* – more specifically to study the ways in which problems of particularism and universalism have been addressed and dealt with *in situ* over the centuries – than to become philosophical partisans in an armchair struggle between relativism and anti-relativism. Undoubtedly, the present concern with relativism is, in part, a manifestation of the cultural heterogeneity of a compressed, globalized world. But our job is to study, not merely echo the process of globalization.

The insertion of Marxism into the Western academy in the mid-1960s also significantly, and not unironically, contributed to a growing concern with culture. That circumstance has, of course, arisen largely in relation to the mainly Marxist problem of the persistence, recently the expansion, of capitalism. Specifically, in so far as capitalism should have collapsed by virtue of its own economic weight, according to most nineteenth- and early twentieth-century Marxist theories, then its continuance and present expansion has to be explained by non-economic factors, of which culture – more narrowly, dominant ideology (Abercrombie et al., 1980) – has appeared as a major candidate, with nationalism and ethnicity being closely related phenomena. Indeed, innovative Western Marxism has been almost entirely centered upon the cultural dimension of social formations (P. Anderson, 1976, 1984). Even what initially appeared to be a major exception to this tendency – Wallersteinian world-systems theory – has, as we will see, taken a cultural turn in specific response to the significance of capitalism at the global level. While much of 'cultural Marxism' has centered on the theme of hegemony, in the form of culture 'holding back' otherwise inexorable economic forces, some brands of modern Marxism or 'post-Marxism' have taken the tack of reconstructing Marxist thought in such a way as to make culture more central to the very idea of historical materialism. Whereas one set of Marxisms sees culture as a recalcitrant epiphenomenon, another set regards 'the problem of culture' as inherent in capitalism (and, perhaps, all other social formations). Baudrillard brought this train of thought to a peak in his argument that the commodification inherent in capitalism has rendered the latter a fundamentally *cultural* phenomenon. More generally and in less clear-cut Marxist vein, mention should be made of those who, like Touraine, tend to deal with the central theme of sociological Marxism – class and class conflict – in terms of the cultural dispositions – or, in Bourdieu's different perspective, the *habitus* – of particular classes. Culture thus becomes a site for what Parsons, in adaption of G.H. Mead, called the definition of the societal situation (cf. Touraine, 1981). It is, however, the *global* situation which is now the most pressing sociological issue. Along somewhat different lines, Marxism has been greatly affected by the cultural factor in Latin America, where the liberation-theology movement has attempted to synthesize forms of Marxism with aspects of Christian thought. In Latin America and elsewhere Gramsci's notion of ideological hegemony has, of course, been a major influence since the widespread stirring of interest in his work in the 1960s.

Another very consequential development, closely related to the fusion of theology and Marxist social science in Latin America during the 1970s, is the increasing salience of religion – or at least the *category* of 'religion' – in the modern world, of which religion–state tensions and the politicization of religion across the globe are major manifestations. The anti-cultural bias of much of modern sociology, a premise of the latter's positivistic tendency, is being strongly challenged by this. Certainly it constitutes a major dimension of the contemporary thematization of culture. One of the more important aspects of that development has to do with the theme of revitalization (Robertson, 1985b). Originating largely in recent social science in the work of Wallace (1956), the notion of revitalization has relevance in the present context because it conveys the idea of reinvigorating 'tired' social structures. Specifically, the theme of revitalization is now increasingly centered on the thesis that periodically all social groups (particularly, in the modern era, total societies) encounter, in diachronically patterned forms, the situational problem of rendering meaningful and redirecting their societally structured forms of socioeconomic routine. The idea that societies need 'cultural transfusions' is what is basically being argued. One important source of both the theoretical idea and the empirical drift in this regard derives mainly, but not only, from the globalization process. In the contemporary global circumstance societies are constrained to 'give life to themselves' and at the same time contribute to the vitalization of the world (Lechner, 1990b) – or, to use Marxist terminology, transform the world from a species in-itself into a species *for*-itself. This is a basis of the contemporary national politicization of culture as is, to be more specific, the disputed penetration of the modern state into more and more areas of social life.

The themes of revitalization (of societies) and vitalization (of the world) may, in turn, be connected to the ideas of paradigm- and problem-shift as developed or inspired by Kuhn. The perspective I take with respect to those well-known, and almost obsessively talked about, ideas is that they are part of a larger, global tendency towards awareness of the relativity of all things. In that connection, it is important to realize that at roughly the same time that Kuhn (1964) was beginning to publish his extremely influential work on scientific revolutions Talcott Parsons (1961) was beginning to adumbrate his own, much more encompassing, theory of cultural reorganization. Parsons's main argument, which in its formal outline was quite similar to but more analytically sophisticated than Kuhn's, was that societies from time to time confront disparities between cultural models and 'realities,' a circumstance yielding the problem of cultural reorganization. (That perspective has yet to be explicitly linked to the analysis of encounters and confrontations between societal and other cultures in the global system.) The greater empirical conspicuousness of religion in many areas of the modern world and the interest in what are basically Durkheimian ideas concerning societal renewal are importantly related to the recent sociological concern with paradigms, frames of reference, and so on. Each of these foci is closely bound up with the problem of what can in the most general sense be called *the terms* in which societies and other collectivities function and change. In this way there is a remarkable degree of convergence in modern sociology. For even though a great deal of sociological theory in the past thirty years or so has been concerned to challenge Parsons's declaration that the central problem of sociological theory is the problem of order, the fact remains that much of the attempt to resist Parsons has consisted of providing *alternative accounts of order*, even though the latter term has rarely been used in recent debates (its foundational significance for ethnomethodology being a major exception). The convergence is seen in one major form, as already noted, in the apparent acceptance by many sociologists, of various schools of modern sociology, of the common culture, or dominant ideology, thesis (Abercrombie et al., 1980), which essentially maintains that the central ingredient of social order is the institutionalization and/or the internalization of cultural values (and beliefs and symbols).

With the specific problem of the adequacy of Abercrombie et al.'s account of Parsons's conception of order I am not directly concerned here. Suffice it to say that Parsons certainly presented a much richer conception of the modes of coherence of collectivities than Abercrombie, Hill and Turner acknowledge and that only for a short period in the early 1950s, if ever, did Parsons come close to claiming that empirical collectivities cohere on the basis of a highly integrated common culture.[3] The main value of the critique of the common culture or dominant ideology thesis is, as I see it, the demonstration of the degree to which a number of strands of modern social theory have converged on a cultural account of the coherence of Western societies. The alternative which is offered by Abercrombie, Hill and Turner raises problems in the present context. (Although see Turner, 1990a.) Their argument is that Marx's notion of 'the dull compulsion of economics' is the most appropriate way of characterizing societal coherence at least as far as modern, mainly capitalist, societies are concerned. Leaving on one side the issue of whether that notion adequately expresses Marx's own conception of the 'order' of capitalist societies (I believe it does not), one has to confront the plausibility of their argument. *How*, to be specific, does 'economics' come to be, and continue to be, 'compulsive'? In raising this question we immediately re-encounter central themes of classical sociology of the period 1890–1920. We are back to Durkheim's interest in the pre-contractual bases of contract and the pre-imperative bases of the imperative, as well as Simmel's attempt, as he put it, to build a storey beneath historical materialism, and Weber's focus on the ethos which sustains the modern monetary economy.

Such matters have recently been addressed in terms of such conceptions as materialist culture, hedonistic culture and the culture of materialism, one increasingly important aspect of the overall trend being the theme of consumerism (Featherstone, 1991a). With the exception of Marx's interest in commodity fetishism, it is not too much to say that pre-classical and classical sociology were almost entirely concerned with 'the supply side' of 'the economic factor'; that is, with the organization and work which goes into the production and offering for sale of economic goods. And with the important exception of Veblen's work on conspicuous consumption there has, at least until rather recently, not been a sociological parallel to the

Keynesian turn in economics; this, of course, involved an emphatic shift to interest in demand for economic goods and services. The contemporary sociological and anthropological interest in 'demand' represents a kind of culture lag, in so far as the significance of aggregate demand has been widely emphasized by economists for about half a century, while the greater part of sociological interest has been devoted, following the Weber thesis about Protestantism and the ethos of capitalism, to the work and production side of economic life. That deficiency is now being rectified, with significant implications for the way in which we think about culture (Campbell, 1987; Featherstone, 1991a). What has happened, to put the matter almost simplistically, is that whereas the focus on 'supply' encouraged the belief that culture is epiphenomenal, the focus on 'demand' now tends to encourage the belief that culture is in some way infrastructural. Be that as it may, it is becoming increasingly clear that the pre-economic basis of 'economic compulsion' is a very significant *Problemstellung* of modern sociology and anthropology.

What seems to be emerging is a kind of solution to – better, a transcendence of – the old materialism–idealism dilemma that has in various forms plagued the history of sociology, and which has also facilitated, until recently, the cleavage between the disciplines of economics and sociology. That 'solution' centers on the idea of *economic culture*, the ideas, values, symbols, and so on, which are more or less directly available for and implicated in economic action. While implied by Marx's concept of commodity fetishism and even more clearly suggested by Weber's devoting most of the last ten years of his life to the analysis of the 'economic ethics' of the major religious traditions, the notion of economic culture has had a surprising ring to many modern ears precisely because it puts together (again) that which had previously been analytically rendered asunder. In so far as we now begin genuinely to acknowledge, not merely rhetorically but also analytically, the sociological relevance of this category the danger remains that we will feel forced into taking sides on opposing claims as to what exactly has brought about this conjunction of the 'material' and the 'ideal.' 'Materialists' will claim that the apparent significance of the 'ideal' is really a consequence of the dynamics of material factors, while, somewhat less predictably, 'idealists' will claim that 'triumph' of the ideal is an immanent issue of 'ideas' or, at least, ideal interests.

Sociology, Cultural Studies and Globality

For the most part, the debate about culture among sociologists has been expressed along remarkably mechanical lines; by which I mean that the debate has continued in terms of choices between whether culture is more or less determined and whether it is determinative. From the pro-cultural side this has been remarkably self-defeating, in the sense that the 'culturalist' has already agreed upon the anti-culturalist rules of argument.

The 'culturalist' agrees to try to prove that culture explains more than the anti-culturalist about allegedly non-cultural matters. He or she (like Swidler, 1986) tries to show that 'social' sociology would be better at what it claims to do if it took culture seriously. I think that is so, but such attempts to legitimize the scientific value of culture are, in a way, anti-cultural. The mechanical orientation to the materialism–idealism problem has persisted, in a sense, as a form of materialism, ever since Marx himself attempted to *overcome* the antimony. In fact exceedingly few general social theorists have made their names since Marx without claiming in one way or another that they were about to solve or had actually solved the materialism–idealism problem or, at least, a problem closely related to it. Recently this has tended to take the form of attempting to 'reconstruct' historical materialism.

In one of his last essays, 'Religious and economic symbolism in the western world,' Parsons (1979) argued that the thematization of the economy, which he periodized as the Industrial Revolution of the late eighteenth and early nineteenth centuries, had identifiable cultural responses, the most fateful of which were and have been utilitarian individualism, '*Gemeinschaft* romanticism,' organic corporatism and Marxist socialism. The general, analytical idea of interpreting responses in pragmatic mode to 'material' change involves systematic rejection of the mechanical infrastructure–superstructure way of looking at things. In particular, what the late-Parsons approach suggests is that while much of culture is 'talk about' the 'productive forces' of human life, that does not entitle us to give greater priority to either 'material' or 'cultural' factors in the mainstream senses. In the frame of the present discussion, the most relevant implication of the late-Parsons conception of cultural responses to axial-global shifts has to do with the phenomenon of globalization as the truly 'post-industrial' phase of world history. In other words, some of the most significant cultural phenomena of our time have to do with responses to and interpretations of the global system as a whole. More specifically, globalization involves pressure on societies, civilizations and representatives of traditions, including both 'hidden' and 'invented' traditions, to sift the global-cultural scene for ideas and symbols considered to be relevant to their own identities. This consumption and syncretization of culture is, perhaps, the most neglected aspect of the revitalization of culture as a sociological motif. Some of these issues have already been raised, and more will be raised in the remaining discussions.

In this chapter I have so far said very little, at least directly, about the ways in which culture has been and is being treated in the expanding field of cultural studies. (It is interesting to note that in her major study of culture and agency Archer (1988) does not discuss developments in the field of cultural studies.)[4] This is primarily because my major concern was to address the theme of culture in fairly well demarcated sociology (and anthropology). But what is currently occurring in cultural studies cannot be relegated to the margins of even that bounded focus. The fact that cultural studies displays in some of its manifestations an aggressive attempt to challenge inattention to, or what are regarded as inadequate treatments of, culture on the part of social scientists makes this inadvisable; as, even more fundamentally, does the cultural studies tendency to reject much of the general thrust of sociology and other social sciences. Moreover, the fact that some workers in the field of cultural studies, as well as in communication studies, have had quite a lot to say about the global scene needs acknowledgment in the present context. Some aspects of that latter focus will receive attention in later chapters.

An indication of what cultural studies appears to 'stand for' is necessary at this point. Such an indication must undoubtedly mention the role of the Birmingham University Centre for Contemporary Cultural Studies, since the cultural studies critique of sociology in particular owes so much to the work of the Centre, notably its most influential figure (no longer at Birmingham), Stuart Hall (Grossberg et al., 1992). The Birmingham School has had what I will call a 'strong program' in cultural studies, 'strong' because of the weight of its critique of the social sciences and its explicit attempt to supplant or transcend them; 'strong' also because of its heavy commitment to the politicization of intellectual analysis – its eagerness, to use a key word employed frequently by many practitioners of cultural studies, to 'intervene' both in the public sphere of ideologies and politics and in the academy. Growing out of a certain strand of British Marxism, cultural studies (or cultural Marxism) has in its most well-known British version had a remarkable impact, particularly in the USA. Needless to say, there have been other influential sources and figures, some of them more traditionally Marxist than Hall's form of Gramscianism, others less so.

'Culture' appears in cultural studies in two major, intersecting forms. On the one hand, cultural studies is cultural in its focus on symbolic expression, text, rhetoric, discourse and so on. On the other hand, it is cultural in its tendency to use the idea of culture to embrace virtually every facet of human life, as when Hall (1986: 26) speaks of culture as 'the actual, grounded terrain of practices, languages and customs of any specific historical society.' The second tendency has much of its origin in the crisis within Marxism of which I have already spoken in this chapter. In any case, cultural studies has both reductionist ('textist') and expansive ('culture is everything') tendencies. A distinguishing feature of most forms of cultural studies is the commitment of many of its practitioners to the expansion of what can be called 'representational space.' Indeed the notion of culture *as* representation is quite strong in cultural studies (Wolff, 1991). Clearly 'representation' of women, gays, lesbians, 'native' peoples, neglected racial and ethnic groups, underprivileged classes and status groups, and so on has not been the unique preserve of cultural studies. But cultural studies has become increasingly conspicuous as a disciplinary site for the creation of representational space. And much of this development has a strong bearing on discussion of the global field – in the concern with perception of the Other, migration and the proliferation of diasporas, postcolonialism, identity formation, and so on.

The fluidity, expansiveness and, in a special sense, anti-disciplinarity of the concern with culture as representation, as well as resistance, has undoubtedly enriched its contemporary treatment and employment, not least through its elevation of the topic of *discourse* to priority status in the interpretation and/or analysis of sociocultural entities, large or small.[5] The constraints exercised by conventional ways of thinking about, or even unconventional ways of discussing, phenomena of interest (or, indeed of no interest) do have to be continuously challenged, nowhere more so than with respect to globality and globalization. Nonetheless, some words of caution are in order with respect to the cultural studies tendency to conflate culture with other dimensions of human life, to operate in terms of a specific ideological agenda and, in particular, with respect to its apparent unwillingness to take the issues of structural contingency and institutional 'reality' seriously, or at least seriously enough.[6]

Notes

1. My own position is partly indicated in Robertson (1974).
2. Norbert Elias's concept of the civilizing process is clearly an exception to the negative conception of civilization. For discussion of this and Elias's relationship to Freud on civilization and culture and the Frankfurt School's critique of the Enlightenment, see Bogner (1987). Aspects of Elias's work are discussed in Chapter 7 of this book. Habermas is also obviously another exception, although for different reasons.
3. The constant repetition of the canard that Parsons saw culture as the source of an unproblematically conceived social order is one of the more striking features of recent sociological writing on culture.
4. Aspects of Archer's book (1988) are discussed in Chapter 6.
5. There is also a contemporary 'anti-culture' intellectual movement (L. Abu-Lughod, 1991) which objects to the tendency to overemphasize the coherence of culture in cultural theories loyally because so many people have mixed ethnocultural origins.
6. Alexander (1990) has discussed some of the issues considered here from a somewhat different, but mainly compatible, perspective. He does not, however, address culture within a global perspective. On the other hand, Arnason has in a number of papers considered culture in a manner that is more directly relevant to global and intercivilizational themes. See in particular his discussion of Castoriadis (Arnason, 1989a). Arnason (1989a: 40) makes a very important point when he argues against Castoriadis's (1987) conception of 'imaginary signification' that 'central significations,' far from having no referent, in fact refer to 'the world with which the society is confronted and of which it nevertheless forms a part and they articulate it from different angles.'

3

MAPPING THE GLOBAL CONDITION

Nothing will be done anymore, without the whole world meddling in it. (Paul Valéry in Lesourne, 1986: 103)

We are on the road from the evening-glow of European philosophy to the dawn of world philosophy. (Karl Jaspers, 1957: 83–4)

Insofar as [present realities] have brought us a global present without a common past [they] threaten to render all traditions and all particular past histories irrelevant. (Hannah Arendt, 1957: 541)

The transformation of the medieval into the modern can be depicted in at least two different ways. In one sense it represents the trend towards the consolidation and strengthening of the territorial state . . . . In another sense it represents a reordering in the priority of international and domestic realms. In the medieval period the world, or transnational, environment was primary, the domestic secondary. (Richard Rosencrance, 1986: 77)

My primary concern here is to continue the discussion of the analytical and empirical aspects of globalization. I also want to raise some general questions about social theory. As far as the main issue is concerned, I set out the grounds for systematic analysis and interpretation of globalization since the mid-fifteenth century, indicating the major phases of globalization in recent world history and exploring some of the more salient aspects of the contemporary global circumstance from an analytical point of view. On the general-theoretical front I argue again that much of social theory is both a product of and an implicit reaction to, as opposed to a direct engagement with, the globalization process.

While there is rapidly growing interest in the issue of globalization, much of it is expressed very diffusely. It has become a widely used term in a number of theoretical, empirical and applied areas of intellectual inquiry, including the various 'policy sciences,' such as business studies and strategic studies. There is also a danger that 'globalization' will become an intellectual 'play zone,' a site for the expression of residual social-theoretical interests, interpretive indulgence, or the display of world-ideological preferences. I think we must take very seriously Immanuel Wallerstein's (1987: 309) contention that 'world-systems' analysis is not a theory about the world. 'It is a protest against the ways in which social scientific inquiry was structured for all of us at its inception in the middle of the nineteenth century.' Even though I do not, as I have said, subscribe to world-systems theory in the conventional sense of the term, primarily because of its economism, and am not pessimistic about the possibility of our being able to accomplish significant theoretical work *vis-à-vis* the world as a whole, I consider it to be of the utmost importance for us to realize fully that much of the conventional sociology which has developed since the first quarter of the twentieth century has been held in thrall by the virtually global institutionalization of the idea of the culturally cohesive and sequestered national society during the main phase of 'classical' sociology. Ironically, the global aspect of that phenomenon has received relatively little attention (Meyer, 1980).

Globalization and the Structuration of the World

The present discussion, in this and the following chapters, is a continuation of previous efforts to theorize the topic of globalization, a task made all the more difficult by the recent and continuing events in the territories of the old USSR, Eastern and Central Europe, China and elsewhere, which have disrupted virtually all of the conventional views concerning 'world order.' At the same time those events and the circumstances they have created make the analytical effort even more urgent. We have entered a phase of what appears to us in the 1990s to be great global uncertainty – so much so that the very idea of uncertainty promises to become globally institutionalized. Or, to put it in a very different way, there is an eerie relationship between postmodernist theories and the idea of postmodernity, on the one hand, and the geopolitical 'earthquakes' that we (the virtually *global we*) have recently experienced, on the other.

We need to enlarge our conception of 'world politics' in such a way as to facilitate systematic discussion, but not conflation, of the relationship between politics in the relatively narrow sense and the broad questions of 'meaning' which can only be grasped by wide-ranging, empirically sensitive interpretations of the global-human condition as a whole. Specifically, I argue that what is often called world politics has in the twentieth century hinged considerably upon the issue of the interpretation of and the response to modernity, aspects of which were politically and internationally thematized as the standard of 'civilization' (Gong, 1984) during the late nineteenth and early twentieth centuries with particular reference to the inclusion of non-European (mainly Asian) societies in Eurocentric 'international society' (Bull and Watson, 1984a).

Communism and 'democratic capitalism' have constituted alternative forms of acceptance of modernity (Parsons, 1964), although some would now argue that the recent and dramatic ebbing of communism can in part be attributed to its 'attempt to preserve the integrity of the premodern system' (Parsons, 1967: 484–5) by invoking 'socialism' as the central of a series of largely 'covert gestures of reconciliation . . . toward both the past and the future' (Parsons, 1967: 484).[1] On the other hand fascism and neo-fascism have, in spite of their original claims to the establishment of *new* societal and international 'orders' (as was explicitly the case with the primary Axis powers of World War II: Germany and Japan), been directly interested in *transcending or resolving* the problems of modernity. That issue has certainly not disappeared. The world politics of the global debate about modernity has rarely been considered of relevance to the latter and yet it is clear that, for example, conceptions of the past by the major belligerents in World War I illustrated a sharp contrast between 'the temporalities of the nations of each alliance system and underlying causes of resentment and misunderstanding' (Kern, 1983: 277), with the nations whose leaders considered themselves to be relatively deprived – notably Germany and Japan – being particularly concerned to confront the problem of modernity in political and military terms.[2] Sociologists and philosophers are familiar with many intellectual developments of the 1920s and 1930s, but these have not been linked to the broad domain of *Realpolitik*. It may well be that the Cold War that developed after the defeat of great-power Fascism constituted an interruption and partial freezing of the world-cultural politics of modernity and that with the ending of the Cold War as conventionally understood those politics will now be resumed in a situation of much greater global complexity, in the interrelated contexts of more intense globalization, the growing political presence of Islam, the discourse of postmodernity and 'the ethnic revival' (A.D. Smith, 1981), which itself may be considered as *an aspect of* the contemporary phase of globalization (Lechner, 1984).

Any attempt to theorize the general field of globalization must lay the grounds for relatively patterned discussion of the politics of the global-human condition, by attempting to indicate the structure of any viable discourse about the shape and 'meaning' of the world as a whole. I regard this as an urgent matter partly because much of the explicit intellectual interpretation of the global scene is being conducted by academics operating under the umbrella of 'cultural studies' with exceedingly little attention to the issue of global complexity and structural contingency, except for frequently invoked labels such as 'late capitalism,' 'disorganized capitalism,' or the salience of 'the transnational corporation.' This is not at all to say that the economic factor is unimportant, or that the 'textual,' 'power-knowledge,' or 'hegemonic' aspects of the 'world system' are of minor significance. Rather, I am insisting that both the economics and the culture of the global scene should be analytically connected to the general structural and actional features of the global field.

I maintain that what has come to be called globalization is, in spite of differing conceptions of that theme, best understood as indicating the problem of *the form* in terms of which the world becomes 'united,' but by no means integrated in naive functionalist mode (Robertson and Chirico, 1985). Globalization as a topic is, in other words, a conceptual entry to the problem of 'world order' in the most general sense – but, nevertheless, an entry which has no cognitive purchase without considerable discussion of historical and comparative matters. It is, moreover, a phenomenon which clearly requires what is conventionally called interdisciplinary treatment.

Traditionally the general field of the study of the world as a whole has been approached via the discipline of international relations (or, more diffusely, international studies). That discipline (sometimes regarded as a subdiscipline of political science) was consolidated during particular phases of the overall globalization process and is now being reconstituted in reference to developments in other disciplinary areas, including the humanities (Der Derian and Shapiro, 1989). Indeed, the first concentrated thrust into the study of the world as a whole on the part of sociologists, during the 1960s (discussed in Nettl and Robertson, 1968), was undertaken, as has been seen, mainly in terms of the idea of the sociology of international relations. There can be little doubt that to this day the majority of social scientists still think of 'extra-societal' matters in terms of 'international relations' (including variants thereof, such as transnational relations, non-governmental relations, supranational relations, world politics and so on). Nonetheless that tendency is breaking down, in conjunction with considerable questioning of what Michael Mann (1986) has called the unitary conception of society. While there have been attempts to carve out a new discipline for the study of the world as a whole, including the long-historical making of the contemporary 'world system' (e.g. Bergesen, 1980a), my position is that it is not so much that we need a new discipline in order to study the world as a whole but that social theory in the broadest sense – as a perspective which stretches across the social sciences and humanities (Giddens and Turner, 1987: 1) and even the natural sciences – should be refocused and expanded so as to make concern with 'the world' a central hermeneutic, and in such a way as to constrain empirical and comparative-historical research in the same direction.

Undoubtedly, as we have already seen, there *have* been various attempts in the history of social theory to move along such lines but the very structure of the globalization process has inhibited such efforts from taking off into a fully fledged research program, mostly notably during the crucial take-off period of globalization itself, 1870–1925. So we are led to the argument that exerting ourselves to develop *global* social theory is not merely an exercise demanded by the transparency of the processes rendering the contemporary world as a whole as a single place but also that our labors in that regard are crucial to the empirical understanding of the bases upon which the matrix of contemporary disciplinarity and interdisciplinarity rests. There has been an enormous amount of talk in recent years about self-reflexiveness, the critical-theoretic posture, and the like; but ironically much of that talk has been about as far removed from discussion of the real world – in the twofold sense of quotidian contemporary realities and differences *and* the concrete global circumstance – as it could be. Much of fashionable social theory has favored the abstract and, from a simplistic global perspective, 'the local' to the great neglect of the global and civilizational contours and bases of Western social theory itself. The distinction between the global and the local is becoming very complex and problematic, to the extent that we should now perhaps speak in such terms as the global institutionalization of the life-world and the localization of globality.

In the second half of the 1980s 'globalization' (and its problematic variant, 'internationalization') became a commonly used term in intellectual, business, media and other circles, in the process acquiring a number of meanings, with varying degrees of precision. This has been a source of frustration, but not necessarily a cause for surprise or alarm, to those of us who had sought earlier in the decade to establish a relatively strict definition of globalization as part of an attempt to come to terms systematically with major aspects of contemporary 'meaning and change' (Robertson, 1978). Nevertheless a stream of analysis and research *has* been developed around the general idea, if not always the actual concept, of globalization. It is my intention here to indicate some of the most pressing issues in this area – not so much by surveying and evaluating different approaches to the making of the contemporary world system, world society, the global ecumene, or whatever one chooses to call the late twentieth-century world as a whole; but rather by considering some relatively neglected analytical and historical themes.

I deal here with relatively recent aspects of globalization, although I want to emphasize as strongly as possible that in doing so I am not suggesting for a moment that moves and thrusts in the direction of global unicity are unique to relatively recent history. I also argue that globalization is intimately related to modernity and modernization, as well as to postmodernity and 'postmodernization' (in so far as the latter pair of motifs have definite analytical purchase). In attempting to justify that proposal I am by no means suggesting that work within the frame of 'the globalization paradigm' should be limited to the relatively recent past. All I am maintaining is that the concept of globalization *per se* is most clearly applicable to a particular series of relatively recent developments concerning *the concrete structuration of the world as a whole*. The term 'structuration' has been deliberately chosen. Although I will shortly consider some aspects of Anthony Giddens's work on 'the global scene,' I cannot address here the general problems which arise from the concept of structuration (Cohen, 1989; Bryant and Jary, 1991). I will say only that if the notion of structuration is to be of assistance to us analytically in the decades ahead it has to be moved out of its quasi-philosophical context, its confinement within the canonical discourses about subjectivity and objectivity, individual and society, and so on (Archer, 1988). It has to be made directly relevant to *the world* in which we live. It has to contribute to the understanding of how the global 'system' has been and continues to be *made*. It has to be focused on the production and reproduction of 'the world' as the most salient plausibility structure of our time (Wuthnow, 1978: 65). The same applies to the cultural-agency problematic which Margaret Archer (1988) has recently theorized.

Human history has been replete with ideas concerning the physical structure, the geography, the cosmic location and the spiritual and/or secular significance of the world (Wagar, 1971); movements and organizations concerned with the patterning and/or the unification of the world as a whole have intermittently appeared for at least the last two thousand years; and ideas about the relationship between the universal and the particular have been central to all of the major civilizations. Even something like what has recently been called 'the global–local nexus' (or the 'local–global nexus') was thematized as long ago as the second century BC when Polybius, in his *Universal History*, wrote with reference to the rise of the Roman empire: 'Formerly the things which happened in the world had no connection among themselves . . . But since then all events are united in a common bundle' (Kohn, 1971: 121).[3] However, the crucial considerations are that it has not been until relatively recent times that it has been realistically thought that 'humanity is rapidly becoming, physically speaking, a single society' (Hobhouse, 1906: 331), and that it has not been until quite recently that considerable numbers of people living on various parts of the planet have spoken and acted in direct reference to the problem of the 'organization' of the entire, heliocentric world. It is in relation to this heavily contested problem of the concrete patterning and consciousness of the world, including resistance to globality, that I seek to center the concept and the discourse of globalization.

The world as a whole could, in theory, have become the reality which it now is in ways and along trajectories other than those that have actually obtained (Lechner, 1989). The world could, in principle, have been rendered as a 'singular system' (Moore, 1966) via the imperial hegemony of a single nation or a 'grand alliance' between two or more dynasties or nations; the victory of 'the universal proletariat'; the global triumph of a particular form of organized religion; the crystallization of 'the world spirit'; the yielding of nationalism to the ideal of 'free trade'; the success of the world-federalist movement; the worldwide triumph of a trading company; or in yet other ways. Some of these have in fact held sway at certain moments in world history. Indeed, in coming to terms analytically with the contemporary circumstance we have to acknowledge that some such possibilities are as old as world history in any meaningful sense of that phrase and have greatly contributed to the existence of the globalized world of the late twentieth century. Moreover, much of world history can be fruitfully considered as sequences of 'miniglobalization,' in the sense that, for example, historic empire formation involved the unification of previously sequestered territories and social entities. There have also been shifts in the opposite direction, as with the deunification of medieval Europe, of which Rosencrance (1986) has spoken – although the rise of the territorial state also promoted imperialism and thus conceptions of the world as a whole.

Nonetheless, when all is said and done no single possibility has, or so I claim, been more continuously prevalent than another. There may have been periods in world history when one such possibility was more of a 'globalizing force' than others – and that must certainly be a crucial aspect of the discussion of globalization in the long-historical mode – but we have not as a world-people moved into the present global-human circumstance along one or even a small cluster of these particular trajectories. Yet in the present climate of 'globality' there is a strong temptation for some to insist that the single world of our day can be accounted for in terms of one particular process or factor, such as 'Westernization,' 'imperialism' or, in the dynamic and diffuse sense, 'civilization.' As I argue more specifically in later chapters, the problem of globality is very likely to become a basis of major ideological and analytical cleavages of the twenty-first century, as the idea of 'the new world order' in its political, military and economic senses, not least because the connotations of that term as used in pre-Axis and Axis contexts are so negative. While I do not subscribe to the view that social theorists should at all costs attempt to be neutral about these and other matters, I am committed to the argument that one's moral stance should be realistic and that one should have no intrinsically vested interest in the attempt to map this or any other area of the human condition. More precisely, I argue that systematic comprehension of the structuration of world order is essential to the viability of any form of contemporary theory and that such comprehension must involve analytical separation of the factors that have facilitated the shift towards a single world – for example the spread of capitalism, Western imperialism and the development of a global media system – from the *general and global* agency-structure (and/or culture) theme. While the empirical relationship between the two sets of issues is of great importance (and, of course, complex), conflation of them leads us into all sorts of difficulties and inhibits our ability to come to terms with the basic but shifting terms of the contemporary world order, including the 'structure' of 'disorderliness.'

Thus we must return to the question of the actual form of recent and contemporary moves in the direction of global interdependence and global consciousness. In posing the basic question in this way we immediately confront the critical issue of the period during which the move towards the world as a singular system became more or less inexorable. If we think of the history of the world as consisting for a very long time in *the objectiveness* of a variety of different civilizations existing in varying degrees of separation from each other, our main task now is to consider the ways in which the world 'moved' from being merely 'in itself' to the problem or the possibility of its being 'for itself.' Before coming directly to that vital issue I must attend briefly to some basic analytical matters. This I do via the statement of Giddens (1987: 255–93) on 'Nation-States in the Global State System.'

Giddens makes much of the point that 'the development of the sovereignty of the modern state from its beginnings depends upon a reflexively monitored set of relations between states' (Giddens, 1987: 263). He argues that the period of treaty making following World War I 'was effectively the first point at which a reflexively monitored system of nation-states came to exist globally' (1987: 256). I fully concur with both the emphasis on the importance of the post-World War I period and Giddens's claim that 'if a new and formidably threatening pattern of war was established at this time, so was a new pattern of peace' (1987: 256). More generally, Giddens's argument that the development of the modern state has been guided by increasingly global norms concerning its sovereignty is, if not original, of great importance. However, he tends to conflate the issue of the homogenization of the state (in Hegel's sense) – what Giddens calls 'the universal scope of the nation-state' (1987: 264) – and the issue of relationships between states.

It is important to make a distinction between the diffusion of expectations concerning the external legitimacy and mode of operation of the state and the development of regulative norms concerning the relationships between states; while readily acknowledging that the issue of the powers and limits of the state has been *empirically* linked to the structuring of the relationships between states and, moreover, that it constitutes a crucial axis of globalization. James Der Derian (1989) has recently drawn attention to an important aspect of that theme by indicating the proximity of the formal 'Declaration of the Rights of Man' that sovereignty resides in the nation to Jeremy Bentham's declaration in the same year of 1789 that there was a need for a new word – 'international' – which would 'express, in a more significant way, the branch of law which goes commonly under the name of the *law of nations*' (Bentham, 1948: 326).

So while the two issues upon which I have been dwelling via Giddens's analysis undoubtedly have been and remain closely interdependent, it is crucial to keep them analytically apart in order that we may fully appreciate variations in the nature of the empirical connections between them. In sum, the problem of contingency arising from state sovereignty and the development of relational rules between sovereign units is not the same as the issue of the crystallization and diffusion of conceptions of national statehood (A.D. Smith, 1979). Nor is it the same as the development and spread of conceptions of the shape and meaning of 'international society' (Gong, 1984). The second set of matters is on a different 'level' than that addressed by Giddens.

My primary reason for emphasizing this matter is that it provides an immediate entry to what I consider the most pressing general problem in the contemporary discussion of globalization. Giddens's analysis is a good example of an attempt to move toward the global circumstance via the conventional concerns of sociological theory. While readily conceding that it was his specific, initial concern to talk about the modern nation state and the internal and external violence with which its development has been bound up, the fact remains that in spite of all of his talk about global matters at the end of his analysis, Giddens is restricted precisely by his having to center 'the current world system' within a discussion of 'the global *state* system' (Giddens, 1987: 276–7; emphasis added). Even though he eventually separates, in analytical terms, the nation-state system (with the ambiguity I have indicated) as the political aspect of the world system from the 'global information system' (as relating to 'symbolic orders/modes of discourse'); the 'world-capitalist economy' (as the economic dimension of the world system); and the 'world military order' (as concerning 'law/modes of sanction') – along lines reminiscent of approaches of the 1960s (Nettl and Robertson, 1968) and, ironically, of a general Parsonian, functional-imperative approach – Giddens ends up with a 'map' of what he reluctantly calls the world system, which is centered upon his conflated characterization of the rise of the modern state system. Giddens (1990) has of course expanded upon, and modified his thinking about what he now calls globalization, in relation to modernity and the idea of postmodernity. That will be the specific focus of Chapter 9.

'Mapping' the world social-scientifically is, of course, a common procedure; it crystallized during the 1960s both with the diffusion of perceptions concerning the existence of the Third World and with polarized First (liberal-capitalist) and Second (industrializing-communist) Worlds. Ever since that period – the beginning of the current phase of contemporary, late twentieth-century globalization – there has proliferated a large number of different and, indeed, conflicting ideological and/or 'scientific' maps of the world-system of national societies, so much so that it is reasonable to say that the discourse of mapping is a vital ingredient of global-political culture, one which fuses geography (as in the use of North–South and East–West terminology) with political, economic, cultural and other forms of placement of nations on the global-international map. Much of this overall effort has resulted in significant work – for example Johan Galtung's *The True Worlds* (1980) and Peter Worsley's (1984) lengthy discussion of the cultures of 'the three worlds.' Indeed, the kind of work which has strongly reminded us of the major cleavages and discontinuities in the world as a whole is a significant antidote to those who now speak blithely in 'global village' terms of a single world. Nonetheless there can be no denying that the world is much more singular than it was as recently as, say, the 1950s. The crucial question remains of the basic form or structure in terms of which that shift has occurred. That that form has been *imposed* upon certain areas of the world is, of course, a crucial issue, but until the matter of form (more elaborately, structuration) is adequately thematized our ability to comprehend the dynamics of the making of the world as a whole will be severely limited.

A Minimal Phase Model of Globalization

I offer here what I call and advocate as a necessarily minimal model of globalization. This model does not make grand assertions about primary factors, major mechanisms, and so on. Rather, it indicates the major constraining tendencies which have been operating in relatively recent history as far as world order and the compression of the world in our time are concerned.

One of the most pressing tasks in this regard is to confront the issue of the undoubted salience of the unitary nation state – more diffusely, the national society – since about the mid-eighteenth century and at the same time to acknowledge its historical uniqueness, in a sense its abnormality (McNeill, 1986). The homogeneous nation state – homogeneous here in the sense of a culturally homogenized, administered citizenry (B. Anderson, 1983) – is a construction of a particular form of life. That we ourselves have been increasingly subject to its constraints does not mean that for analytical purposes it has to be accepted as *the* departure point for analyzing and understanding the world. This is why I have argued not merely that national societies should be regarded as constituting but one general reference point for the analysis of the global-human circumstance, but that we have to recognize even more than we do now that the prevalence of the national society in the twentieth century is an aspect of globalization (Robertson, 1989a) – that the diffusion of *the idea of* the national society as a form of institutionalized societalism (Lechner, 1989) was central to the accelerated globalization which began to occur just over a hundred years ago. I have also argued more specifically that the two other major components of globalization have been, in addition to national systems and the system of international relations, conceptions of individuals and of humankind. It is in terms of the shifting relationships between and the 'upgrading' of these reference points that globalization has occurred in recent centuries. This pattern has certainly been greatly affected by and subject to all sorts of economic, political and other processes and actions; but my task here is to legitimize the need for an overall comprehension of the global circumstance.

I now propose, in skeletal terms, that the temporal-historical path to the present circumstance of a very high degree of global density and complexity can be delineated as follows:

Phase I: The Germinal Phase Lasting in Europe from the early fifteenth until the mid-eighteenth century. Incipient growth of national communities and downplaying of the medieval 'transnational' system. Expanding scope of the Catholic church. Accentuation of concepts of the individual and of ideas about humanity. Heliocentric theory of the world and beginning of modern geography; spread of Gregorian calendar.

Phase II: The Incipient Phase Lasting – mainly in Europe – from the mid-eighteenth century until the 1870s. Sharp shift towards the idea of the homogeneous, unitary state; crystallization of conceptions of formalized international relations, of standardized citizenly individuals and a more concrete conception of humankind. Sharp increases in legal conventions and agencies concerned with international and transnational regulation and communication. International exhibitions. Beginning of problem of 'admission' of non-European societies to 'international society.' Thematization of nationalism–internationalism issue.

Phase III: The Take-off Phase   Lasting from the 1870s until the mid-1920s. 'Take-off' here refers to a period during which the increasingly manifest globalizing tendencies of previous periods and places gave way to a single, inexorable form centered upon the four reference points, and thus constraints, of national societies, generic individuals (but with a masculine bias), a single 'international society,' and an increasingly singular, but not unified conception of humankind. Early thematization of 'the problem of modernity.' Increasingly global conceptions of the 'correct outline' of an 'acceptable' national society; thematization of ideas concerning national and personal identities; inclusion of a number of non-European societies in 'international society'; international formalization and attempted implementation of ideas about humanity. Globalization of immigration restrictions. Very sharp increase in number and speed of global forms of communication. The first 'international novels.' Rise of ecumenical movement. Development of global competitions – for example the Olympics and Nobel prizes. Implementation of world time and near-global adoption of Gregorian calendar. First *world* war.

Phase IV: The Struggle-for-Hegemony Phase   Lasting from the mid-1920s until the late-1960s. Disputes and wars about the fragile terms of the dominant globalization process established by the end of the take-off period. Establishment of the League of Nations and then the United Nations. Principle of national independence established. Conflicting conceptions of modernity (Allies v. the Axis), followed by high point of the Cold War (conflict within 'the modern project'). Nature of and prospects for humanity sharply focused by the Holocaust and use of the atomic bomb. The crystallization of the Third World.

Phase V: The Uncertainty Phase   Beginning in the late 1960s and displaying crisis tendencies in the early 1990s. Heightening of global consciousness in late 1960s. Moon landing. Accentuation of 'post-materialist' values. End of the Cold War and manifest rise of the problem of 'rights' and widespread access to nuclear and thermonuclear weaponry. Number of global institutions and movements greatly increases. Sharp acceleration in means of global communication. Societies increasingly facing problems of multiculturality and polyethnicity. Conceptions of individuals rendered more complex by gender, sexual, ethnic and racial considerations. Civil rights become a global issue. International system more fluid – end of bipolarity. Concern with humankind as a species-community greatly enhanced, particularly via environmental movements. Arising of interest in world civil society and world citizenship, in spite of 'the ethnic revolution.' Consolidation of global media system, including rivalries about such. Islam as a deglobalizing/reglobalizing movement. Earth Summit in Rio de Janeiro.

This is merely an outline, with much detail and more rigorous analysis and interpretation of the shifting relationships between and the relative autonomization of each of the four major components to be worked out. Some of this is attempted in the following chapters. Clearly one of the most important empirical questions has to do with the extent to which the form of globalization which was set firmly in motion during the period 1870–1925 will 'hold' in the coming decades. In more theoretical vein, much more needs to be done to demonstrate the ways in which the selective responses of relevant collective actors, particularly societies, to globalization play a crucial part in the making of the world as a whole. Different forms of societal participation in the globalization process make a crucial difference to its precise form. My main point is that there is a general autonomy and 'logic' to the globalization process, which operates in *relative* independence of strictly societal and other more conventionally studied sociocultural processes. The global system is not simply an outcome of processes of basically intra-societal origin (*contra* Luhmann, 1982b) or even a development of the inter-state system. Its making has been and continues to be much more complex than that.

Notes

1. It is of more than passing interest to note that in speaking of communism as a radical branch of one of 'the great "reform" movements of postmedieval Western history' – socialism – Talcott Parsons said in 1964 that 'it seems a safe prediction that Communism will, from its own internal dynamics, evolve in the direction of the restoration – or where it has yet not existed, the institution – of political democracy' (1964: 396–7). On the other hand, Parsons insisted, problematically, that the *internationalism* of communism had made a crucial contribution to world order.
2. Ronald Inglehart (1990: 33) observes in the course of his empirical analysis of culture in advanced industrial societies 'that the publics of the three major Axis powers, Germany, Japan, and Italy, all tend to be underachievers in life satisfaction. The traumatic discrediting of their social and political systems that accompanied their defeat in World War II may have left a legacy of cynicism that their subsequent social change and economic success has still not entirely erased.'
3. I owe the precise phrases 'local–global nexus' and 'global–local nexus' to Chadwick Alger (1988).

4

WORLD-SYSTEMS THEORY, CULTURE AND IMAGES OF WORLD ORDER

The overall process of globalization, and the resulting single global arena, can best be treated in terms of what may be called a 'voluntaristic' theory. That theory rests upon the following main points. First, the global 'system' is not reducible to a scene consisting merely of societies and/or other large-scale actors. Thus individuals, societies, the system of societies, as well as mankind, are to be treated in terms of one coherent analytical framework, but reductionism – notably functionalist, utilitarian and materialist forms thereof – must be avoided.[1] The global field as a whole is a sociocultural 'system' which has resulted from the compression of – to the point that it increasingly imposes constraints upon, but also differentially empowers – civilizational cultures, national societies, intra- and cross-national movements and organizations, sub-societies and ethnic groups, intra-societal quasi-groups, individuals, and so on. As the general process of globalization proceeds there is a concomitant constraint upon such entities to 'identify' themselves in relation to the global-human circumstance. In addition, globalization also yields new actors and 'third cultures' – such as transnational movements and international organizations – that are oriented, negatively or positively, to the global-human circumstance. But while I advocate a specifically global point of view, this does not force us to account for globalization only in terms of entities at a particular level – be it global or sub-global. In principle, a multidimensional theory ranges across levels of analysis, precisely to examine new global constraints and involvements of the social entities sociology has traditionally dealt with.

Second, it is equally important to avoid reductionism in dealing with the analytical dimensions of the process of globalization. Thus far, the emergence of what some call the modern world-system has been discussed in either political or economic terms. I want to go beyond relatively simple models of a 'world polity' or a 'world economy' by pointing to the independent dynamics of global culture and to the problematic status of the 'culture factor' in much of current world-systems theory (Wallerstein, 1990). In particular, I will argue that cultural pluralism is itself a constitutive feature of the contemporary global circumstance and that conceptions of the world-system, including symbolic responses to and interpretations of globalization, are themselves important factors in determining the trajectories of that very process.

Finally, one of my aims is to raise what may be called the 'problem of global order,' in addition to, or perhaps even instead of, the old problem of social and societal order. But rather than emphasizing the crystallized structure of the world-system, a voluntaristic theory remains sensitive to empirical developments, and thus stresses the processes of globalization and the continuing contentiousness of global order. One of my basic points is that varying responses to globalization influence that very process, so that its direction and outcome, and hence the shape of the global field itself, are still very much 'up for grabs.'

Modernity – Recent and Classical Themes

The waves of interest in sociologies of global and international structures and processes that occurred in the 1960s such as expressed by Lagos (1963), Galtung (1966), Horowitz (1966), Moore (1966), Nettl and Robertson (1968), Frank (1969), and Parsons (1971), was developed in significant part in relation to the more well-tried themes of development, industrialization and modernization. In their different ways the 'globalists' of the 1960s argued that approaching the theme of the trajectories, characteristics and dynamics of societal change in the modern world in solely comparative terms involved a highly unrealistic neglect of global or, at least, intersocietal constraints. In other words, the study of 'modernization,' 'development' and so on was being undertaken as if there were no concrete relationships between societies, let alone the possibility that over and beyond the phenomenon of societal interaction there was a global circumstance *per se*.

The analysis of societal change – and, more diffusely, of sociocultural change in general terms – that was paradigmatically dominant in the 1950s and 1960s was a truncated version of the image of change that had been crystallized in the period of classical sociology (1890–1920). Western social scientists of the 1950s and 1960s basically worked with a three-types, sequential image of change: primitive or traditional; developing; and developed societies. That image – whether explicitly acknowledged or not – followed to a significant degree images which had been quite elaborately explicated in the late nineteenth and early twentieth centuries. The image of the 1950s and 1960s echoed in part such well-known conceptions as the shifts from societies based on status to those based on contract; from societies characterized by mechanical solidarity to those characterized by organic solidarity; from feudal societies to capitalist societies and, as in the most sociologically invoked conception of all, from *Gemeinschaft* to *Gesellschaft*. That the proponents of those older images disputed – often sharply – with one another is of little consequence in the immediate context. They shared the view that – whatever the sociocultural dynamics and determinants involved and the existential problems raised – a 'Great Transformation' had occurred in the Western world between the medieval period and the late nineteenth century (Polanyi, 1957). Their particular interest was in the full flowering of the new form of society during the so-called *fin-de-siècle*, which meant that a large number of aspects of the new societal form received attention. Those aspects included, quite significantly, various fundamental problems in the formation of that new type of society. *Gesellschaft* was by no means taken for granted.

Although one should be wary of exaggeration on this point, it may be said that the years between World War I and the years immediately following World War II constituted a parenthesis in social-scientific (and related modes of more ideological) thinking along the lines suggested by the progressivist thinkers of the nineteenth century and the *fin-de-siècle* writers of the early twentieth century. It might not be too much to say that 'the long war' lasting from 1914 until 1945 itself partly involved an ideological conflict over the rival merits of the diagnoses of the past and the prognoses which had been generated in the debate about the transition to modernity that had reached its first culmination in the years before 1914. The point of more direct significance is that when thinking on a large scale about long-run trajectories of societal change was resumed in the West (to use the latter term very flexibly) in the late 1940s and early 1950s the frame of reference was in one sense much narrower than it had been before the parenthesis, yet in another respect much broader.

The revival of interest in large-scale transformation of societies in the late 1940s and, more particularly, the early 1950s was mostly framed by concern about the condition of what increasingly became known from the mid-1950s onwards as the Third World. The interest in societal transformation in those years was particularly focused on economic and 'quality of life' matters of a relatively tangible kind (such as education and physical health).[2] The focus was narrower than the classical interest, in so far as the latter had been as much if not more concerned with diffuse issues such as modes of individual existence, new forms of social solidarity, the degree of meaningfulness of modern life and the attributes of social interaction in the new form of society. In other words, whereas the late nineteenth- and early twentieth-century interest in the Great Transformation was largely dictated by considerations of the breakup of 'old European' styles of life and what the future held for Western societies in that regard, the interest in societal transformation that crystallized in the 1950s hardly touched such issues. In so far as it touched them at all it was in terms of how 'primordial' attachments to traditional forms of community and culture had to be severely and problematically attenuated in order that Third World societies might be able to 'modernize' along paths resembling those supposedly taken in the past by the 'more developed' societies (see Geertz, 1963). Relatively little attention was being paid at that time to older, classical problems posed by the family of concepts centered upon *Gesellschaft*, the only fairly conspicious exception being those promoting (and then only in a highly Western focus) the revival of the concerns expressed in the 1930s by members of the Frankfurt School. In contrast to some of the better-known – but by no means all of the – images of the Great Transformation produced in the nineteenth and early twentieth centuries, the Third World focused analyses that rapidly developed in the 1950s and remained conspicuous up to at least the early 1970s tended to include a third form of society which was considered to be transitional between two polar types. It may be added that in such analyses *Gemein-schaft* aspects of the 'least-developed' type were regarded as problematic in the development toward a more *Gesellschaft*-like society.

But in one respect the work on 'modernization and development' was broader in orientation or, at least, encouraged perspectives which became broader than the direct concerns of the classical sociologists, namely, in its near global foci. I have, however, acknowledged certain 'global openings' in the work of late nineteenth- and early twentieth-century sociologists.

For the most part the concern with modernity (or, in somewhat different but still very significant form, modernism) has not been coordinated analytically with the phenomenon of 'globality.' Few of those concerned with the crystallization of the globe as a single place or of the entire world as a sociocultural system have clearly expressed interest in the kinds of theme first explicitly expressed by the writers of the *fin de siècle* and continued most clearly in Frankfurtian and post-Frankfurtian critical theory.[3] On the other hand, few of those who have been concerned with the tradition established by the classical sociologists have considered the 'deep' features of modernity in systematic global terms. Berger (Berger et al., 1973; Berger 1974) has dealt with both modernity in the classical sense and modernization in the more contemporary sense. With special sensitiv-ity to the symbolic dimensions of the modern experience, he has emphas-ized the costs of modernity/modernization in the forms of 'homelessness' and 'sacrifice.' However, Berger does not by any means, even in his recent work, directly treat the global condition as such, and overemphasizes the costs and discontents of modernity – the side of the classical tradition which is fundamentally critical of *Gesellschaft*. Habermas (1974, 1981a) also deals with both classical themes and the contemporary sociocultural condition. The apparent aim of his reconstruction, critique and extension of classical theories is to provide a more comprehensive assessment of the domination of meaningful life-worlds by the operation of functionally rationalized systems in capitalist societies. Although his theory of communicative rationality is certainly not simply a romantic critique of the discontents of capitalist modernity, Habermas's treatment of the life-world in opposition to system functioning is rather one-sidedly critical of the accomplishments of modern societies, and at least runs the risk of being equated with a *Gemeinschaft*-oriented attack on an alienating *Gesellschaft*-type of society. In addition I would agree with Lyotard (1984) to the extent that the consensus envisioned by Habermas may be impossible to achieve in view of the modern differentiation of life-spheres and language-games – a point that will be reinforced below in the discussion of global cultural pluralism.

Nevertheless, what may be the most significant feature of modern history – the 'creation' of a world 'system' – has largely been attended to in terms of its 'hard realities' (economic or political), to the neglect of interest in the relevance of some of the central themes involved in the birth of modern sociology (Robertson, 1977, 1983a, 1983b). Even to that conclusion there are, fortunately, exceptions.[4] The most relevant of these in the immediate context emerge from debates which have arisen within Wallerstein-centered world-systems theory.

Wallerstein and Beyond

The development of Wallerstein's work which, it should again be noted, initially centered on modernization in the more conventional sense (see Hopkins and Wallerstein, 1967), fits the trend I described earlier of an increasingly global orientation emerging in the discourse of societal modernization. Although various sociologists had established an interest in global analysis in the 1960s, Wallerstein's work in the 1970s and early 1980s contributed much to the 'global shift' in sociological theory. Throughout most of his writing, as critics have pointed out, the logic of his explanations is functionalistic, in so far as units' roles in the system account for their actual operation; and his explanatory factors are mostly 'material' and 'objective,' even when it comes to explanation of disequilibrium, conflict and, at least until recently, cultural variety and continuity.[5] Actions of collective units on the global scene are generally explained in terms of their knowledge of the situation, their given means and interests, and their differential capacity to seize varying opportunities – indeed, a utilitarian approach (cf. Bergesen, 1980a).

Wallerstein might claim, of course, that this type of analysis is required to capture the working of the modern world system itself, on the grounds that the modern world system has been driven by primarily economic processes (see Robertson, 1985c). Much can be granted to that argument and few of the extended critiques of Wallerstein's work have done much more in that regard than maintain (very plausibly) that Wallerstein has granted insufficient autonomy to the state – and, more particularly, interstate, or international, relations *per se*.[6] In any case, even if we were to agree about the prime-mover significance of 'the economy' in the making of the modern world, that does not in and of itself lead to the simple conclusion that – to take up the major problem – 'culture' has been epiphenomenal. Wallerstein's record with respect to that central issue is not entirely clear-cut. For long, he explicitly stated that 'culture' is to be regarded as epiphenomenal. Yet he has devoted significant portions of his major works to discussion of cultural, particularly religious, matters (Wallerstein, 1974a, 1980) and, indeed, acknowledged the significance of cultural variety as part of his initial definition of the modern world-system (Wallerstein, 1974a) and as an empirical aspect of world-systemic order (Wallerstein, 1979).

But the explicit treatment of culture as epiphenomenal involved, *inter alia*, the overlooking of the fact that the thematization of the economy – particularly in the Western world from approximately the late eighteenth to the late nineteenth century – was accompanied by quasi-religious (as well as straightforwardly religious) attempts to give it meaning. Among the more significant of those symbolic constructions were economistic socialism; utopian socialism; economistic individualism; and traditionalistic communalism (see Dumont, 1977; Parsons, 1979; Bourricaud, 1981; Robertson, 1982; Seidman, 1983). To imply that each of these (conflicting) orientations was and/or has since become epiphenomenal is, to put it mildly, to underestimate their significance. Specifically it is misleading to imply that cultural responses to and interpretations of the autonomization of the economy are to be regarded as epiphenomenal.

All of this is to leave, for the moment, on one side the issue of the degree to which the economization of the world has proceeded without 'cultural guidance.' Assuming that we can speak of the different symbolic constructions put upon the various clusters of meanings ascribed to the 'liberation' and recognition of the increasingly global strength of the economic factor, the most pressing need now becomes to address systematically the contemporary global human circumstance in similar terms (Robertson, 1982). In other words the thematization of globality, not simply the global economy, is at present the object of symbolic constructions. Just as, according to the classical authors, the analysis of modernity required that close attention be paid to cultural modes of dealing with emerging *Gesellschaft*, a multidimensional perspective on global modernity should include paying substantial attention to symbolic modes of dealing with the rapidly emerging global field. Indeed, one of the main thrusts of the present discussion consists in the proposition that the problem of modernity has been expanded to – in a sense subsumed by – the problem of globality. Many of the particular themes of modernity – fragmentation of life-worlds, structural differentiation, cognitive and moral relativity, widening of experiential scope, ephemerality – have been exacerbated in the process of globalization, while the threat of species death has been significantly added to them.[7]

Wallerstein's functional-utilitarian approach – whatever its virtues in accounting for particular processes – has also produced certain dilemmas in world-systems theory, which have to do especially with the issues just raised. For example, in essays written during the 1970s Wallerstein (for example, 1979) became aware of tensions between 'subjective' and 'objective' aspects of the world-system – as in the case of ascribed status groups v. class. Universal dimensions were seen to conflict with more particularistic ones, as in the case of classes economically orientated to the world-system as such and politically orientated to particular states, or in the tension between 'social' and 'national' movements. These and other cracks in the objective-functionalist, world-systemic framework have increasingly given rise to interest in 'epiphenomenal' matters *per se*. The ongoing debate concerning the problem of the role or function of socialist states in the (capitalistic) world-system and the closely related issue of the prospects for and paths to a world socialist system is an important manifestation (Chase-Dunn, 1983, 1989). Another is the strong trend among 'revisionists' in the world-systems camp – in particular Meyer (1980) – to emphasize political and cultural aspects of the global system (Meyer and Hannan, 1979; Bergesen, 1980b). Revisionism, in this sense, thus backs away from both the utilitarian and the materialist objectivist thrusts in Wallersteinian theory, in the direction of a voluntaristic world-system theory.

More importantly, in this context it is worth noting the degree to which we find Wallerstein himself recently shifting away from determinism and materialism in the direction of voluntarism and 'idealism.' Specifically, we find him talking about both the 'metaphysical presuppositions' which, he maintains, have played a crucial part in the crystallization of the modern world system and the degree to which socialistic voluntarism has a necessary part to play in its transformation (Wallerstein, 1982a, 1982b, 1983a), and also about the challenges to those presuppositions from the 'renaissance' of other 'civilizations' (Wallerstein, 1982b). In analytical terms, this shift in a more multidimensional direction is similar to, though not yet as refined as, the one that took place generally in the classical period with respect to analysis of what we are, in its more than Toenniesian sense, calling *Gesellschaft* in more intra-societal terms. For example, both Weber (1978) and Simmel (1978) sought to use the latter term to discover the presuppositions underlying the monetary economy.

'Metaphysical presuppositions' became an important consideration because, according to Wallerstein, even 'anti-systemic' movements – i.e. movements, including whole societies and clusters of societies, which move against the 'logic' of the world capitalist system – are nonetheless, but perhaps decreasingly, subject to basic assumptions about the world-system.[8] In ways highly reminiscent of previous (and continuing) debates among Marxists about the degree of autonomy of 'the cultural factor' Wallerstein is now apparently willing to agree that all actors on the global scene are 'permeated by the latter's metaphysical presuppositions' (Wallerstein, 1983a) or 'operating myths' (Wallerstein, 1983b). To be more precise, there are three major arenas of struggle from an activist, world-systemic standpoint: the economic, the political and the cultural. The second and the third of these arenas are, says Wallerstein, in particular 'turmoil' and will be ever more so 'in the next 30 to 50 years.' (See also Wallerstein, 1990.)

Culture has thus become a significant consideration in world-systems theory. Indeed we are approaching the point where it has become an accepted part of some world-system theorizing to include culture as a critical variable. That this is the case can be seen not merely in recent writings of Wallerstein but also in writings of 'revisionists.' However, such acknowledgment does not in itself guarantee systematic incorporation. Wallerstein's own interest in culture is skewed in a rather standard Marxist direction – which is to say that 'culture' appears as an ideological impediment. In the form of metaphysical presuppositions or organizing myths, world-system analysis is concerned with the ways in which cultural conceptions of the world-system *per se* have acted as empirical or analytical barriers to the rapid development of anti-systemic movements (which have sought to speed the magnification of world-system contradictions and the supersession of the existing world-system). From that point of view the main cultural problem is the persistence, indeed the growing strength of world capitalism, while the force and content of various forms of cultural resistance must ultimately remain puzzling. The fact that in fairly recent publications Wallerstein sees civilizational cultures as potential resources of opposition to the cultural premises of the core societies seems only to derive from an impasse inexorably created by a theory which began by seeing culture as an impediment to the breakdown of a system whose 'real' logic indicated its inevitable demise. (See Wallerstein, 1984b.)

However, even in this Marxist view (although, of course, the 'problem' of the persistence of capitalism does not have to be treated along Marxist lines), there must surely be problems other than those which center on the failure of anti-systemic movements (those which are, in Wallerstein's terms on the 'right side' of history) to throw off their cultural chains. It must be worth considering, even from the Wallersteinian standpoint, a range of other 'cultural possibilities.' And this is precisely where – to invoke Parsons's macrostructural interpretation of Thomas's notion of the definition of the situation – the issue of 'real' definitions of the global situation comes analytically to the fore.

Cultural Aspects of Global Order

Wallerstein's acknowledgment of the importance of presuppositions and cultural movements leads to the question of what definitions of the global situation are to be expected, assuming that the global 'system' is still in the process of crystallization. If anti-systemic movements attack the world-system within the constraints of traditional presuppositions, then we need to look for possible alternative presuppositions; otherwise they remain, so to say, cognitively victimized by the traditional presuppositions – as they now are, according to Wallerstein. By analogy with the classical tradition, which showed *Gesellschaft* to be more than an 'iron cage' – especially because of varying important symbolic interpretations of the emerging sociocultural order – I suggest that globalization involves the crystallization of both relatively dominant presuppositions and alternative presuppositions – presuppositions that especially concern what the world is and should be and which themselves influence the trajectories of globalization.

However, I argue that looking for alternative presuppositions cannot (even in a Wallersteinian perspective) be limited to the search for a single 'correct' set of presuppositions. Why is that so? First, because it is extremely doubtful whether it could be shown that a single set of presuppositions has sustained the empirical operation of the expanding global field. I have already indicated the importance of considering the different cultural interpretations of the modern global circumstance. At this point I should particularly emphasize the fact that Wallerstein's own brief statements on world-system presuppositions (or myths) have been confined to presuppositions of the core countries of the world-system. That Islamic or Hindu-Indian or Chinese presuppositions have simply yielded to core presuppositions over the centuries – to the point where they play virtually no role in the cultural construction of the modern world-system – is, on the face of it, an unacceptable line of argument. In other words (and this is virtually a truism across the board of modern global commentary) the expansion of the world-system in economic and political terms has not involved in a symmetrical relationship the expansion of world culture to the point where all major actors on the global scene share the same presuppositions.

Second, I draw attention to the fact that the main theme of one form of 'revisionism' is that the prevalence in the modern world of strong, formally sovereign states cannot be explained by primary reference to the development of world capitalism *per se*. The proliferation of – in many ways similar – nation states in the twentieth century has, in this view, to be explained in reference to the crystallization of global political culture. Following that idea I should remark, however, that there is much to suggest that the development of the modern state has also entailed the 'nationalization' of culture – in the sense that the modern state is impossible without its becoming heavily involved in the production of a 'high culture' which is necessary not merely in order for the state to undertake its internal-administrative affairs (Gellner, 1983), but also to deal with its 'identity problems.' So it is not enough to point to the ways in which the global system has constrained societies to participate in that system along the 'acceptable' lines of possessing relatively homogeneous state apparatuses. One has to go a crucial step further and consider the possibility that the modern global circumstance facilitates the proliferation of competing societal (and other) definitions of the global situation, which is also to go much further than Wallerstein's long-held view that the modern world-system is marked by cultural diversity. Such competing definitions can perhaps be seen as the cultural analogues to mercantilist strategies in the economic sphere (see Wallerstein, 1982a), in that a world-system containing relatively independent politically organized units stimulates, or even 'requires,' the development of culturally protectionist strategies – in the form of attempts to close a national culture to external influences and claims in the global arena which may at least appear 'fundamentalist.' Still further, it would seem that the search for national identity (which has in Wallersteinian theory, at least until very recently, largely been regarded as an epiphenomenon in relation to position in the world economy) encourages conflicts within societies, because the increasing significance of the problem of societal order in relation to global order almost automatically means that political-ideological and religious movements arise in reference to the issue of defining societies in relationship to the rest of the world and

the global circumstance as a whole. This applies particularly to a number of
the 'fundamentalist' politicoreligious movements which have become so
active and conspicuous around the world.

Wuthnow is one of the few sociologists (see also Nettl and Robertson,
1968) to have paid systematic attention to competing definitions of the
global situation – for example by interpreting Reformation-like movements as attempts from relatively peripheral areas in the world-system to
challenge sacred assumptions in the prevailing world order and provide a
globally relevant new vision of ultimate reality (Wuthnow, 1980: 64). In
Wuthnow's work the correlation between cultural movements and the
dynamics of the world economy – for example between cultural developments and patterns of expansion, polarization and reintegration – may be
too 'tight' (Wuthnow, 1980, 1983; cf. Wuthnow, 1978). But by pointing out
the very significance of cultural developments and by emphasizing cultural
diversity as a constitutive feature of the world-system (as broadly conceived), his work moves in the direction of the multidimensionality I am
advocating here.

Third, and this follows from the two points I have just made, the global
field is highly 'pluralistic' in that there is a proliferation of civilizational,
continental, regional, societal and other definitions of the global-human
condition as well as considerable variety in identities formed in those
respects without direct reference to the global situation. But full-blown
pluralism would have to pivot on the global generalization of the value of
cultural diversity with particular reference to the idea that such diversity is
in and of itself good both for the system and for units within the system; as
well as involving elements of a shared global culture in terms of which the
plurality of entities could minimally communicate. However, such maximal
pluralism clearly does not obtain in global terms. 'Mere' cultural diversity
can be seen as analogous to 'mere' global-utilitarian mercantilism. A
multidimensional (and non-idealist) view of globalization implies that a
viable global order does require the actual generalization of the legitimacy
of diversity and of contending presuppositions.

In his attempt to provide an alternative set of presuppositions for the
world-system – an attempt which, as I have just argued, is as such quite
problematic – Wallerstein has stated, following Prigogine, that non-
equilibrium rather than equilibrium is more frequently a source of order.
The point Wallerstein seeks to make in this regard is not entirely clear. On
the whole, however, it would seem that because of his opposition to the
prevailing form of world order he wishes to show that much of the activity
of anti-systemic movements actually contributes to the maintenance of the
present world-system, his major example being the socialist movement
which seizes state power and then conducts the relevant society as a regular
member of the system. Thus, to all intents and purposes, disruptive
movements create a disequilibrium which itself contributes to order. While
not for a moment maintaining here that only 'anti-systemic' movements
create world order, I tend to agree with Wallerstein that such movements

often do contribute to world order, although what seems to be missing from his account is a recognition of the significance of movements which are directly rather than indirectly oriented to the global circumstance. Among the latter are the anti-global movement within American fundamentalism, the Unification Church, the Green movement, certain strands of the Latin American liberation-theological movement, and tendencies within radical Islam.

The main problem here is that while Wallerstein wishes to overthrow prevailing social-scientific and philosophical presuppositions about the world as a whole (such as universalism and rationalism) all he can say about movements that are directly or indirectly oriented to the global condition is that they should do only those things which increase the degradation of the modern world-system. There is explicit recognition neither of existing and competing conceptions of the world order which are greatly opposed to the direction in which Wallerstein's anti-systemic movements are supposed to be facing, nor of the fact that even Western intellectual thought has produced a variety of conceptions of order. But given Wallerstein's own particular interest – in the form of theory and practice – in the promotion of world-system disorder it is, perhaps, not surprising that he has shown little explicit interest in order other than in that kind which is, from his standpoint, undesirable; although he has indicated that a socialist world order would need its own 'cultural expressions' (Wallerstein, 1982b).

Wallerstein argues that the socialism towards which the world-system as a whole is moving 'will be what we make it through our collective expression, the world of anti-systemic movements' (1982a: 278). With only a little reservation, he encourages a 'voluntarist' orientation to the world-system. However, the voluntarism inheres only – at least as far as I can see – in the making of the new world. Whether the new order should or should not itself be voluntaristic is undisclosed. There is, of course, no shortage of intellectually produced alternative images of future world order, but there is a paucity of academic discussion of rival images of world order among the movements of our time.

Wallerstein's Prigogine-based approach is reminiscent of some aspects of classical thinking about *Gesellschaft* at the societal level. For Weber, meaning complexes are always a rich texture, a tug of war, and a struggle between various 'gods.' For Simmel, the contents of the life process are themselves un- or even dis-ordered and exist in constant tension with ordering forms. So we can think of globalization as a process which involves, *inter alia*, movements and other actors on the global scene creating 'non-equilibrium,' in terms of differing images of the global condition, thus both challenging and constructing structural aspects of the world-system. In the process, various problems of meaning emphasized by the classical *fin-de-siècle* generation (with particular but, as I have pointed out, not exclusive reference to the intra-societal *Gesellschaft* circumstance) will be found to be 'translated' to the global level. Similarly, concepts used to analyze the possible outcomes of the Great Transformation must now be translated to deal with possible outcomes of globalization.

As suggested above, world-systems theory itself has produced a *Gesellschaft*-like image of the globe, which follows the view of classical political economy. It has been used as a form of critique of the existing world situation, redefining exploitation and a problematic mastery of nature as global problems. I suggest that world-systems theory, in a diffuse sense, has also (and not undeliberately) become ideology, and one possible definition of the global situation, a 'party' in global cultural conflict. According to the world-systems model of the world, a formally rational core operates on the basis of given interests in a hierarchical structure. Units of the system, particularly those on the 'periphery,' suffer, both by being reduced to mere cogs in the machine and by objective domination from the core. Many local traditions are obliterated; only residual cultural resources can be mobilized in the interest of materially based opposition to core domination. On the basis of a new global mode of production and unfettered, free individuals and societies, the alienation inherent in the present global *Gesellschaft* can, however, be resolved. Free rational activity, by individuals and societies, would then lead to a 'spontaneous' global solidarity and 'democratic' world-socialist government. The liberating transformation of hierarchical global *Gesellschaft* would be replaced by a non-ascriptive, egalitarian association of free men and women. Such ideas have been incorporated to some extent in other globe-oriented movements such as 'base-community' liberation theology in Latin America, and have been used as intellectual legitimation of the global actions of communist or neo-communist states. Redefining capitalist *Gesellschaft* at the global level, as well as the discontents inherent in it and the appropriate alternative, the rationalist-universalist thrust in such movement-like phenomena is still in line with more traditional Marxist views of emancipation – notwithstanding Wallerstein's objections to 'universalism.'

Another image of the globe has been used to redefine two other problems addressed in the classical phase: the problem of meaningful solidarity under conditions of differentiation, and the problem of individual identity in the face of an institutionally differentiated state-organized society. Global *Gesellschaft* can also be seen as a system of states, a global polity in which particular independent administrative units are loosely interrelated. Such a global polity legitimizes the independence of such units – including their monopolization of force and thus their potential for the destruction of the human species – and the priority of strategic interests over others. Such units are expected to operate in formally rational fashion, both internally and externally, but they can have varying substantively rational orientations. In other words, in such relatively prevalent images the globe is seen as an *association* of diverse units, operating within an encompassing economic division of labor. Only 'rules' to guide contractual and strategic relations are shared; otherwise mere cultural diversity and absence of collective identity is to be expected.[9] Within such a system of societies there may, of course, emerge a hierarchy of collectively valued criteria, but attempts to impose symbolically or structurally a social-systemic form on the globe will be resisted.[10] However, assuming for the moment that some such associational-*Gesellschaft* image of the globe is fairly prevalent, various problems may come to be perceived in it which may become the basis for anti-systemic movements.

For example, the problem of individual identity can be raised not merely *vis-à-vis* a particular state but also *vis-à-vis* the global circumstance. Some movements may see global *Gesellschaft* as the systemic oppression of an authentic personal or communal life and the systematic endangerment of the species. Resistance to such a system may become an effort to reduce the complexities of *Gesellschaft* on the basis of that which individuals have in common in opposition to the system of states: their common humanity. So traditional communalism and utopian socialism concerned with meaningful individuality can now be generalized to the level of the species. Radical parts of the pre-1989 peace movement constituted a case in point (involving a reification of the concept of 'peace').

The more collectivist variant of romanticism, concerned with preserving and restoring 'warm' communities in the face of a formally rational system, can similarly be generalized by proposing replacement of objective state structures with communally rooted entities. Against the universalistic tendencies of global *Gesellschaft* particularistic communal closure is advocated. Against the functional differentiation and technical rationalization of existing societies on the basis of a formal-legal code a more *Gemeinschaft*-like globe is presented as an alternative. In so far as, for example, ethnic movements reach a truly global conception of *Gemeinschaft* (and very few actually have), they would at least symbolically go beyond both *Gemeinschaft* in the traditional sense and *Gesellschaft* in its global sense (see Lechner, 1984).

The classical problem of creating meaningful order in terms of a more or less coherent meaning complex becomes the problem of restoring an objective global value-basis in terms of which societies are to operate. Against the 'disenchanted' operation of societies and the cultural diversity allowed in global *Gesellschaft*, efforts will be made to assert the primacy of a particular encompassing ideology, covering all dimensions of life and relativizing the independent operation of societies. In such 'fundamentalist' approaches to the globe the proposed alternative takes on a more hierarchical, social-systemic form on the basis of a substantive definition of what the globe stands for. Compared with the universalistic emancipation orientation, or the more extra-societal orientation to identity and common humanity, or the particularistic *Gemeinschaft* orientation, the last approach is a more universalistic and hierarchical attempt to resolve global culture conflict and remake the world.[11]

Thus in the classical period a 'multidimensional' view of modernity was made available, which provided an analytical framework for the interpretation of the discontents of modernity and various anti-modern responses, but which also transcended the intellectual limitations of the latter. Similarly, in the contemporary period a major task for social theory is to account for the trajectories of globalization in a multidimensional fashion, to treat the problem of global order with special sensitivity to its cultural dimensions, and to provide an analytical framework that can both interpret various symbolic responses to globalization and overcome their particular limitations. By analyzing globalization in relation to the theme of modernity and through a critique of world-systems theory and its treatment of culture I hope to contribute to that overall task.

Various post-classical theorists have contributed at least elements of a more comprehensive theoretical approach to globalization that would at the same time help account for the problematic nature of the radical attempts to deal with global problems of meaning by constructing counter-images to the world-systemic *Gesellschaft* that was discussed in the previous section. I will mention a few here.

First, Parsons has come closest to endorsing a 'liberal' interpretation of global *Gesellschaft* in which – by analogy with the main trend at the societal level – organized collectivities would operate in a framework of 'institutionalized' norms with consensus only on very broad principles. In this view global-fundamentalist movements that attempt to define the globe exclusively in terms of one set of value-principles are to be expected. Parsons would also have emphasized that such attempts must be internally unstable and will not lead to a viable form of global order. I would emphasize, with Parsons, the importance of principles legitimizing plural-ism, but also the very contentiousness of global order. Second, according to Luhmann (1976, 1982b) world society is the only possible one, since communication processes and functional differentiation of systems have made 'societies' and shared culture obsolete. So to attempt to restore a societal identity in any traditional sense or a global culture that can be shared across the boundaries of differentiated systems is essentially self-defeating. While agreeing with Luhmann on that point, I would emphasize that such differentiation still needs to be symbolically anchored, and that precisely in the present situation presumably 'obsolete' societies must become culturally active. Third, according to Habermas, a substantive collective identity for world society is neither possible nor necessary; universalistic participation in global communicative action is the maximum attainable (cf., in contrast, Dumont, 1980). Although I would agree that a collective identity in any traditional sense is indeed unlikely and unnecess-ary (short of the discovery of life on other planets), I would nevertheless be more sociologically concerned with the global preconditions of such 'universal communication' – if only because it is precisely such universalism which now seems to be vulnerable.

In addition, I would also argue that, in the modern world 'system,' societies as such are relativized, but also made possible as parts of a system in which both political and cultural 'power' are dispersed (Robertson and

Chirico, 1985; Robertson, 1985, 1986). Following my argument about global cultural pluralism I would add that such dispersal is a constitutive feature of the globe, and is itself an object of contention among conflicting cultural approaches to the global circumstance. Despite the qualifications just mentioned I suggest that the implication of recent general theorizing with respect to the globe is that pluralism must be a constitutive feature of the global system, and has to be legitimized as such. Of course this leads to the traditional problem that that very proposition may itself be seen as a 'dominant presupposition,' one originating in the 'core' civilization. However, I am pointing to the pre-conflictual elements in global-cultural conflict rather than a single, global dominant ideology. It is precisely the search for such a dominant ideology – by movements and societies – and the accompanying attempt to establish one, at least symbolically, that can be seen as contravening possible requirements of a viable global order. Such efforts are, in that sense, global attempts to reach postmodernity via anti-modernity (see Habermas, 1981b). Thus we find the cultural predicament inherent in the Great Transformation, to which much of classical sociology drew attention, generalized to the global level. As the problems of order and meaning so central to the classical analyses of modernity have become essentially global ones, the need for a distinctly global type of sociological theory has dramatically increased, while the stakes in modern cultural conflict have been raised (Wallerstein, 1990).

Images of the World: An Application of the Basic Model

As we have seen Wallersteinian (and other Marxist, or Trotskyist) theories of the world economy and their sociocultural ramifications have – at least until very recently – largely chosen to ignore (or, at least, play down) the idea that not merely are there ideal as well as material interests of great sociocultural significance but that 'world images' play a crucial role in framing the directions in which these interrelated sets of interests will be pursued. In the present context the concept of world images has to be taken very seriously and employed more literally than it was in Max Weber's work; for I use it here mainly in the sense of images of global order. (In a more technical, neo-Kantian sense, I am addressing from a different angle the issue of how the world is variously and often conflictfully regarded as *possible*.) Whereas Weber's concept of world images referred mainly to very general orientations to and conceptions of the human condition (particularly to the theme of the relationship between the 'intramundane' and the 'supramundane' aspects of the cosmos), the concept of world images as it is employed here refers more concretely to conceptions of how the intramundane world is actually and/or should be structured (Robertson, 1985c). This does not mean, however, that the wider cosmic aspect of the concept of world images is irrelevant.

Weber's work as a whole was, of course, directed largely at issues centered on the crystallization of modern rationalism. His interest in world images was largely dictated by his concern to comprehend the historical circumstances of the rise of rationalism in the Occidental world. A rather different, but not incompatible, orientation to the phenomena of central significance to Weber was promoted, as we have seen, in one of Parsons's very last essays. In 'Religious and economic symbolism in the western world' (1979) Parsons discussed *the cultural interpretations* of what, for the sake of brevity, he called the Industrial Revolution. This constituted a very significant turn in Parsonian action theory, but one which has received exceedingly little attention (Robertson, 1991c). Parsons argued that the Industrial Revolution of the late eighteenth century stood diachronically in line with the thematization of the erotic-sexual aspect of human life which had occurred in the period of early Christianity and the shift from ancient Judaistic particularism to early Christian universalism. In ancient Judaism, he said, the sexual-erotic dimension of life had been, so to say, hidden by laws and rituals concerning familial relationships and the Deuteronomic distinction between in- and out-group relations (Nelson, 1969); whereas early Christian doctrinal obliteration of the in-group/out-group distinction involved a more direct confrontation with the 'dangers' of sexuality and eroticism. (This is, almost needless to say, a controversial assertion in light of the actual history of Christian attitudes toward the Jews.)

Parsons claimed that the Industrial Revolution of the late eighteenth century was both a diachronic-functional equivalent and an evolutionary upgrading of the mission to the Gentiles. It constituted another crucial stage in the odyssey of particularism–universalism, involving the 'revelation' of the economy as a potentially autonomous realm. The market economy represented at one and the same time a vehicle of universalistic, potentially global social interaction and exchange, and a 'dangerous' intrusion upon traditional forms of sociality and solidarity. It was part of Parsons's argument that the general character of modern social theory, ideology and political culture was largely shaped by the early nineteenth-century response to the thematization of the economy as a relatively autonomous realm of life.[12] To this I add the claim that responses to *globality* are very likely to frame the character of social theory, doctrine, ideology and political culture in the decades ahead. The meanings ascribed to 'the dangers' of the world as a single sociocultural entity (notably, concerns about threats to humanity as a whole, and the massive relativization of identities and traditions) constitute the crucible in which major ideas of great potential significance are being formed. More than that, they are potentially the focal point of the social movements of the future. The revelations of the productive forces of sex and then of the economy have been followed by the baring of the global human-species condition itself (Robertson, 1982). However, that does not by any means suggest that those productive forces have diminished in sociocultural significance. On the contrary, they have now acquired explicitly *global* significance – as current problems of and controversies about global economic justice, the environment and the rights to 'indigenous' and local identities demonstrate. A particularly significant example is provided by the recent United Nations declaration of environmental principles in preparation for the Earth Summit in Rio de Janeiro.

To a small, but not insignificant, degree the perspective I am here bringing to bear upon the contemporary world as a whole *is* partly in line with certain analytical trends within the general world-systems theoretical framework. For example, Jameson (1986: 68) – a literary critic and interpreter of culture who attunes much of his current work to Wallerstein's ideas – in his plea for 'the reinvention, in a new situation, of what Goethe long ago theorized as "world literature,"' argues that contemporary 'cultural structures and attitudes' of relevance to the *world* cultural scene were 'in the beginning vital responses to infrastructural realities (economic and geographic, for example).' Such cultural structures and attitudes should, he insists, be seen initially as 'attempts to resolve more fundamental contradictions – attempts which then outlive the situations for which they were devised, and survive, in reified forms as "cultural patterns"' (Jameson, 1986: 78). Jameson then goes on to argue that 'those patterns themselves become part of the objective situation confronted by later generations, and . . . having once been part of the solution to a dilemma, then become part of the new problem.' His argument is not entirely unpersuasive, but at the same time it illustrates some of the problems in the world-systems perspective on culture to which I have been drawing attention. In one sense Jamesons's observations are clearly compatible with the way in which Parsons treated Western cultural responses to and interpretations of the onset of the Industrial Revolution. However, the term 'infrastructure' gives the impression of cultural responses being essentially secondary to material factors. Moreover, Jameson appears to be trying to sustain the view that in a globalized world the major point of reference is *still* the economic 'infrastructure,' rather than globality itself, which – as I have been insisting – transcends, although it certainly includes, the global economy. On top of that, in a situation of increasing consciousness of the world as a whole one would expect civilizational conceptions of the entire world which *pre*date the 'emergence' of the 'infrastructure' to be activated. In other words, even though national, regional and other 'cultural patterns' have undoubtedly been formed partly as responses to the growth of the capitalist world-system, the contemporary concern with the world as a whole – with *globality* – recrystallizes, in varying degrees, the historic philosophies and theologies of ancient civilizations concerning the structure and cosmic significance of the world. The critical difference between, for example, traditional Islamic or Chinese conceptions of the world and present ones is that the latter, unlike the old worldviews, are being reformulated or upgraded in terms of a very concrete sense of the structure of the entire world in its modern (or postmodern) form.

Together *societies, individuals, the system of societies and mankind* constitute the basic and most general ingredients of what I call the global-human condition, a term which draws attention to both the world in its contemporary concreteness and to humanity as a species. 'Globality' refers to the circumstance of extensive awareness of the world as a whole, including the species aspect of the latter. This set of major components of the global-human condition may be used to treat responses to and symbolic constructions of the thematization of globality in the same analytical spirit as that in which Parsons typified responses to the thematization of the economy in the late eighteenth and nineteenth centuries. I depart slightly from Parsons in producing a typology of general images of the contemporary world as a whole (or the global-human condition), rather than the specific social-theoretic and ideological responses which he delineated in respect of the Industrial Revolution (his types being socialism in its more economistic forms; *'Gemeinschaft* romanticism'; what I will summarize as corporatism; and utilitarian individualism). Moreover, I do not in the present context press so hard as Parsons the idea that each response when it explicitly rejects all of the remaining three constitutes a form of reductionism or avoidance of complexity in the mode of *fundamentalism* (see Robertson, 1983a). That is not because of disagreement with Parsons on this interpretive matter but because my primary concern here is simply to map, describe and provide a rationale for the very idea of analyzing major general responses to globalization and globality. (For an entirely different, indeed a materialist account, of what are here called responses to globality, see Harvey, 1989.)

Four types of image of world order are first presented in relatively formal terms. Some empirical flesh is then added.

Global Gemeinschaft 1 This conception of the global circumstance insists that *the world should and can be ordered only in the form of a series of relatively closed societal communities*. The *symmetrical* version of this image of world order sees societal communities as relatively equal to each other in terms of the worth of their cultural traditions, their institutions and the kinds of individual produced in them. The *a*symmetrical version, on the other hand, regards one or a small number of societal communities as necessarily being more important than others. Those who advocate global 'relativism' based upon the 'sacredness' of all indigenous traditions fall into the symmetrical category; those who claim that theirs is 'the middle kingdom,' 'the society of destiny' or 'the lead society' fall into the second category. In the late twentieth-century world both versions tend to seize upon the idea that *individuals* can only live satisfactory lives in clearly bounded societal communities. That does *not* mean that this image emphasizes individual*ism* or individual*ity*. Rather, it involves a particular concern with the problem of the 'homelessness' of individuals confronting the 'dangers' of globalization.

Global Gemeinschaft 2 This image of the world situation maintains that *only in terms of a fully globewide community per se can there be global order*. Corresponding to the distinction between symmetrical and asymmetrical versions of *Gemeinschaft 1*, there are *centralized* and *decentral-ized* forms of this image of the world as almost literally a 'global village.' The first insists that there must be a globewide Durkheimian 'conscience collective,' while the second maintains that a global community is possible on a much more pluralistic basis. Both versions of this second type of *Gemeinschaft* stress *mankind* as the pivotal ingredient of the world as a whole. Thus the dangers of globalization are to be overcome by commitment to the communal unity of the human species.

Global Gesellschaft 1   This variant of the image of the world as a form of *Gesellschaft* involves seeing the global circumstance as *a series of open societies, with considerable sociocultural exchange among them*. The *symmetrical* version considers all societies as politically equal and of reciprocally beneficial material and cultural significance; while the *a*symmetrical version entails the view that there must be dominant or hegemonic societies which play strategically significant roles in sustain-ing the world and, indeed, that that is the primary mechanism of world order. In both cases national *societies* are regarded as necessarily constituting the central feature of the modern global circumstance. So the problem of globalization is to be confronted either by extensive societal collaboration or by a hierarchical pattern of inter-societal relationships.

Global Gesellschaft 2   This conception of world order claims that it can only be obtained *on the basis of formal, planned world organization*. The *centralized* version of *Gesellschaft 2* is committed to a strong supra-natural polity, while the *decentralized* form advocates something like a federation at the global level. Both variants take the *world-system* of societies as constituting the major unavoidable dimension of the contem-porary global-human condition. They share the view that the only effective way of dealing with the dangers of globalization is by systematic organization of that process.

In attempting shortly to provide empirical nuance to each of these four major types of orientation to world order, it should be emphasized that I am particularly interested, given my continuing insistence upon the fairly recent emergence of globality as an aspect of contemporary consciousness, in explicitly *globe-oriented* ideologies, doctrines and other bodies of knowledge. I define an explicitly globe-oriented perspective as one which espouses as a central aspect of its message or policy a concern with the patterning of the entire world. In so doing I allow room for perspectives which, while concerned about the phenomenon of globality, may actually be militantly opposed to those who urge study of – and certainly to those who appear to embrace – the globality of contemporary life.

A significant example of what has sometimes been described by its proponents as 'anti-globalism,' counterposed to 'one-worldism,' is provided by recent (nationally organized) attempts in parts of the American South to limit the exposure of children in public schools to ideas that might involve relativization of American culture and citizenship. What is of particular interest in the present context about these occurrences is that they have grown almost directly out of reference to an older opposition to the alleged dangers of 'secular humanism.' Anti-globalism thus becomes a symbolic vehicle for generalizing beyond the dangers of intra-societal secular *Gesellschaft* so as to deal with perceived threats from other cultures and the world *per se*. Initially the objection was to a 'national' secularity which was at best indifferent to religion and local custom; now the objection, in the face of the relativizing and intrusive dangers of globalization, is also – perhaps even more – to the contaminating effects of exposure to alien doctrines and philosophies, such as those of Islam. In other words, the shift from the problem of the making of the modern West to the problem of the world as a single place is not simply a focus of intellectual social theory but of 'real-world' practice (and certainly not only in the West itself).

So anti-global trends and sociocultural tendencies are to be included conceptually in the family of globe-oriented movements. Their growth is just as symptomatic of the development of consciousness of globality as is the more often studied rise of movements that are concerned in one way or another with organizing what are perceived to be crucial aspects of the entire world (such as Greenpeace and Friends of the Earth) or, indeed, the world in its entirety (as is apparently the case with some religious movements such as the South Korea-centered Unification Church and the Japan-based Soka Gakkai). Moreover, even though anti-global perspectives are not necessarily concerned with the theme of world order *per se* they are surely held to a significant degree in 'subliminal thrall' by that which they oppose. They address the problem of the world as a whole negatively, yet their attitude toward it tends to imply a conception of how the contemporary global-human circumstance is possible, although in the case of some American Christian fundamentalist groups there is evidence that the world as a whole is considered to be *im*possible – a view which is expressed in apocalyptic symbolism.

Views of the world as a whole as consisting of a series of relatively closed societal communities (*Gemeinschaft 1*) – with each as preciously unique – became evident in the West toward the end of the eighteenth century, notably in the writings of Herder. The symmetrical version of this view has found twentieth-century expression in anthropological relativism and within certain contexts of the apparently worldwide ethnic revival (A.D. Smith, 1981; Lechner, 1984). The asymmetrical version – which insists upon the greater worth of one or a small number of societal communities in comparison to others – is much older, paradigm cases being the classical (Chinese) conception of China as the Middle Kingdom at the center of a world structured as a series of concentric circles of communal forms of life. Historically there have also been strong parallel versions of this kind of conception in Islam. In the modern period of increasingly mature globality the asymmetrical, dispersed *Gemeinschaft* worldview is to be seen in the large number of politicoreligious 'fundamentalist' movements which have arisen around the world. Many of these advocate the 'restoration' of their own societal communities to a pristine condition, with the rest of the world being left as a series of closed communities posing no threat to the 'best' community. This involves a kind of 'apartheid' conception of the world, although it does not necessarily rest on principles of racial superiority *per se*.

The idea of the world as being in and of itself a single community (*Gemeinschaft 2*), or at least having the potential for so becoming, has a very long history, having been expressed in such notions as worldwide earthly paradise and the Kingdom of God on earth. In the modern period a number of new religious movements have arisen which, as I have already noted, advocate and are taking concrete steps toward nothing less than the global organization of the entire world, while the movement which can surely lay legitimate claim to being the oldest significant globe-oriented organization – the Roman Catholic Church – has recently become a particularly effective globe-oriented and politically influential actor across most of the world, claiming mankind to be its major concern. Perhaps the most striking of the new religious movements tend to be of East Asian origin, where the idea of *harmonizing* different worldviews has a very long history. For the most part such movements should be associated with the centralized version of global *Gemeinschaft*, since they often appear to seek global harmonization of existing worldviews under a theocratic umbrella of 'absolute values' (that being particularly true of the Unification Church). The more decentralized vision of the view of the entire world as a single community was to be found until very recently in many strands of the peace movement, and in romantic Marxism (Williams, 1983). It is also to be found in much of the current environmental movement, for example in ecofeminism (Diamond and Orenstein, 1990). In such cases the response to globality is to argue, in effect, that the only way to save the world from extreme complexity and turmoil is the establishment of a global community which is highly respectful of local tradition and cultural variety. So whereas the centralized version of globewide *Gemeinschaft* seeks a 'harmonizing theocracy' at the global level, the decentralized version is at most what might be called 'concultural' in its conception of world order (Mazrui, 1980). The concultural view characterizes cultural traditions as constituting a set of indigenous variations on the condition and predicaments of mankind. Some of the numerous movements centered on theologies of liberation which have arisen in many parts of the world (often through emulation of the most solidly established of such – the Latin American) appear to subscribe to this perspective on world order.

The image of world order which emphasizes the pivotal significance of national societies (*Gesellschaft 1*) involves in its symmetrical version the idea that, to all intents and purposes, we should see the world as a kind of aggregate of all societies. This is what might be called the small-society view of the world, although one finds strands of such thinking in societies which are certainly not small geographically or in terms of resources, Canada being a major candidate for inclusion here. This orientation seems to constitute a societal parallel to the decentralized version of *Gemeinschaft 1*, in that it would seem to advocate a kind of global consociationalism – whereby very different interests are more or less systematically combined to realize the interests of the whole. In contrast, as I have suggested, the asymmetrical version of *Gesellschaft 1* rejects the view of a world order centered upon all societies. It stands in the tradition of international *Realpolitik* and needs no further elaboration here. It may be added, however, that social movements can and do directly advocate this standpoint (quite apart from its advocacy by politicans and rulers in great-power societies). For from certain religious and ideological points of view it is considered that the great-power arrangement of the world is the only one which prevents cultural contamination. Thus, for example, *Gesellschaft 1* in its asymmetrical form may be combined with the asymmetrical version of *Gemeinschaft 1*, the former being instrumental in relation to the consummatory significance of the latter.

The *Gesellschaft 2* image of world order, it will be recalled, considers the world to consist primarily in its thoroughly systemic nature – or at least advocates that only formal systemicity can, so to say, save the world from the chaos of globality. In its centralized form this image involves a conception of strong world government, an idea which has been most frequently proposed during the present century by groups of liberals, on the one hand, and Marxists, on the other. The difference between the two is that the first sees a potential world government as necessary mainly to prevent global chaos, whereas the second seeks to capitalize upon it to usher in and sustain world socialism (often leaving open the question of whether the world state should wither away in favor of another type of global order). Finally, the decentralized form of the image of the world as a *Gesellschaft* is best exemplified by some of so-called world federalists; although, in ideological terms, the Wallersteinians' view of the present condition of the world also fits here. The major difference between the two is, of course, that whereas the former aspire to overcome the problems of globality by federalizing a disorderly world-system, the latter see the present world-system as ordered but with dynamic contradictions that will eventually transform it to a higher and preferable form of order.

In this section I have attempted to develop some ideas concerning global culture, particularly in the form of cultural responses to and interpretations of globality and globalization. That has involved using the term global culture in a way which, to a considerable extent, parallels the use of the term economic culture as a concept referring to culture that has a specific bearing on economic action and institutions. Thus, as I have used the term *here*, global culture refers primarily to culture which has a close bearing on the phenomenon of globality as a 'dangerous' phenomenon of world-historical significance. Globality is, I argue, a virtually unavoidable problem of contemporary life. The perspective I have expounded with reference to general images of world order has a number of further possible applications, including the analysis of the terms in which *societies* formulate (and display internal conflicts with respect to) their modes of participation in the modern global-human circumstance.

In reference to earlier parts of this chapter concerning Wallerstein's notion of anti-systemic movements, I want to point out that many papers currently being written in the increasingly large number of journals, as well as books, devoted to such themes as 'historical consciousness and the culture of late capitalism' (Chakrabarty, 1992), are in fact attempts to change or reconstruct the presuppositions of the contemporary world-system and shape its future. The general thrust of much of the 'subaltern work' which is being undertaken at the present time, challenges the allegedly dominant cultural underpinnings of the 'actually existing world.' Intentionally or not, many of the recent contributions to 'cultural studies' read as if they had been written in specific reference to Wallerstein's claim that culture is the 'ideological battleground of the modern world-system' (Wallerstein, 1990; cf. Boyne, 1990). Wallerstein has in effect encouraged and 'legitimized,' somewhat paradoxically, the growth of cultural studies. The 'analytic participant' in contemporary globality and globalization is in any case faced with a formidable, but very interesting, task.

The present discussion is by no means intended to exhaust the meaning of the term 'global culture' (Featherstone, 1990). Other aspects have been encountered in the preceding chapters, while still others will be considered in the chapters that follow. In the concluding section of this chapter I have concentrated on the relatively neglected theme of global culture as consisting in conceptions of the world as a whole, describing them as 'images of world order,' but not thereby committing myself to a strong sense of 'order.' This word has acquired a pejorative meaning in some quarters of social and cultural theory, and I am prepared, with some misgivings, to state in 'the last analysis' that I am just as much concerned with 'the order of global disorder' (cf. Featherstone, 1991b; Appadurai, 1990) as I am with global order *per se*. This has, in any case, been an attempt to push forward with issues raised in previous chapters about the inevitability of societies, movements and so on becoming involved, in some cases anti-globally, in global matters. Again, it should be said that the general idea of conceptions of world order, *including* negative and latent ones, is certainly nothing new under the sun. Although I have concentrated here on recent and present images it should be clear that, in varying degrees of crystallization, images of 'the world' have been operative in and often very consequential throughout 'world history.' In the 'post-communist' global circumstance the idea of world order in its 'world politics' sense has loomed large.

Notes

1. In this general respect my approach here to globalization coincides with one proposed by Bergesen (1980a) under the heading of 'globology,' although from the points made below it will become clear that the analytical scope of the voluntaristic type of approach I propose is much broader than Bergesen's.
2. There was also a somewhat less conspicuous, but still significant, concern with aspects of 'political modernization' and 'nation-building.'
3. It is readily conceded that world-systems theory has been original in its systematic coordination of the study of the Third World with the study of European history (Hopkins, 1982). However, in spite of the insights that have resulted, that coordination has been undertaken – and deliberately so – with primary reference to economic history.
4. Quite apart from the work of theologians and philosophers of religion who have become increasingly interested in 'world religion' (W.C. Smith, 1981) during the past thirty years or so.
5. Wallerstein's work has thus largely been functionalistic because it has both sought explanations in functional terms and concentrated on a limited set of functions (mainly economic-adaptive and, secondarily, political).
6. Of course this does not mean that the work of Wallerstein's 'political' critics, such as Modelski (1978, 1983) and Zolberg (1981, 1983), does not contain interesting material on the political dimension of what I have called globalization.
7. That globality is the more general and formidable problem is emphasized in right-wing, ideological terms in Bowen (1984), who rails against 'globalism' as an expansion of 'secular-humanist' modernism.
8. For an early formulation of societal orientations to the world-system with particular reference to the idea of a world culture of modernity and modernization, see Nettl and Robertson (1968).
9. I should point out that both the 'political' type of world-system theory advocated by Modelski (1978, 1983) and Zolberg's (1983) critique of that approach in principle leave room for a more sensitive treatment of culture.
10. I am using the adjective 'social-systemic' in Swanson's sense; he distinguishes between 'social system' and 'association' as two distinct forms of social organization – the former is the more holistic-hierarchical type, while in the latter priority is given to constituent parts (Swanson, 1968). For suggestions on the application of Swanson's concepts in global analysis, see Robertson and Lechner (1984).
11. This is not to subscribe to ethical relativism (cf. Dunn, 1979: 106–7). Pluralism does not entail the view that all cultures are equally 'right.' Moreover, as indicated, I insist that pluralism involves the grounding of variety.
12. Parsons's analysis appears in some respects to be continuous with Smelser's (1959) extended discussion of situational responses to structural differentiation in the early English Industrial Revolution.

5

JAPANESE GLOBALITY AND JAPANESE RELIGION

As I announced in the Prologue, in the present book I am not concerned directly with the theme of globalization and religion in the double sense of religion as 'the way' (to invoke an East Asian term) and religion as a globalized category for the structuring of societal, as well as inter-societal affairs. However, for a number of reasons it is appropriate to discuss globalization and religion at this point. Particularly, I do not believe that one can discuss Japan and globalization without considering the role and function of religion. In terms of the 'official-global' definition of 'religion,' Japan has presented itself as a basically secular society. This is, in one sense, a matter of 'public relations,' just as the self-presentation of the USA as simultaneously a religious *and* a secular society is also part of the global politics of collective identity presentation. (The culture of politics and the politics of culture are particularly evident in the contemporaneously crucial axis of Japan–USA relations: Robertson, 1990a.) It follows that, in certain circumstances, religion – more generally, the debate about secularization – is a strategic resource in world politics. At the same time, Japan is a vital and unavoidable topic for theorists of globalization. Japan is often, but perhaps shortsightedly, considered to be a 'late entrant' to the 'world-system,' a 'newcomer' which for relatively unexplored reasons has been able both to 'modernize' and, in a certain way, 'become global' (in spite of Western complaints about its failure to participate fully in the international system). But, against that view, it can be argued that Japan's isolation from the international system – particularly during the Tokugowa period – was, in a way, a preparation for the extensive global involvement of the twentieth century and beyond. In other words, Japan's 'isolation' from the global circumstance was a globally oriented gesture; Japan's long separation from the world was a circumstance of 'world watching.' Many countries have also, in terms of the old model of modernization, been isolated or 'withdrawn.' The present discussion of Japan is partly intended to demonstrate the narrowness of conventional ideas about 'latecomers' and 'laggards.' By now Japan has become a society which is to be emulated, not because of its self-proclaimed uniqueness, but largely because of its orientation to the world. In particular, East Asian and South-East Asian societies have learned from Japan how to *learn how to learn*. Why, in contrast, Latin American countries have been much less successful in this respect is an interesting topic.

A particular world-systems view is that Japan did not even enter 'the world' until forced to do so by the Western powers, in particular by US Commodore Perry's 'black ships' in the 1850s. In contrast, my argument centers on a certain kind of reversal of the world-systems perspective. In this discussion I insist upon the relatively autonomous significance of 'culture' and of 'voluntaristic,' societal transitions; although that is certainly not to say that objective, economic and world-systemic factors are unimportant. My position rests on the essentially, but also differentially, reflexive nature of modernization. The central problem with purely economic historical sociology is that it makes no allowance for seriously pragmatic reflection on economic circumstances. Japan is of great sociological interest not because it is 'unique' and 'successful,' but because it fulfills the function in the contemporary world of the society from which 'leaders' of other societies can learn how to learn about many societies. *That* is what makes Japan a global society, in spite of claims to the contrary.

The Specific Problem: Globality and Japan

During the most crucially formative decades of sociology (1890–1920) Durkheim, Simmel and, more ambiguously, Max Weber argued that growing intellectual concern with the economic factor and the rise of economistic doctrines, notably Marxian socialism, were symptomatic rather than genuinely analytical of the changes sweeping the Western world at that time. Along similar lines, I suggest that in registering with excitement the increasing prominence of, and interest in, religion in many parts of the world, contemporary students of religion should be exceedingly careful about producing 'religious readings' of contemporary circumstances, particularly readings that show that there is an inevitability about the apparent upswing of religion. Far too much attention has been paid by sociologists of religion to issues which center upon the problem of whether religion is rising or declining. The debate about secularization has clearly been the most visible form of such concern but many other interests of sociologists of religion have been driven by that question. Far more appropriate, I suggest, is the strategy of exploring the ways in which religion and related phenomena are significantly implicated in historical and sociocultural contexts whose significance can be justified on firmer ground than is involved in the implicit claim that for a student of religion something is of potential interest merely because it falls into the category of religion. Besides which the very category of religion is bound up, as I have argued, with global and international issues (Robertson, 1988, 1990b).

The firmer ground from which the substantive thrust of the present discussion proceeds consists above all in the increasing salience of the problematic phenomenon of globality in the affairs of individuals, societies and civilizations. The fact and the perception of ever-increasing inter-dependence at the global level, the rising concern about the fate of the world as a whole and of the human species (particularly because of the threats of ecological degradation, nuclear disaster and AIDS), and the 'colonization' of local by global life (not least, via the mass media) facilitate massive processes of relativization of cultures, doctrines, ideologies and cognitive frames of reference. At the same time, there are problems about the ways in and degrees to which individuals and sociocultural entities of various kinds and sizes should relate to the world as a whole. One of my main arguments in relation to these developments is that the problem of the shift from the mechanical to the organic, the feudal to the capitalist, *Gemeinschaft* to *Gesellschaft*, status-based society to contract-based society and so on, has been subsumed, but not eliminated, in recent decades by the problem of globalization. Yet the problem of globality is not simply a direct extension of the problem of the Great Transformation (Polanyi, 1957). It is not to be regarded simply as a long-term result of the forces which initiated the destruction of European feudalism. This is largely the view of the Wallersteinians, who specifically see what they call the modern world-system as having been wrought by the economic changes which propelled the overthrow of European feudalism by nascent European capitalism and which necessitated economic expansion on an increasingly global scale. This is not to deny that the modern global circumstance has been in large part made from the West. But it is to reject the idea of the almost absolute significance of the economic factor in this development and the insistence that the modern global circumstance is only an outcome of an initially European development.

Regardless of the question of the 'deep' historical embryo of the modern world as a whole, it would seem that as the latter has been constituted there have been a number of trends at work, each with its own, varying, degree of autonomy. Thus there is a 'logic' of the development of the modern form of the state, a 'logic' of development of formal education, and so on. Moreover, and of particular relevance in the present context, there has been a variety of responses to the onward march of the overall globalization process toward the making of the entire world into a single place. And just as the cultural aspects of the socioeconomic changes central to the Great Transformation became vital ingredients of the Western world in the nineteenth and early twentieth centuries, in such forms as Marxism, the ideology of capitalism, anti-modernist Catholicism and Protestantism and so on, so are responses to and interpretations of the facticity of globality becoming central, relatively autonomous ingredients of the contexts in which modern men and women live and in terms of which contemporary societies move and have their being.

It is along these lines that we may begin to situate the significance and character of religion in the contemporary circumstance, not so much in terms of its status as either consequence or cause but rather as a critical ingredient of globalization. In the present discussion, however, I am not concerned with laying out the full range of ways in which religion has been historically or is contemporaneously bound up with the globalization process. Instead I am concerned with one specific theme – the contribution of religion to the structuring of a mode of societal involvement in the global situation. I focus on one particular society – Japan – and I address the problem of the relationship between the religion of Japan – more accurately, Japanese religion – and Japan's involvement in the contemporary global circumstance.

I select Japan for a number of reasons. The most obvious and general of those centers, of course, on the sheer conspicuousness of Japan in the contemporary world. In recent years Japan has become the object of globewide, but perhaps most acutely and explicitly American, interest and concern. Generally this has arisen from Japan's external success in economic growth, but in the USA's case it has arisen particularly from the absence of the USSR as a focal Other and as a focus of internal integration and national identity, in conjunction with the fear of American decline relative to Japanese ascent in the global system. Notwithstanding periods of Japanese respect for and selective emulation of the USA in the twentieth century, there is a long history of tension between the two societies, which in various ways are polar sociocultural opposites in the contemporary global field. This 'international culture' of increasingly explicit and comparative-interactional oppositions includes such variables as cultural heterogeneity v. homogeneity; large v. small; importation of people v. exclusion of people; internal generation of new ideas v. importation of ideas; and so on. This 'econocultural' axis of tension in the global system is likely to be of pivotal significance in the culture of world politics (in conjunction with issues centered on Europe and the Muslim nations).

One basis of primarily intellectual interest in Japan consists in the proposition that contemporary Japan constitutes the new 'lead society' of the world and the new major mode of modernization, or 'postmodernization,' an idea which is of considerable interest in Japan itself (Miyoshi and Harootunian, 1989). 'Internationalization' and, more recently, 'globalization' have become central themes in Japanese public life.[1] And it is important to note that 'internationalization' is a significant part of the *religious* scene in contemporary Japan. While the idea that Japan is or has the potential for becoming the religious center of the world is old, it has become particularly evident, in a number of different forms, since the beginning of the Meiji era in 1868; even more so since the military defeat of Japan in 1945. There has been a tendency to attribute the large number of new religious movements which have developed since what the Japanese call the Pacific War to stresses and strains inside Japanese society (McFarland, 1967). Only now are we beginning to see that the most prominent of the new religious movements, such as Soka Gakkai and its rival lay-Buddhist movement Risso Kosei Kai, are, in their different ways, frequently global in a very significant way. Both movements have definite conceptions of a Japan-centered world, although they differ with respect to the incorporation of non-Japanese into that world, with Soka Gakkai (which also has its own party in the Japanese Diet) being by far the more 'aggressive' and far-reaching. Both have developed explicit 'foreign policies,' policies with respect to particular governments in both East and West and, not least, both have pivoted their public activities on the idea of peace.

The circumstance of Japan's final defeat in 1945 – the dropping by the USA of atomic bombs on Hiroshima and Nagasaki – has made the pursuit of peace a central, and highly manipulable, theme in Japanese society. Both Soka Gakkai and Risso Kosei Kai have made much of their dedication to peace, not least in the Western world, by sponsoring conferences, giving awards to international statesmen, and so on. In Soka Gakkai's case there is, intentionally or not, a clear continuity with the wartime Japanese notion of 'the world under one roof,' even though it has ostensibly inverted its 'doctrinal' emphasis since its pre-war nationalism. The general point here is that some of the new religious movements (a term which in the Japanese context actually includes movements which have developed since the mid-nineteenth century) have been clearly implicated in Japan's involvement in the world since the Meiji period. They partly gain their (sometimes controversial) legitimacy in such terms, while at the same time contributing both to Japan's extensive involvement in the world and to the generation of ideas about world order. Part of this overall effort is centered on the attempt to incorporate academics in their worldview, for example by holding conferences and developing journals, which involve non-Japanese, especially Western, scholars in their intellectual activities. In reference to the Unification Church, a South-Korea-centered movement with Japanese connections, I have characterized this policy as 'philomandarin' (Robertson, 1985a). The policy appears to rest on a somewhat mistaken assumption that Western academics are politically influential. It may, on the other hand, rest on an acute insight, to the effect that the long-run shaping of cultural ideas is of great significance.

The conventional way of considering the relevance of religion to Japan's post-1868 attempt to modernize in relation to Western society, its subsequent expansionist moves in Asia and the Pacific, and its rise from the ashes of defeat in the Pacific War to a position of increasing strength and impact in the 1970s, 1980s and 1990s is to focus only on the part played in the expansionist phase by State Shinto as an imperial 'civil' religion. For much of the time between the 1880s and 1945 State Shinto was constitutionally and strategically pronounced by Japanese regimes to be a moral, specifically a Confucian, rather than a religious institution, partly in order to accommodate Western views on the differentiation of church and state. At the same time, there has been a well-developed view that since the abolition of State Shinto and the enforcement of religious freedom by the American occupiers after World War II Japanese religion has been at best an epiphenomenon of an increasingly secularized culture, a view which Japanese political leaders have not discouraged. Indeed, in all of the outpouring of books and essays on 'the Japanese miracle' in recent years surprisingly little sustained attention has been paid, except in celebratory and stereotypical terms, to Japanese culture and related matters, let alone to Japanese religion. However, recent interest has been stirred with respect to Shinto beliefs and practices as an ingredient of Japanese commercial and manufacturing activities. (To which New Age involvement in the 'enterprise culture' of Western, including East European, capitalism is probably a response. It is certainly a parallel phenomenon.)

The problem concerning the bases of Japan's virtual uniqueness in having over many centuries – but, to Western observers most conspicuously since the 1860s – calibrated its relations with the rest of the world so carefully remains to be satisfactorily explored, in spite of the considerable literature on it. So we must still ask: what are the internal sources of and resources for Japan's high degree of careful selectivity concerning what is to be accepted or rejected from without? How has a society which is, in some respects, the epitome of insularity and post-primitive mechanical solidarity become, while not substantially relinquishing those characteristics, a society whose elites are almost obsessed with Japan becoming an international, or a global, society? My interest in such issues runs in parallel to the way in which I have tried to link the relationship between the old Great Transformation problem and the new globality-and-globalization problem. In other words, whereas the old, but still surviving, way of considering Japan was in terms of its externally stimulated internal transformation along an objective path of modernization, the new, more appropriate form of consideration should take as its starting point Japan's relatively great capacity not merely to adapt selectively to and systematically import ideas from other societies in the global arena but also, in very recent times, to seek explicitly to become, in a specifically Japanese way, a global society.

I suggest that the kinds of question asked in the old but strongly surviving way will be better answered by the new, global type of query. Japanese 'success' will not be accounted for by focusing simply on endogenous structural transformation; even when that is supplemented by attention to the mere fact of Japan having opened itself selectively to the world in the late nineteenth century (after more than two hundred years of voluntary, but 'world sensitive,' isolation) and having been forced to reconstruct itself in the late 1940s and the early 1950s, plus a vague interest in 'the Japanese mind.' Rather, we should provide an account of the features of Japanese life in relation to globality which have historically facilitated and are currently facilitating a carefully calibrated rhythm with respect to external involvement. Since religion in Japan has, perhaps more than in any other society, been almost continuously subjected to political modulation – from 1945–52 by an external agency and since then in subtle Japanese–governmental ways – it is reasonable to assume that Japanese religion will provide some major clues.

Modernization, Globalization and Societal Selectivity

At the risk of repetition, it is worthwhile restating my general argument concerning globalization and modernization. In the earliest phase of this enterprise (the mid- and late 1960s) prevailing conceptions and theories of societal modernization were rejected in favor of an approach which considered modernization as a process of catching up with and/or surpassing another society or set of societies with attributes deemed to be in whole or in part desirable. Employing a mixture of Parsonian action and system theory, symbolic-interactionist ideas concerning identity and reflexivity, Schutzian insights relating to multiple realities, and conceptions of the structure of the 'international system,' Nettl and I tried to recast the field of modernization theory so as to avoid what poststructuralists and post-modernists now call a 'grand narrative' account of the past, present and future (Nettl and Robertson, 1968). In place of theories that stood more or less directly in line with nineteenth-century philosophies of history indicating a definite, progressive movement of societies and civilization along a particular path, we offered an image of what at the time we called the international system as a place in which societies – more accurately, the influential and powerful elites within societies – in different degrees and with greatly varying degrees of success construct their own and other societal identities in tandem with constructions of the entire system. In that perspective societal modernization was not to be largely considered as consisting in a more or less inexorable move (with deviant or pathological exceptions) in a 'progressive,' Western direction – or, at the most, moves in either First or what used to be called Second World directions. Rather it was to be regarded as indicating a field of definitions both of the global situation and of societal self-definitions.

To all intents and purposes the theory of modernization which was proposed was voluntaristic, in the special sense that Parsons had introduced that term (Parsons, 1937). While acknowledging, indeed emphasizing, that the global inter-societal system possessed its own structural properties and thus that societies acted under the constraints of global (as well as internal) constraints, it was also maintained that there was a strong element of choice involved as to the direction(s) of societal change and the form(s) of global involvement. That element was seen to be centered upon an emergent global culture of modernization, a global culture which demanded that all extant societies adopt an orientation to, if not necessarily an acceptance of, the idea of modernization. What was taken to be modern – or, more loosely, what was taken to be a worthy direction of societal aspiration – was something which was constructed in the global arena in relation to the constraints upon societies to maintain their own identities and senses of continuity. It was not just a case of the presentation of images of trajectories of modernization to Third (or Fourth) World societies, but a much more complex picture of globewide 'reality construction.'

Japanese Religion: A Refocusing

One of the reasons for our relative inability to comprehend the modern 'Japanese phenomenon' is that the fathers of modern scholarship did not prepare us well for this.[2] If we look, for example, to Max Weber, who has been the single most influential figure in the modern study of the cultural dimensions of socioeconomic change and modernization, we get little help. Indeed, for Weber, Japan was a kind of cultural dumping ground. Beginning in the sixth century, Buddhism (in highly magico-animistic Mahayana form), Confucianism, aspects of Taoism and yin-yang thought, and, to a tiny degree, Christianity were simply deposited there on top of a primitive, Shintoist folk religion. That appears to have been Weber's view. Indeed, most of what Weber said directly about Japan is contained in the 'mission chapter' of his book on India (Weber, 1958). In that perspective Japan was a relatively passive receiver of, but was not greatly penetrated by, Indian, Chinese and Korean religions. For Weber, Japan seems to have been perhaps the only exception to his general rule that religion and culture have played a crucial part in what we now problematically call the modernization of societies and civilizations. Roughly speaking, his argument was that the otherworldly elements of Oriental religion did not take very strongly in Japan and that the completeness and the specific circumstances of the Meiji-imperial overthrow of the feudal Tokugawa system enabled it, given late nineteenth-century technological and economic conditions, to instigate capitalism 'from above.' But that view almost renders Japan as a society without religion of general-societal relevance. Certainly, it begs the question as to *why* Japan was and has been not merely such a systematic selector of ideas for import (Westney, 1987) but also increasingly a shaper of the global field.

Bellah (1957) subsequently attempted, *without* attempting to incorporate Weber's own writings on Japan, to produce something like a Weberian analysis of Japan's modernization; discovering, in effect, a functional equivalent of the Protestant Ethic. His position was thus Weberian in a general sense, in so far as he sought to show that there *were* strong religiocultural trends, notably among and in the period of the decline of the samurai, which encouraged a basically political-national manipulation of and positive orientation to economic productivity. But that still does not assist us much in posing the question which I have raised, particularly in view of the fact that Bellah now argues, in the 1985 preface of his *Tokugawa Religion* (1957), that 'the problem' with modern Japan is its utilitarianism and absence of identity-conferring, meaning-bestowing civil religion (Bellah, 1985).[3] His view is echoed by those many writers on 'the Japanese economic miracle' who barely mention 'religion' as a crucial factor in Japanese history, ancient or modern. It is as if they are saying that with the Allied Occupiers' abolition of State Shinto and the cult of the Emperor after the Pacific War, religion was effectively cancelled as a critical factor in Japanese society (even in Japanese history, except – of course – for its ignominious role in the period which culminated in the defeat of 1945, when it was used by military, economic and political elites to legitimize itself internally and mobilize the Japanese for economic and military advance). Those who have studied religion in Japan, whether historically or along contemporary-sociological lines, in recent decades have done so mainly without attention to Japan's 'subjective' position in the world. The main sociological interest has been in the internal significance of the new religions, particularly those which have developed since the summer of 1945, plus a less conspicuous focus on Japanese civil religion, or the lack thereof. In sum, with a few important exceptions, notably the work of Murakami (1980), the study of Japanese religion has been separated both from the study of Japan *per se* and the world as a whole, except in terms promoted by some Japanese religions themselves.[4]

What, then, are the major features of Japanese religion, apart from its political calibration and the sensitivity about 'the world' on the part of some lay Buddhist movements, that have a strong bearing on the seemingly unique tendency of the Japanese to assimilate so many sets of ideas from the outside and, at the same time, maintain or invent a continuous and resilient national-societal identity? In one sense I can only answer that question tautologically, since for at least fifteen hundred years Japanese culture and identity have been, in significant part, *constituted* by 'alien' religious ideas and practices (Pollack, 1986).[5] In other words, if we consider why it is that modern Japan exhibits a particular proclivity for adopting and adapting externally generated ideas for its own specific purposes we are inevitably tempted to say simply that that *is* a central feature of Japanese society. It is even, so the argument would go, an aspect of Japanese identity itself, an identity formed by encounters with the outside world. Nevertheless, important questions would remain. How has an identity that has been formed from such a remarkable mixture of religious and philosophical worldviews actually been maintained? Does the very form in which that configurational identity is sustained itself constitute the basis for the tendency to incorporate ideas from outside?

I suggest that there are two relatively unique features of Japanese religion which have a great bearing upon these puzzles and which, at the same time, make it necessary to speak of Japanese religion as being a cohesive, relatively autonomous whole in spite of its superficial heterogeneity. I refer, first, to the particular nature of Japanese *syncretism* and, second, to the resilience of what I call the *infrastructure* of Japanese religion and the *infrastructural significance* of religion itself. I also invoke the significance of pollution/purification rituals throughout Japan's history, rituals which are central to the 'native,' Shinto tradition, marking the boundaries between the inside and the outside of numerous relationships and circumstances.

The concept of syncretism is extremely slippery. (As with many concepts of Western origin it has been resisted by Japanese intellectuals.) Nevertheless, it is fairly safe to say that it refers loosely to the mingling of two or more religious traditions. In that respect, Japanese religion is a calibrated syncretic mixture of interpenetrating religions of Indian, Chinese, Korean and, to a much smaller degree, Christian origins plus indigenous religious tendencies, of which Shinto and shamanism are the most important. What, however, marks the uniqueness of religious 'syncretism' in Japan is that it is indeed an 'ism' – in the sense that it is a kind of 'ideology,' even though that term is not actually used. (Along such lines we might say that we find an ideology of religious plural*ism* in the USA, but not nowadays in Lebanon.) The central feature of this strong sense of the term syncretism when applied to Japan is that religious traditions have historically been used, often by governments, to legitimize each other. Examples of what might well be called *interlegitimation* abound, a form of legitimation which differs from Western notions of legitimation that depend upon 'vertical' validation. Whereas the Western notion of legitimation rests considerably upon justification of a regime in terms of an 'external' view on the part of the relevant populace, an important part of Japan's mode of legitimation consists in 'horizontal' legitimation of one aspect of the society by another, and vice versa. After the introduction of Confucianism and then Buddhism an indigenous Japanese religion was 'discovered'; and it was given the name of Shinto: 'the way of the gods.' But of course the concept of 'the way' was of external, *Chinese* origin. Along somewhat parallel lines, following the introduction of Buddhism to Japan, buddhas came to be regarded as protectors of native deities and forces. In one respect buddhas were superior, but in another sense the gods and spiritual forces (*kami*) were more fundamental. A much more recent example is to be found in the way in which State Shinto was promoted during the Meiji period largely in order to legitimize a basically *Confucian* code of ethics of loyalty, at the apex of which was the Emperor system. Such examples form only the tip of the iceberg of the phenomenon of interlegitimation in Japanese history.

But there is another crucial aspect of Japanese syncretism, pertaining more directly to the lives of individuals and families. The most visible demonstration of this dimension is the fact that in Japan individuals frequently adhere to more than one religious orientation. Even though there are exclusivist movements (most of them of recent origin) which discourage involvement in the affairs and rituals of other movements, Buddhist temples and Shinto shrines, the majority of the Japanese people are not merely free to partake of what seems to suit their religious 'fancy' according to their particular life circumstances, but there is a diffuse ethos which indicates that the individual *should* regard different components of overall Japanese religion as catering to different needs. A common saying is that Shinto is for life and Buddhism is for death. A more elaborate version would include Confucian ethics and folk magic. A yet more elaborate one would incorporate the increasing tendency for marriage ceremonies to occur in Christian but very secular form. In any case, the critical point is that the very structure of Japanese religion as a whole *and* the syncretism of everyday individual life are both based upon and encourage the tendency to make an identity from various sources, which themselves vary in terms of 'native' and 'foreign' references. Thus the popularity of 'Christian' marriages ritualistically confirms selective Japanese orientations to the West, while involvement in Buddhism confirms, *inter re*, an orientation to the universal and to humanity in general.

In raising the theme of the Japanese religious infrastructure I deliberately counterpose it to the well-worked concept of civil religion. There has been considerable debate about the degree to which State Shinto performed, and whether disestablished Shinto still performs or should perform (should even be re-established at the level of the state in order to serve), that function. I would claim, however, that regardless of that kind of problem, there is a basic solidity to the syncretic nature of Japanese religion, in both of the senses that I have described it, which is more central to the solidarity of Japanese society and its external relationships. The main feature of that infrastructure resides in the essential, but nonetheless disputed, polytheism of Japanese religion – having its deepest roots in ancient beliefs in a multitude of *kami* – which, in turn, has facilitated a highly instrumental, functional conception of religion. (Here again, Japanese scholars have disputed the concept of polytheism as being applicable to Japan.) Indeed, since at least the introduction of Buddhism into Japan there has been a continuing series of 'multireligious policies,' which have in one way or another reconciled the nativistic Japanese tradition with the universal claims of other religions and worldviews (Kitagawa, 1987). That since the Pacific War there has been a modulated religious freedom in Japan makes little difference to the general point; for even though since that time ostensible state calibration of the relationships between religions has been considerably reduced, individual Japanese people have had such 'policies' in their everyday lives. In any case, I suggest that the thoroughly institutionalized 'polytheism' of Japanese religion greatly encourages the view that many different kinds of worldview can, indeed should, be coordinated, reconciled and functionalized.

Another important aspect of the religious infrastructure has to do with the salience of rituals of purification in Japanese society, rituals which mark boundaries between the sacred and the profane and which also demarcate the 'inside' from the 'outside.' The great concern with purification itself is a religiocultural basis of the capacity to reject some externally generated ideas and to 'purify' those that are imported. So when ideas have been imported, most dramatically during the early Meiji period (Westney, 1987), they have been 'decontaminated' and rendered Japanese through a variety of practices, including the practice of not importing many sets of ideas concerning the establishment of new institutions from a single foreign source.

These, then, are some reflections on the specific puzzle of Japan's great proclivity for rhythmically opening and closing itself and being able systematically to import ideas with relatively little 'contamination.' Of course, a number of explanations of that phenomenon have been offered from outside and from within Japan, but I have been concerned specifically with religion. I certainly do not claim that a focus on religion is a substitute for other approaches, but I do suggest that it must play a part. Much more needs to be done, particularly to facilitate comparisons with other societies, in order that we may develop a comprehensive account of the part played by societal patterns of 'religioculture' in shaping societies' modes of participation in the global context. Such a perspective will surely assist in the understanding of the formation of the contemporary world and will help to counteract the view that the contemporary global field is simply a consequence of capitalism, modernity, imperialism, or whatever. The 'internal' features of societies greatly affect their forms of global involvement, and in a certain sense those features are an aspect of the overall global circumstance. Japan is an effective generator of specific conceptions of world order.

Notes

1. The term 'internationalization' – more recently, 'globalization' – has many different meanings in contemporary Japan, ranging from almost nationalistic conceptions to those which stress the desirability of Japan becoming much more open to the world. The 'compromise' is that Japan should become so integral to the world at large that it is 'indispensable.'
2. The sources upon which I draw in this section are far too numerous to list here. Among the more relevant are: Kitagawa (1966, 1987); McFarland (1967); Hori et al. (1972); Woodward (1972); Murakami (1980); Thompson (1983); Hardacre (1986) and Inoue (1991). Hardacre's work generally is especially illuminating with respect to what she calls Japanese religious 'worldviews.' See also W. Davis (1992).
3. Actually Bellah (1965: 170) once emphasized that modernization involves the capacity to 'learn to learn,' but he seems not to have applied that idea to Japanese religion.
4. A major exception among Western analysts is Wolferen (1989: 273–94), who argues that religion in Japan is closely interwoven with 'the enigma of Japanese power.' According to Wolferen, religion in Japan is based on expedience. He argues that 'the ideology of Japaneseness' consists in the overall religious attributes of 'the Japanese system.' From Wolferen's standpoint Japan is *so* religious that it is resistant to internal analysis. It is, he says, 'insidiously religious' (1989: 277). This is, of course, to take Durkheim to the extreme.
5. For a harsh critique of Pollack, see Sakai (1989: 99–105).

6

THE UNIVERSALISM–PARTICULARISM ISSUE

The nationalisms of the modern world are not the triumphant civilizations of yore. They are the ambiguous expression of the demand both for . . . assimilation into the universal . . . and *simultaneously* for . . . adhering to the particular, the reinvention of differences. Indeed, it is universalism through particularism, and particularism through universalism. (Immanuel Wallerstein, 1984a: 166–7)

Modern societies are characterized less by what they have in common or by their structure with regard to well-defined universal exigencies, than by the fact of their *involvement in the issue of universalization* . . . . The need, even the urgency, for 'universal reference' has never been felt so strongly as in our time . . . . The process of modernization is . . . the challenge hurled at groups closed in by their own contingencies and particularities to form themselves into an open ensemble of interlocutors and partners . . . (François Bourricaud, 1987: 21; emphasis added)

Like nostalgia, diversity is not what it used to be; and the sealing of lives into separate railway carriages to produce cultural renewal or the spacing of them out with contrast effects to free up moral energies are romantical dreams, not undangerous . . . . [M]oral issues stemming from cultural diversity . . . that used to arise . . . mainly between societies . . . now increasingly arise within them . . . . The day when the American city was the main model of cultural fragmentation and ethnic tumbling is quite gone. (Clifford Geertz, 1986: 114–15)

I have already indicated that the relationship between the universal and the particular must be central at this time to our comprehension of the globalization process and its ramifications. Here I consider that issue even more directly, and continue to explore the theme of global culture and global cultures. Much has been written about universality and universalism in recent years. On the one hand, those ideas have been looked upon with skepticism by communitarians, who are generally resistant to the claim that there can be viable bodies of universalistic ethics and morals. On the other hand, universalism has been rejected by many poststructuralist and postmodernist theorists. Such rejection constitutes a vital feature of the critique of foundationalism. At the same time, much has been written about particularity and particularism, difference, locality and, of course, community. A primary concern of the present chapter is to bring these two sets of interests – which are usually counterposed – into alignment.

The title of the symposium in which an early version of this chapter was presented contained three key terms: culture, globalization and world-system.[1] Each of these is in one way or another problematic and contestable and it is, I think, desirable not merely to identify the main problems involved in the uses to which they may individually be put but also to address the issue of their constituting an analytical package. To some extent the rationale in the latter respect was provided by the subtitle of the symposium. 'Contemporary conditions for the representation of identity' suggests that we should consider the ways in which 'the representation of identity' is intimately bound up, first, with cultural aspects of and responses to processes which can be identified as global in their reach and significance and, second, with an entity which has been conceptualized as the world-system. That stipulation does constitute a relatively sharp focus; and while I will not confine myself slavishly to it I will bear it carefully in mind as a directive for a general, theoretical discussion.

I begin by formulating a general position with respect to the issue of universalism and particularism in global context, to which my opening quotations draw attention, adding some reflections on gender and globalization. I then move to a discussion of our social-theoretical resources for the analysis of global complexity, with special reference to the concept of culture. Much of that exercise involves a continuation of my attempt to loosen the notion of culture, but not to the extent that culture becomes everything and everything becomes culture, which is a strong tendency in a lot of recent work under the headings of poststructuralism, postmodernism and, more diffusely, cultural studies.

Identity and the Particular–Universal Relationship

In addition to the ideas of culture, globalization and world-system, the concept of identity is, of course, also problematic (Holzner and Robertson, 1980; Robertson, 1980).[2] I cannot get involved directly in that thorny issue here, but will instead simply take the approach that, in a world which is increasingly compressed (and indeed often identified as *the* world) and in which its most 'formidable' components – nationally constituted societies and the inter-state system – are increasingly subject to the internal, as well as external, constraints of multiculturality or, which is not quite the same thing, polyethnicity, the conditions of and for the identification of individual and collective selves and of individual and collective others are becoming ever more complex.

What Bernard McGrane (1989: x) calls 'the authoritative paradigm for interpreting and explaining the difference of the other' has undergone mutation, so that increasingly ' "Culture" accounts for the difference of the other.' McGrane (1989: ix) is concerned with 'the history of the different conceptions of difference from roughly the sixteenth to the early twentieth century' – almost entirely in the West. He sees a shift from 'the alienness of the non-European Other' being interpreted 'on the horizon of Christianity' in the sixteenth century through an Enlightenment concern with the Other as Ignorant, a nineteenth-century use of *time* as 'lodged . . . between the

European and the non-European Other, to the twentieth-century employment of Culture' (McGrane, 1989: x). This approach is important in that it
draws specific attention to the civilizational paradigms for identity construction and representation. Yet it tends to neglect Oriental and other
civilizational interpretations *of* the West; as well, for the most part, as what
Benjamin Nelson (1981) called 'intercivilizational encounters.' It also does
not explicitly address the crucial contemporary question of the emergence
of a *globally* 'authoritative paradigm' or globally *contested* paradigms for
'interpreting and explaining the difference of the other.' McGrane is
nonetheless aware of such issues. Indeed he makes them relevant to his
critique of anthropology as a discipline.

Let me make this issue even more explicit. No matter that personal and
collective identity is largely constructed, but not of course without some
constraints and ascriptive fixities, there are nonetheless dominant, but
certainly not consensual, ways of 'doing' identity in any given period and
place. As the entire world becomes more compressed and singular the
bases of doing identity are increasingly, but problematically 'shared,' even
though they may at the same time collide. Thus, for example, in
multicultural educational programs there is an ongoing struggle for the
presentation of identity claims, but a condition of the operation of such
programs is the operation of something resembling a shared basis of
identity presentation (a pre-conflictful basis of conflict). This is a somewhat
different matter from the issue raised by Beck and Giddens (Giddens,
1991; Beck, 1992) in terms of the 'risk society.' Giddens (1991: 28)
describes the latter as involving 'living with a calculative attitude to the
open possibilities of action, positive and negative, with which, as individuals and globally, we are confronted in a continuous way in our
contemporary social existence.' I myself have also discussed the reflexive
choicefulness of contemporary life with particular reference to religion in
the light of 'economic' models of choice and ideas about postmodernity
(Robertson, 1992b). But diagnosis of such tendencies of what Giddens
calls 'high modernity' do not in and of themselves relate to the question of
the cultural bases of doing identity (Holzner and Robertson, 1980;
Robertson, 1978: 148–222).

The overall circumstance of identity representation in conditions of great
global density and complexity poses large analytical problems, to which
there have been a number of responses. Among the most immediately
relevant and 'extreme' of these are what I will for the sake of convenience
call *relativism*, and *worldism*. Relativism – which term covers a multitude
of 'sins,' including postmodernism, as an ideology of the intelligentsia, and
'the new pragmatism' – involves, for the most part, refusal to make any
general, 'universalizing' sense of the problems posed by sharp discontinuities between different forms of collective and individual life. In the
fashionable phrases, this perspective is anti-foundational or anti-totalistic;
and one of its offshoots is the view that talking about culture – certainly in
global perspective – almost inevitably involves participation in a game of

free-wheeling cultural politics, in which culture is regarded as being inextricably bound up with 'power' and 'resistance' (or 'liberation'). Worldism is, in contrast, foundational. It is based upon the claim that it is possible and, indeed, desirable to grasp the world as a whole analytically; to such an extent that virtually everything of sociocultural or political interest which occurs around the globe – including identity presentation – can be explained, or at least interpreted in reference to, the dynamics of the entire 'world-system.' However, that does not preclude analyzing the formation or representation of identity in terms of cultural politics; for many of those who emphasize culture as a 'privileged area' at the present time make diffuse, highly rhetorical claims as to its grounding in a world-systemic, economic realm.[3]

My own argument involves the attempt to preserve direct attention *both* to particularity and difference *and* to universality and homogeneity. It rests largely on the thesis that we are, in the late twentieth century, witnesses to – and participants in – a massive, twofold process involving *the interpenetration of the universalization of particularism and the particularization of universalism*, a claim that I will flesh out in reference to the three quotations with which I began this chapter.

Speaking specifically of recent nationalism – which is, in a number of respects, paradigmatic of contemporary particularism – Wallerstein insists, in my view correctly, on the simultaneity of particularism and universalism. However, I do not think he goes far enough in addressing the issue of their direct interpenetration, a shortfall which can be largely attributed to Wallerstein's (1984a: 167) adamance in grounding the relationship between them in 'the genius and the contradiction of capitalist civilization.' While I think there is much to the view that capitalism *amplifies* and is bound up with 'the ambiguous expression of the demand both for assimilation into the universal and for . . . adhering to the particular,' I do not agree with the implication that the problematic of the interplay of the particular and the universal is unique to capitalism. Indeed, I would claim that the differential spread of capitalism can partly be explained *in terms of its accommodation to* the historical 'working out' of that problematic. Nor do I agree with the argument that we can, in an explanatory sense, trace the contemporary connection between the two dispositions directly to late twentieth-century capitalism (in whatever way that may be defined). Rather, I would argue that the consumerist global capitalism of our time is wrapped into the increasingly thematized particular–universal relationship in terms of the connection between globewide, universalistic supply and particularistic demand. The contemporary *market* thus involves the increasing *interpenetration* of culture and economy: which is not the same as arguing, as Jameson (1984) tends to do, that the production of culture is *directed by* the 'logic' of 'late' capitalism. More specifically, the contemporary capitalist creation of consumers frequently involves the tailoring of products to increasingly specialized regional, societal, ethnic, class and gender markets – so-called 'micro-marketing.'

Wallerstein (1984: 167) also argues that 'capitalist civilization . . . as it hurtles towards its undoing . . . becomes in the interim stronger and stronger.' This is undoubtedly both a more sophisticated and a 'safer' point of view than that of another prominent advocate of world-systems analysis, namely Christopher Chase-Dunn, who had the misfortune to have the following statement published in late 1989: 'The revolutions in the Soviet Union and the People's Republic of China have increased our collective knowledge about how to build socialism despite their only partial successes and their obvious failures. Their existence widens the space available for other experiments with socialism' (Chase-Dunn, 1989: 342). The difference between Wallerstein and Chase-Dunn is important, because it illustrates the contrast between sophisticated and simplistic forms of world-systems analysis. Whereas the apparent collapse of much of communistic socialism in 1989 (and subsequently) surely came as a great disappointment to utopian members of that school of thought, there is nothing about 1989 and its aftermath which should embarrass 'true Wallersteinians.' In fact there is a crucial sense in which Wallerstein predicted the collapse of in-one-country 'socialism.'

Bourricaud, although less specific in that he does not indicate a 'driving mechanism,' comes closer to the mark in suggesting that there has emerged a globewide circumstance involving the spatial and temporal compression of the world, which increasingly constrains multitudes of groups and individuals to face each other in what he calls an 'open ensemble of interlocutors and partners.' This is what gives rise to *the issue* of 'universalization' and also accentuates *the issue* of particularization. Bourricaud draws attention to a critical matter which must surely lie at the center of any discussion of globalization and culture – namely, the ideational and practical aspects of interaction and communication between collective and individual actors on the global scene. This is an aspect of global 'reality construction' which has been almost continuously neglected. However, Bourricaud does not go far enough. Missing from his formulation is concern with *the terms* in which interaction between different particularisms may occur. To him the issue of universalization is apparently a more or less purely contingent matter arising from the problem of 'how to get along' in a compressed world, and thus has little or no cultural autonomy; although, in all fairness, it should be said that Bourricaud is mainly trying to move us away from the purely logical or ideal solutions to the problem of world order which some of the more philosophically minded anthropologists and sociologists have offered in recent years in the face of sharp cultural discontinuities, in particular Louis Dumont (1983).[4]

I am emphasizing two main points with respect to the interesting ways in which Wallerstein and Bourricaud have raised the universalism–particularism issue. First, I am arguing that the issue is a basic feature of the human condition, which was given substantial and extremely consequential historical thematization with the rise of the great religiocultural traditions during what Karl Jaspers (1953) called the Axial Age. Those traditions were, in large part, developed precisely around what has come to be called the universalism–particularism theme and their significance in that regard has continued into our time. A major example of great contemporary relevance, which I have already mentioned, has to do with the way in which Japan acquired the substantive theme of universality through its encounters with and modifications, along nativistic lines, of Confucianism and Mahayana Buddhism. Japan's crystallization of a form of 'universalistic particularism' since its first encounter with China has resulted in its acquiring paradigmatic, global significance with respect to the handling of the universalism–particularism issue. Specifically, its paradigmatic status is inherent in its very long and successful history of selective incorporation and syncretization of ideas from other cultures in such a way as to particularize the universal and, so to say, return the product of that process to the world as a uniquely Japanese contribution to the universal.[5]

Second, I am arguing that in more recent world history the universalism–particularism issue has come to constitute something like a global-cultural form, a major axis of the structuration of the world as a whole. Rather than simply viewing the theme of universalism as having to do with principles which can and should be applied to all, and that of particularism as referring to that which can and should be applied only 'locally,' I suggest that the two have become tied together as part of a globewide nexus. They have become united in terms of the universality of the experience and, increasingly, *the expectation of* particularity, on the one hand, and the experience and, increasingly, the *expectation of* universality, on the other. The latter – the particularization of universalism – involves the idea of the universal being given global-human concreteness; while the former – the universalization of particularism – involves the extensive diffusion of the idea that there is virtually no limit to particularity, to uniqueness, to difference, and to otherness. (One aspect of the latter tendency is conveyed by Jean Baudrillard's (1988: 41) aphorism concerning our present condition: 'It is never too late to revive your origins.')

I suggest that along these lines we may best consider contemporary globalization in its most general sense as a form of institutionalization of the two-fold process involving the universalization of particularism and the particularization of universalism. *Resistance* to contemporary globalization – as, for example, some consider to be involved on the more radical side of the general Islamic movement – would thus be regarded as opposition not merely to the world as one, homogenized system but also – and, I believe, more relevantly – to the conception of the world as a series of culturally equal, relativized, entities or ways of life. The first aspect could well be regarded as a form of anti-modernity, while the second could fruitfully be seen as a form of anti-postmodernity. Put another way, it is around the universalism–particularism axis of globalization that *the discontents of globality* manifest themselves in reference to new, globalized variations on the oldish themes of *Gesellschaft* and *Gemeinschaft*. The *Gemeinschaft–*

Gesellschaft theme has been a primary focus for the critique of modernity (most directly in Germany). It is now increasingly interwoven with the discourse of globality in the sense that it has been 'upgraded' so as to refer to the general relationship between the particular and the communal, on the one hand, and the universal and the impersonal, on the other. This issue is closely related to what Arjun Appadurai (1990: 5) calls 'the tension between cultural homogenization and cultural heterogenization,' which he regards as 'the central problem of today's global interactions.'

Appadurai (1990: 17) argues that 'the central feature of global culture today is the politics of the mutual effort of sameness and difference to cannibalize one another and thus to proclaim their successful hijacking of the twin Enlightenment ideas of the triumphantly universal and the resiliently particular.' This evocative interpretation is, it should be noted, connected by Appadurai (1990: 20) to his suggestion that 'the theory of global cultural interactions . . . will have to move into something like a human version of the theory that some scientists are calling "chaos" theory.' While this cannot be the place for an adequate discussion of this complex issue, it should be said that Appadurai's advocacy of a *chaos*-theoretic approach to global culture – which he sees more specifically in terms of a 'disjunctive' series of 'scapes' (ethnoscapes, technoscapes, finanscapes, mediascapes and ideoscapes) – clearly involves rejection of the idea of the global institutionalization of the relationship between universalized particularism and particularized universalism.

While not denying the fruitfulness of Appadurai's ideas about the existence of empirically disjunctive relationships between different cultural 'scapes' at the global level, I do insist upon the general structuring significance of the particular–universal connection – its crystallization as 'the elemental form of global life.' Some of my differences with Appadurai may arise from his suggestion that the Enlightenment ideas of universalism and particularism were necessarily incongruent. My own interpretation is that they were basically complementary. As Anthony Smith (1979: 2) has written of the late eighteenth century, '[A]t the root of the "national ideal" is a certain vision of the world . . . . According to this vision mankind is "really" and "naturally" divided into distinct . . . nations. Each nation . . . has its peculiar contribution to make to the whole, the family of nations.'[6] Or, to put it more incisively, *the idea* of nationalism (or particularism) develops *only* in tandem with internationalism. This way of looking at the issue is compatible with Simon Schama's (1991) analysis of the origins in the West of the association between land and homeland. We now, of course, tend to take such an association for granted but, as Schama (1991: 13) points out, 'for much of Western history [it] was not at all axiomatic.' Schama traces the beginning of the association, at least in image making, to the later years of the European Renaissance in northern Europe and in the Netherlands. That period and region witnessed the development of landscape as an autonomous form, rather than as a supplement to sacred or classical narratives. Schama (1991: 13) is interested in 'the moment of alteration from the universal to the particular, from world to home.' His specific point is that images in Dutch painting involved a differentiation of 'visual parochialism' from a wider universalistic and imperialistic culture.

Finally, as far as fleshing out in relation to my introductory quotations is concerned, the citation from Geertz reminds us strongly of the fact that globalization is not simply a matter of societies, regions and civilizations being squeezed together in various problematic ways but also of this occurring with increasing intensity *inside* nationally constituted societies. Nowadays, to quote further from Geertz (1986: 112), 'foreignness does not start at the water's edge but at the skin's . . . the wogs begin long before Calais.' Published in 1986, Geertz's suggestions have since acquired poignant relevance to current trends in Central and Eastern Europe and the former Soviet Union, for in those areas the problems of old ethnic identity are being played out within the context of increasing global thematization of ethnicity-*within*-humankind, although there are undoubtedly elements of relatively raw atavism involved.

Geertz's observations press us, *inter alia*, to take seriously into account the position of *individuals* in the globalization process. (I return briefly to the issues of multiculturality and polyethnicity raised by Geertz at a later point.) There has been a marked tendency in many discussions of the world-system, world society or whatever, to ignore individuals – more precisely, the contemporary construction of individualism – for the apparent reason that globalization of alleged necessity refers to very large-scale matters, in contrast to the 'small-scale' status of individuals. This bow in the direction of the textbook wisdom which distinguishes microsociological from macrosociological approaches in terms of naive conceptions of scale and complexity is, I believe, misplaced. I insist that individuals are as much a part of the globalization process as any other basic category of social-theoretical discourse. I have argued that there are four elemental points of reference for any discussion of contemporary globalization – national *societies*; *individual selves*; *the world system of societies* (international relations); and *humankind*. My general argument in making this set of distinctions is that globalization increasingly involves thematization of these four elements of the global-human condition or field (rather than the world-system). Any given element is constrained by the other three. For example, individuals as such are increasingly constrained by being members of societies, members of an increasingly thematized and endangered human species and greatly affected by the vicissitudes of international relations. Thus late twentieth-century globalization involves the institutionalization of both the universalization of particularism and the particularization of universalism and can be more specifically indicated as consisting in the interpenetrating processes of societalization, individualization, the consolidation of the international system of societies, and the concretization of the sense of humankind.

Returning directly to the individual, my primary claim is that globalization has involved and continues to involve the *institutionalized construction* of the individual. Even more specifically, we must recognize that world-political culture has led to a globewide institutionalization of 'the life course' – which has, John Meyer (1987: 243–4) maintains, two dimensions: 'aspects of the person that enter into rationalized social organization' and 'the public celebration of . . . the "private" or subjective individual.' Much of that has been and continues to be mediated by state structures, but international *non*-governmental organizations have also increasingly mediated and promoted individualism in the areas of education, human rights, the rights of women, health, and so on. In sum, the globewide encouragement of individualism in association with increasing polyethnicity and multiculturality – themselves encouraged by large migrations and 'diasporations' – has been crucial in the move towards the circumstance of 'foreignness' described so well by Geertz. At the same time, what Meyer calls the celebration of subjective identity *relative to* involvement in 'rationalized social organization' has played a major part in the virtually globewide establishment of various 'minority' forms of personal and collective identification – among which gender has been of particular significance. This has a considerable bearing on the question raised earlier about identity, particularly personal identity, in the current condition of late twentieth-century life.

A Note on Women and Gender

This may be the best place to raise the question of my conception of women in relation to globality and globalization. While I cannot present here a comprehensive exploration of that theme, some reflections are in order. In loosely empirical terms, it should be said that my own experience of women's responses to the analysis and interpretation of globalization is that women participate in it as eagerly as men. This is probably most clear with respect to the *humankind*, particularly the environmental, aspects of my model; the latter tendency having been confirmed to me by others, including female teachers working in the field of international (or global) education. But it can be reasonably argued that this 'fact' should not be regarded uncritically. Is not the assignment of women to the most 'familial' aspect of the globalization process a reproduction of the historically subordinate status of women inside societies and communities? My answer to that is ambiguous, for who can tell where the maximum leverage is going to be as far as the patterning of the world as a whole is concerned? Certainly the entire question of global ecology and the fate of humankind as a species will be increasingly important in the politics of the global-human condition in the coming decades. It *could* be the case that concern with humankind will be established as a predominantly 'feminine' issue; but yet it could, alternatively, come to be a powerful basis for feminism. (Cf. Diamond and Orenstein, 1990.) In any case, the ways in which women, in all their variety, *participate in* the discussion of globalization is a particularly significant factor.

The issue of gender and globalization is very relevant to one of the most pressing problems in contemporary feminist theory: whether women should emphasize their equality with men, or whether they should emphasize difference. Among those who have stressed difference a particular interpretation has been given to the feminine experience of childbearing and mothering. For example, Sara Ruddick (1989) has argued that women, regardless of whether they actually bear children, share a commitment to the nurturing of life and, by the same token, a natural opposition to its destruction. On the other hand, Elizabeth Fox-Genovese has issued a sharp critique of the tendency among many contemporary feminists to operate within what she describes and analyzes as the constraints of a critique of individualism. Remarking at the outset that 'no politics remains innocent of that which it contests' (1991: 17), Fox-Genovese concludes her discussion with the argument that 'feminism, in all it guises, is itself the daughter of that (male) individualism which so many feminists are attacking' (1991: 243). Speaking specifically of feminists' attempts to reshape the canonical curriculum, particularly in American universities, she cogently points to the irony of women ostensibly opposing 'the tradition' but actually articulating 'the view of themselves that it propounds' (1991: 174). This means that, for the most part, the project of identifying a uniquely feminine tradition has led to the identification of women with values which are presumed to be the exact opposites of male values, such as nurture, community and pacifism (Janeway, 1980). In this regard it is interesting to note that Auguste Comte, who was arguably not only the first fully-fledged sociologist but also a globalist, accorded a special place to women, not as 'active participants in the basic public roles,' but as representatives of 'ultimate goodness' (Fox-Genovese, 1991: 175). Women were, in that perspective, 'relegated to the margin where they could be celebrated – even worshipped, as Clothilde de Vaux was to be worshipped in [Comte's] Religion of Humanity' (1991: 175).

In *Feminism without Illusions* Fox-Genovese (1991) frequently characterizes the feminist tendency, at least in the USA, to celebrate women's maternal roles and instincts and their disposition to favor *Gemeinschaft* over *Gesellschaft* as basically nostalgic. 'Most feminine theorists who criticize male individualism . . . end by embracing the sentimental view of community' (Fox-Genovese, 1991: 52). On the other hand, 'the path that feminism is treading leads inexorably to the final erosion of community, nor will any amount of nostalgic rhetoric be able to wish it back' (1991: 53). Fox-Genovese is generally very persuasive, at least to this writer, in her critique of many feminists' acceptance of a prevailing, and mostly male-contrived, distinction between feminine *Gemeinschaft* and male *Gesellschaft* and their failure 'to elaborate a theory that would justify radical interventions in social policy' (1991: 51). She is equally cogent in her claim that even though there are those such as Gayatri Spivak (1987, 1990) who 'avoid the worst pitfalls of a complacent celebration of the existence of community among women' (Fox-Genovese, 1991: 51) they too tend to 'avoid the central political issues' (1991: 51). Of course, it could well be argued that 'post-colonial' or 'subaltern' feminists such as Spivak (who certainly does not speak only as a feminist) in addressing the positions of women throughout the world in a distinctively non-sentimental way, are simply but boldly attempting 'to render visible the historical and institutional structures of the representative space from which [they are] called to speak' (Harasym, 1990: vii). Even though this may not directly enhance our understanding of global complexity it may make some contribution to that task; besides which Spivak seems to subscribe to the view that opening up and rendering visible a variety of 'post-colonial' spaces *is* a distinctively political project, even if it only 'deconstructs' conventional, 'colonial' standpoints. In any case, Fox-Genovese (1991: 150) is certainly correct when she says that 'a privileged position in academia ought to make us all shrink from pretending that we are somehow the voice of the downtrodden.'

My main concern here, however, is to consider the relationship, actual and potential, between women and globalization. The rise of a diverse international women's movement and that movement's particular concern with the theme of 'women and development' (Goetz, 1991) is relevant to, and a manifestation of, globalization. Indeed it is one among many movements and organizations which have helped to compress the world as a whole. What seems to be emerging from that movement is an increasing recognition of the diversity of women's experiences and a recognition that the perspective of Western, more specifically American, women is by no means of universal applicability.

One of the few attempts to address directly the issue of 'international politics' from a feminist point of view is Cynthia Enloe's *Bananas Beaches and Bases* (1990), the central claim of which is that women have, for the most part, been global victims of an essentially patriarchal international system. 'The national political arena is dominated by men but allows women some select access; the international political arena is a sphere for men only, or for those rare women who can successfully play at being men, or at least not shake masculine presumptions' (Enloe, 1990: 13). Having thus set the tone for her discussion Enloe proceeds to an exploration of various sites upon which women have been used and victimized by or collaborated in the operation of the international system: tourism; foreign bases of armed forces; diplomacy; cross-national and global advertising; global consumerism; and the trade in domestic servants. Throughout these discussions Enloe is concerned to make 'feminist sense' of international politics (although her empirical focus is somewhat larger than this term suggests). Enloe (1990: 18) rightly argues that an international feminist alliance, which appeared to become a real possibility at the Nairobi conference in 1985, marking the conclusion of the United Nations Decade of Women, 'doesn't automatically weaken male-run imperialist ventures.' Specifically, 'a feminist international campaign lacking a feminist analysis of international politics is likely to subvert its own ultimate goals' (1990: 18).

A definite move has already been made in the direction of a feminist approach to international politics in the volume edited by Grant and Newland, *Gender and International Relations* (1991). The contributors to this volume are, for the most part, concerned to theorize the place of gender in the discipline of international relations and consider the prospects for explicit feminist perspectives. Among the themes discussed is the extent to which 'normal and patriarchal' international relations is, to quote Grant, 'ensnared by the trap of dividing the domestic and the international' (1991: 22). This view is strongly in line with the emerging anti-nostalgic, anti-'micro' thrust in some strands of contemporary feminist theory, involving the reformulation and 'modernization' of the concept of community so as to make it refer to *the world as a whole* in all its difference and variety. This focus is, in turn, congruent with my own conceptualization of the global field, or the global-human condition. One of my continuing and strongest claims is that if we are to 'map' the global situation seriously we must do so comprehensively. We should have an image which both fluidly and systematically connects the series consisting (in no particular order) of individuals, humankind, societies and international relations. Even though relative autonomy is accorded in principle to each sphere, the basic point is this: that what are often considered to be strictly internal-societal matters (or epiphenomenal, or even irrelevant phenomena) are in my scheme rendered *as part of* the complex global circumstance.

The most important point in the present context is that, during the crucial take-off period of globalization, women were thematized as a 'natural' aspect of societal life, while men were thought of as self-reflexive, extra-social subjects (Baykan, 1992) standing in problematic relationships with the increasingly standardized conception of society (Boli, 1980). Inspired by Riley (1988), Baykan (1992) argues that it was in this respect that, in the West, women came to accept their modern self-definition, and placed this definition in relation to, actually in distinction from, the 'political.' Riley and Baykan thus contribute to the thesis that twentieth-century conceptions of gender are the outcome of a globalized process of society construction. 'Women' were constructed specifically in reference to 'the communal essence' of non-Western societies.

Sociological Theory and Global Culture

There seems to be something of a consensus among those sociologists who have been doing work directly on the global circumstance that the main traditions of social theory are inadequate to the task of illuminating discussion of the world as a whole and the making thereof. As I have said, Wallerstein (1987: 309) has probably put the matter most sharply in arguing that 'world-systems analysis' is a protest against the received tradition of social science as a whole. I have great sympathy with the general, if not the specific, thrust of that claim and I will now outline some of my own main views on this, in relation to the substantive task at hand and mainly in reference to my own 'official' discipline of sociology. Sociology has played a significant role in the patterning of twentieth-century globalization; but it has not done much in its mainstream to focus analytically and interpretively *on* globalization as an historical phenomenon of increasingly salient contemporary significance.

There can be little doubt that sociology took its classical shape during the declining years of the nineteenth century and the first quarter of the present century in primary reference to what has come to be called the problem of modernity, on the one hand, and to the mode of operation of the nationally constituted society, on the other – with the society–individual problematic being central to both. In such a perspective there was little or no room for the analysis of cultural differences except in terms of analytical contrasts between civilizations and civilizational traditions, since it was widely assumed that the modern form of society was culturally homogeneous or had to become so in order to achieve viability. Certainly Max Weber had no clear sociological sense of, certainly no liking for, what we have come to call, in reference to ethnicity, culture and race, a pluralistic society. In one way or another the leading classical sociologists promoted the idea, if only implicitly, that what later came to be called a central value system was an essential feature of viable national societies and that in external terms each society should develop a sense of its own collective identity. In this respect some sociologists of that period became very influential outside Western Europe.

Social-scientific ideas, notably those of the English utilitarians and the French positivists, had, of course, been influential among dominant, 'liberal' elites in newly independent Latin American societies during the nineteenth century; but such turn-of-the-century people as Durkheim, Toennies, Spencer and Max Weber had a particular impact in European and Asian countries in terms of their ideas concerning such matters as culture and national identity, as well as those relating to the issue of what form a modern national society should take. For example Spencer, whose work was influential in late nineteenth-century Japan and China, explicitly advised the Meiji political elite to establish a firm tradition-based Japanese identity; Durkheim's ideas on the theme of civil religion were influential in the establishment of the new Turkish republic in the 1920s; while the German theme of *Gemeinschaft* v. *Gesellschaft* (or culture v. civilization) was widely manipulated in East Asia and elsewhere. The Meiji elite decided quite early to erect a nationally organized community, or 'national household' – to try to have both *Gemeinschaft* and *Gesellschaft*.

So even though it is conventional to think of Western social science as having developed more or less solely in the West itself (with the partial exception of its Marxian component), the fact of the matter is that in a great array of different juxtapositions it found its way into the life-courses of a large number of non-Western societies well before the peaking of Western social-scientific theories of societal modernization in the late 1950s and early 1960s (in relation to the emergence of the Third World as a global presence). By the end of the first quarter of the twentieth century Western social science had become a 'cultural resource' in a number of global regions – perhaps most notably in East Asia, where there was a long-standing cultural tendency to juxtapose superficially contradictory sets of ideas in syncretic form. Thus while Western social scientists, most significantly Max Weber, were busy *comparing* East and West as an analytical exercise (with political and ideological overtones), the objects of the comparison (more accurately, intellectual and political elites) were busy sifting and implementing packages of Western ideas for very concrete political, economic and cultural reasons.

The irony in this is, of course, that in spite of the diffusion of their ideas to the very societies which they were contrasting with the West, there was little sense among the leading sociologists of the classical period that an increasing number of societies around the world were in varying degrees subject, often very willingly, to their ideas concerning the functioning and operation of modern, nationally consituted societies; although those ideas were invariably recast for local purposes. In other words these sociologists, with the possible exception of Durkheim, had little sense of the possibility of national societies being subject to *generalized, external* expectations of how societies could establish and maintain viability, that they themselves were actually central to the formation of an increasingly global sense of how societies should be constructed. They were, in brief, relatively insensitive to what has come to be called globalization, particularly cultural aspects thereof.

To be sure, Durkheim became increasingly concerned with what he called 'international life' to which individual societies became subject, and he was actually engaged at the time of his death in work on the more or less logical, rather than the contingent-sociological, question of how culturally different societies could form an ensemble of societies in moral terms. For the most part, however, the dominant idea in the foundational period of academic sociology was – in so far as international or global matters were attended to at all – that societies were engaged in something like a Darwinian struggle, a view which was to be found particularly in those quite numerous societies which were directly influenced by so-called Social Darwinism and, less explicitly, in the orbits in which Max Weber was particularly influential.[7] My main point here is thus that not merely has sociology suffered greatly from its inattention to extra-societal issues but that it still remains ill equipped to deal with inter-societal let alone global matters, although considerable effort is currently being exerted to rectify this. As I have said, one of the major liabilities has been sociology's general acceptance of something like a dominant ideology or common culture thesis at the level of nationally constituted societies. It is to that specific issue which I now turn.

As Margaret Archer (1988) has argued, sociological discussion of cultural phenomena has been plagued by 'the myth of cultural integration,' according to which all societies that are considered to be viable are normatively integrated, with culture performing the major function in this regard. Archer's primary concern is to distinguish culture as an objective, ideational phenomenon – possessing considerable autonomy in terms of its own inner 'logic' (but not necessarily consistency) – from agents who, in specific circumstances, seek to comprehend, invoke, manipulate and act in reference to systems of ideas. Those analysts who consider culture to be almost exclusively of significance in terms of its capacity to *constrain* action (and social structure) are classified by Archer as 'downward conflationists.' The basic myth of cultural integration derives mainly from the latter, particularly from anthropological functionalists of the 1930s, and was incorporated, in Archer's view, into sociological structural-functionalism in the 1940s and 1950s.

Yet we have also, according to Archer, witnessed more recently another form of the myth of cultural integration, arising from Marxist and neo-Marxist schools of thought. Deeply concerned about the problem of the persistence of capitalism, a considerable number of Marxist social scientists have produced their own versions of 'the myth' (cf. Abercrombie et al., 1980, 1990). Archer classifies this as 'upward conflationism,' on the grounds that in contrast to downward conflation it involves the notion of culture deriving from and being imposed by one set of agents upon other members of a collectivity and pays little attention to the idea of culture having some kind of inner logic. ('Strong' cultural studies programs belong in this category.) In both downward and upward conflation the upshot is, to all intents and purposes, the same, in spite of differing conceptions of how the result is achieved. Culture is to be considered primarily as a constraint; although in some of the more radical forms of cultural studies this situation is reversed, with culture seen as representative and constitutive of subaltern groups and movements.

Archer also deals with a third approach, which involves the refusal or analytical inability to distinguish between culture and action (or between culture and social structure). 'Central conflationism,' of which Anthony Giddens's structuration theory is provided as a major example, is the target of much of Archer's harshest criticism, since it leaves room neither for action in relative independence of culture nor for the objective, ideational status of the latter. My primary reason for rehearsing the central thrust of Archer's argument is that she helps clear the way for a definite sociological move away from the old culture-as-integrating approach. In particular, she draws attention to the issue of the different ways in which ideational patterns may be interpreted, employed, reconstituted and expanded in a variety of situational circumstances. Nevertheless, there are, most certainly, weaknesses in Archer's *Culture and Agency*. Probably the most significant is her rationalistic bias, which precludes her from attending to expressive meaning and to morality. She also sets up an implausible distinction between social and cultural action and does not attend directly to interaction and interpenetration of societal and civilizational cultures. Moreover, Archer tends, ironically like cultural studies 'interventionists,' to see action as 'something which is . . . opposed to institutionalized cultural codes' (Alexander, 1992: 2; see also Holzner and Robertson, 1980; Robertson, 1978: 148–222).

It would seem that the declining myth of cultural integration is, indeed, closely bound to the perception of the national society as a homogenized entity, and so it needs to be periodized just as much as does the idea of the culturally homogeneous, state-governed society. In the latter respect I can do no better than invoke William McNeill (1986: 33), who has provided three reasons for 'the prevalence of polyethnicity in civilized societies before 1750 . . . [C]onquest, disease, and trade all worked in that direction, most pronouncedly in the Middle East, and somewhat less forcefully towards the extremities of the Eurasian ecumene.' In the latter 'ethnic diversity diminished, though even in remote offshore islands, like medieval Japan and Britain, aliens played significant roles as bearers of special skills' (1986: 33). McNeill argues generally that the idea of an ethnically homogenous society is fundamentally 'barbaric.' In any case, with the French Revolution and the new conception of citizens constituting a single nation and possessing rights and duties to participate in public life, nationalism triumphed as, to quote McNeill (1986: 34), *'the* central reality of modern times.' The major issue in the present context is whether and in what ways we can develop modes of understanding of the modern circumstances of polyethnicity and multiculturality, on the one hand, and globality, on the other, which will not involve repetition of mainstream sociology's enchantment with the national society.

Let me emphasize here that I am *not* arguing that the nationally constituted society is about to wither away. On the contrary, it is being revamped in various parts of the world as the multicultural society, while 'old European' and other nationalisms have reappeared – but in new global circumstances – in the context of the world-political ferment of 1989 and subsequent years. I have insisted that 'societalism,' the commitment to the idea of the national society, is a crucial ingredient of the contemporary form of globalization (the rendering of the world as a single place). My point is that we should not carry into the study of globalization the kind of view of culture that we inherit from the conventional analysis of the national society. Much of our difficulty in thinking about culture at the global level stems from that view, from conceiving of societies as unitary and larger units, including the world as a whole, as lacking in such. To a significant extent the unitary view of the nationally constituted society is an *aspect* of global culture. Even more specifically, the state is in large measure a cultural construct.

Apart from limitations stemming from the derivation of the notion of culture from a particularly unitary notion of society (one which was also projected by anthropologists on to primal societies during the crucial take-off phase of recent globalization, 1870–1925), the other main problem about thinking of culture in global terms derives from the fact that the dominant image of what is often called global interdependence has been centered on the global *economy*, although the self-serving idea of 'the global village' promoted by television commentators remains a close and also misleading contender, as does 'planet earth.'

The main difficulty with the primarily economic attitude parallels the problem arising from our having been held in thrall by the idea of the homogeneous national society. Because there has, indeed, occurred a very rapid crystallization of a global economy in relatively recent times we are tempted into thinking that that is what defines or determines globalization in general. Such a view, unfortunately, overlooks a number of historical developments which, however loosely, are bound up with the notion of global culture. Moreover concentration almost exclusively on the global economy exacerbates the tendency to think that we can only conceive of global culture along the axis of Western hegemony and non-Western cultural resistance. While it would be extremely foolish to reject the relevance of that perspective it has a number of serious liabilities.

There has recently been considerable expansion of the rhetoric of globality, globalization, and internationalization. In fact there appears to have rapidly developed across the world a relatively autonomous mode of discourse concerning such themes. Put another way, 'globe talk' – the discourse of globality – has become relatively autonomous, although its contents and the interests that sustain them vary considerably from society to society and also within societies. The discourse of globality is thus a vital component of contemporary global culture. It consists largely in the shifting and contested terms in which the world as a whole is 'defined.' Images of world order (and disorder) – including interpretations of and assertions concerning the past, present and future of particular societies, civilizations, ethnic groups and regions – are at the center of global culture.

Along such lines we can readily conceive of global culture as having a very long history. The idea of 'humankind' is at least as old as Jaspers's Axial Age (Eisenstadt, 1982) in which the major world religions and metaphysical doctrines arose, many centuries before the rise of national communities or societies. Throughout that long period civilizations, empires and other entities have been almost continuously faced with the problem of response to the wider, increasingly compressed and by now global, context. The ways in which such entities (in relatively recent history, national societies in particular) have at one and the same time attempted to learn from others and sustain a sense of identity – or, alternatively, isolate themselves from the pressures of contact – also constitute an important aspect of the creation of global culture. More specifically, the cultures of particular societies are, to different degrees, the result of their interactions with other societies in the global system. In other words, national-societal cultures have been differentially formed in interpenetration with significant others (Robertson, 1990a). By the same token, global culture itself is partly created in terms of specific interactions between national societies.

The issue of 'selective response' is particularly important in any attempt to grasp what might be meant by the term 'global culture,' because it indicates the contemporary phenomenon of particular national societies becoming positive or negative paradigms as far as involvement in globalization is concerned.[8] The global thematization of the ill-fated Soviet perestroika/glasnost motif may have played a large part in this respect. It may have brought to the forefront of global discourse the problem of the relationship between societal identity, societal restructuring and participation in the globalization process. The global diffusion of the perestroika/glasnost motif in the second half of the 1980s reminds us that all societies have been under the constraint to institutionalize a connection between inwardness and outwardness.

In combination with my discussion of the universalism–particularism issue I have indicated some of the more neglected aspects of the analysis of global culture. Commitment to the idea of the culturally cohesive national society has blinded us to the various ways in which the world as a whole has been increasingly 'organized' around sets of shifting definitions of the global circumstance. It would not be too much to say that the idea of global culture is just as meaningful as the idea of national-societal, or local, culture.

Notes

1. This chapter has grown out of a paper delivered at a symposium held at the State University of New York at Binghamton in April, 1989. I am grateful to the organizer, Anthony King, for inviting me and also to Janet Wolff, another participant, for prodding me into making my views on gender and globalization a little clearer (in spite of her unwarranted claim, among others, that I am interested only in *the experience* of globalization: Wolff, 1991).
2. Among the most important recent studies of *national*-identity formation are A.D. Smith (1981, 1983); B. Anderson (1983); Gellner (1983); Hobsbawm and Ranger (1983); Gluck (1985); Nairn (1988); James (1989); Kierney (1989); Hobsbawm (1990).
3. A major example is Fredric Jameson (1986). Also see Lash and Urry (1987) and Harvey (1989).
4. This, however, is not intended as a pejorative comment on Dumont's pioneering work on what he calls, in a very abstract manner, (civilizational) ideologies. See Kavolis (1986).
5. For a provocative discussion of this aspect of Japanese identity, see Pollack (1986). For a strong critique of Pollack, see Sakai (1989: 99–105).
6. See also Hans Kohn (1971) and, for more recent period, Emerson (1964).
7. For an instructive discussion of the Japanese reception of Max Weber's ideas in Japan, see Ishida (1983).
8. For an excellent study of what is called 'selective receptiveness,' see Cohen (1987). Also see Robertson (1987a).

7

'CIVILIZATION,' CIVILITY AND THE CIVILIZING PROCESS

Humanity is simply another word for the totality of human societies, for the ongoing process of the figuration which all the various survival units form with each other. . . . In former days, the term humanity often served as a symbol of a far-fetched ideal beyond the reach of social science inquiries. It is far-fetched no longer nor is it an ideal. At a time when all the different tribes, all states of the world, are drawn together more closely, humanity increasingly represents a purely factual frame of reference of sociological inquiries into past no less than present phases of social development. (Norbert Elias, 1987: 244)

In this chapter I consider the general relevance of Norbert Elias's work to the current concern with globalization, making some comparisons with Parsons. Specifically I consider the degree to which Elias's work is relevant to *world*, as relatively distinct from *state*, formation. Although I concentrate here upon inter-state relations I obviously deny that the conception of the world is by any means exhausted by such relations. In my discussion I draw considerably upon Gong's (1984) analysis of 'the standard of "civilization",' to a lesser degree on Cuddihy's (1987) work on civility, and to a small extent on Parsons's (1977b) concepts of differentiation, normative upgrading, inclusion and value generalization.

I am primarily concerned with one particular aspect of the making of the contemporary world, that which for a significant period of time in the late nineteenth and the early twentieth century centered on the international-legal ramifications of the concept of 'civilization'. This concept has undoubtedly enjoyed a problematic career. Indeed in many quarters it has become a thoroughly discredited notion, on the grounds that it often suggests superior 'moral sensibility' (Mazrui, 1990: 30). Such a suggestion has been increasingly and understandably rejected by intellectuals and others outside the West, as well as by many within it. On the other hand, there have been those who have spoken emphatically of civilizations in a neutral way to refer to the major sociocultural and symbolic centers in world history (e.g. Kavolis, 1986, 1987, 1988). In the latter perspective the category of civilization refers generally to the distinctive 'richness' and historical 'depth' of particular configurations or sociocultural patterns. Without denying in any way the appropriateness of that approach to the analysis of civilizational configurations, I want to focus on the way in which the idea of civilization became for a critical historical moment a, perhaps the, central ingredient in the globalization process, not least because it was largely in terms of that idea as a legal notion that the fundamental form of the dominant globalization process was established on a near-global basis (Lechner, 1991).

Elias and Globalization

Few of Elias's interpreters or critics have attended directly to the relevance of his work to the theme of globalization, Mennell (1990) being a significant exception.[1] Mennell in fact discusses what he explictly calls Elias's theory of globalization. This, however, is somewhat misleading, for Mennell does not suggest what Elias might have made of nor what he himself precisely means by that concept. Nor does he specifically link Elias's work to any of the current literature on that theme. Yet it is certainly necessary to attend to his interesting arguments. Haferkamp (1987a) also focused briefly in a review essay on Elias's ideas concerning inter-state relationships, arguing that around 1980 Elias became so much concerned with inter-state 'civilization' that post-1980 work constituted a new phase, virtually a 'new Elias.' Haferkamp argued that

> the 'new' Elias set inter-state-societal processes in the centre of the stage, that these processes were no longer a starting mechanism for a new level of civilization as they had been earlier. Certainly they *may* have this effect but they *could* just as well be a completion process, leading to the downfall and destruction of civilization. (1987a: 546)

Haferkamp went on to argue that Elias underestimated the effects of intra-societal civilizing processes on inter-state-societal processes and that Elias reified 'hegemonical regularities' (Haferkamp, 1987a: 555). Arguing against what he saw as undue pessimism and/or lack of insight on Elias's part, Haferkamp asks 'how Elias would explain the widespread acceptance of human rights, the international rejection of slavery, the codifying of the crime of genocide' (1987a: 555). These are, I believe, important criticisms, although Haferkamp inevitably had to situate his critique within the bipolar superpower world of the 1980s. His assessment was also, in my judgement, insufficiently adventurous.

On the other hand, Mennell has argued that there was no 'new Elias,' that Haferkamp set up 'a false polarity between intra-state and inter-state processes, which have always been two sides of the same coin in Elias's thinking' (1987: 559). Elias simply paid more attention to inter-state processes in his later years. Mennell points out that in *The Civilizing Process* (Elias, 1978, 1982) 'inter-state processes are discussed in considerable detail,' the leading argument being (in Simmelian mode) that the reduction of intra-societal violence went hand in hand with 'the relatively unbridled persistence in violence between states' (Mennell, 1987: 559); although, as Haferkamp (1987b) pointed out, there is an aspect of Elias's work which points to the ways in which the area of 'civilization' is *enlarged* by inter-state conflict. In a separate paper, the one in which he talks more directly about Elias's ideas on globalization, Mennell (1990: 369) agrees that 'Elias's own writing about the globalization of human society had centered mainly on the chances of nuclear war,' but that there is much in Elias's work, 'in his underlying theoretical strategy,' which will be of great help to those now analyzing 'other aspects of global society.' Mennell (1990: 369) provides as an example Elias's early work on manners, asking about 'the prospects for the globalization of manners.' This is indeed a significant topic, to which I will briefly return. For the moment I want to deal with a much more general issue.

The present discussion is part of a larger project in which I am attempting to connect important and influential ideas within a number of sociological traditions to the contemporary discussion of globalization. Elias's work obviously has to be considered in any such exercise. His long interest in what he called the civilizing process and his figurational sociology generally were clearly based on a profound concern with and for what I have often called the global-human condition. My opening quotation draws sharp attention to that concern. In that connection it may be worth saying that Elias has from time to time been characterized, pejoratively of course, as a 'Comtean.' While I am not directly interested here in either the substance or the academic politics of that charge, it is worth saying that the 'global' perspectives of Comte, as well as those of Saint-Simon, appear in a new and somewhat more appreciable light as the debate about globalization gains momentum (Albrow, 1990; Turner, 1990b). One aim of the present discussion is the modification of Elias's alleged evolutionism or developmentalism by a more epigenetic and comprehensively global perspective, which allows for the emergence of increasingly global constraints from 'above' and 'below' *on* the affairs of 'survival units'; although it does seem that Elias recognized that through historical time it is *the world*, or 'humanity,' as a whole which becomes the dominant survival unit. My main concern is to add to, modify and connect Elias's work to relevant others.

It is not my purpose here to present a general assessment of Elias's theory of the civilizing process nor certainly of his figurational sociology as a whole. I want, as I have indicated, to consider strengths and weaknesses in particular reference to the rapidly increasing interest in globalization. In general I consider Elias's ideas concerning the contingent internalization of restraint within societies – or survival units – to be equally applicable to inter-societal systems, indeed to *the* contemporary globewide inter-societal system. As Mennell implies, Elias himself more than hinted at that in the second volume of *The Civilizing Process*, but he did not, in my view, make enough of it, even in his phase of direct concern with Cold War inter-state relations. Indeed, Mennell (1990: 368) says that Elias remained skeptical of ideas that appeared to flow from what he had to say about inter-state relations in his early work. Bentham van den Bergh (1983, 1990) has, according to Mennell (1990: 367), perceived an analogy between Elias's basically intra-societal civilizing processes and the function of nuclear weapons as '*an external constraint towards self-restraint* in international relations' (Mennell, 1990: 367; emphasis in original). Thus the 'principle' of mutually assured destruction could have come to acquire what Mennell (1990: 367) calls 'a civilizing function in international politics.' Citing Goudsblom, Mennell invokes the notion of 'mutually expected self-restraint.' Apparently Elias was not convinced by this line of thinking.

To some extent these considerations have been relativized and altered by the severe attenuation of the communist presence – more specifically, by the demise of Soviet strength *per se* – in the contemporary world since 1989. 'The hegemonical fevers,' to use Elias's phrase, are not what they used to be. Nonetheless the general problem of thermonuclear destruction has become much more complicated and unpredictable. Speaking in reference to nuclear tension centered on USA–USSR conflict Elias argued, again according to Mennell (1990: 368), that humanity appeared to stand at a saddle point: 'the possibility of global pacification on the one side, and on the other the chances of destruction through nuclear holocaust or ecological disaster – both produced by the globalization of human interdependence.' However, in the changed inter-state situation of the 1990s a different prospect emerges (leaving the important ecological issue on one side). While always present since the acquisition of nuclear weapons – first by the USA and then by Britain, the USSR, France, the People's Republic of China and almost certainly a number of others – there now veers more clearly into view the problem of the global 'democratization' of nuclear, as well as biological and chemical, weaponry. In some respects, as many have noted, this is probably more dangerous, certainly less controllable and predictable, than the Cold-War-centered global situation. From one, somewhat perverse, perspective the Cold War circumstance came, in a neo-duopolistic, way to resemble Elias's hope for 'a single central political institution and thus for the pacification of the earth' (quoted in Mennell, 1990: 364). (In the McLuhanite way of thinking 'the Cold War bomb' performed the function of God.) Elias would, clearly, have resisted this idea. But I would still insist that the world 'learned' something about what has been called 'mutually expected self-restraint' during the Cold War period; although that is not to say that the use of nuclear weapons can be avoided.

In the world of the 1990s – the world in which there emerges, not for the first time, the so-called problem of 'the new world order' – the situation has changed drastically. Regardless of the possibility of what is left of the old USSR reasserting itself in a Cold War posture, there has arisen as an object of very direct concern the problem of 'rights' to the manufacture of and threat to use nuclear and other weapons of mass destruction. Whereas previously it was taken for granted that 'the great powers' had such weapons and that there was a problem of deciding whether or not to enter or admit others to 'the nuclear club,' the problem has now become much more delicately balanced. In spite, in a sense because, of almost worldwide prognoses to the contrary, the USA has emerged unambiguously – at least for the time being – as the strongest military power. Its attempt, after many years of being more or less anti-UN, to fuse the future of the United Nations with American self-interest has resulted in a situation in which the world is now on a rather different saddle point. The USA now has the problem of legitimizing its position as the guarantor of 'world peace,' of denying to every additional nation the right to overwhelming warlike nuclear and 'post-nuclear' power. For the moment, and it will almost certainly be only a brief world-historical moment, the USA – in part via the United Nations – bears some resemblance (not that he would have liked it) to Elias's hope for 'a single central political institution and thus [?] for the pacification of the earth.' At the time of writing (early 1992) the brevity of the moment becomes increasingly clear, not least because of the expanding international presence of Japan and Germany.

But where does all of this leave the civilizing process, self-restraint and so on? Mennell (1990: 368) is almost certainly right in claiming that the dominant motif in Elias's work has been 'the long-term integration of humanity and the obstacles it encounters.' And he is correct in emphasizing that 'interdependence is Elias's central category' (Mennell, 1990: 369). Yet there are a number of lacunae in the Eliasian program. One of these has to do with the relative autonomy of inter-state and trans-state norms and practices. Without denying the horrors of the history of inter-state warfare and genocide, particularly during the twentieth century, we should not forget that there is, to take a major aspect of the problem, a remarkably complex body of international law. As Lechner (1991: 268) has written: 'By analogy with normative order within societies we can say that international law provided for many centuries and even before the official "start" of the Wallersteinian world system, the pre-conflictual elements in international conflict and the pre-contractual elements in trans-societal contracts.' Lechner notes that apart from the hundreds of international governmental and non-governmental organizations there are also more than 20,000 treaties and conventions. Citing Harold Berman (1982), Lechner (1991: 266–7) also observes that commercial law has become 'an intricate, autonomous legal order on a transnational scale, developed over many centuries by participants in a truly international community.' Parallel comments could be made about other spheres, perhaps most notably science.

Whatever Elias may have written in conceptual detail about the problematic and uncertain move towards a unified humanity there can be no doubt that he did so without unpacking the idea of 'the pacification of the earth.' Rather like Comte, Elias seemed to hope for a final jump into 'peace,' a utopian end to global *complexity*. This arises, in Elias's case, from his basically intra-societal, or at the most, intra-civilizational, way of thinking. He did indeed talk a lot about inter-societal, occasionally about inter-civilizational, relations, but he seems not to have had any realistic conception of the relative autonomy of the globalization process. He did not seem to appreciate that in so far as the world moves toward unicity (Archer, 1990) it does so in significant part on 'its own' terms. While Eliasian theory may be able to accommodate Giddens's (1987) notion of 'self-reflexive monitoring' on the part of nation states it is not equipped to deal with the proposition that, in part, globality preceded societality, as well as modernity. More specifically, he ignored the relative autonomy, and the history, of the 'culture' of inter-state relations.[2] Elias (1987) demanded that we do not 'retreat into the present,' but in spite of such cogent injunctions he failed to recognize that the world has become, or is becoming, 'one' along a somewhat more global, as opposed to societal, path than he, and many others, have acknowledged. Elias shared with many others who have labored recently in the vineyards of Western theory a tendency to emphasize 'the continuity of European history and the postponement of any detailed comparison with other civilizations' (Arnason, 1987a: 450), as well as the reception of Western theory in non-Western societies.

Some aspects of the issue of globality can be expressed in terms of the relationship between the ideas of institutionalized individualism and institutionalized societalism. Whereas the Durkheimian–Parsonian idea of institutionalized individualism is compatible with, although not as rich as, Elias's idea of the civilizing process, there is nothing really in Elias's work which corresponds to institutionalized societalism. The problem of globally institutionalized societalism (Lechner, 1989; Robertson, 1991b) has become particularly evident in the current phase of post-communism and post-colonialism and the ending of the 'old-style' Cold War between the USSR and the USA. Both rapidly increasing global interdependence and the fluidity and multipolarity of international relations increase the 'necessity' for widespread societal self-restraint – a restraint which was in a sense not so 'necessary' *across the globe* in the classic phase of the Cold War. As I have said, Elias wrote virtually all of what he had to say about inter-state relationships in embryonic or actual Cold War circumstances and that, I believe, partly explains his view of long-term trends; although he was most certainly not uninterested in the matter of self-restraint at the inter-state level. At the same time Elias had only a limited conception of what has come to be called the globalization process, in which he is certainly not alone. In spite of being much more aware than many contributors to the debate about globalization that globalization has been 'a very long-term social process' (Mennell, 1990), Elias appears not to have appreciated that globalization has, at least in recent centuries, acquired a specific, if malleable, *form* which is certainly not reducible to his particular conception of the civilizing process.

By broadening the scope of the idea of the civilizing process, I believe that it can be made central to the discussion of globalization. It is in this respect that Gong's work on 'the standard of civilization' becomes relevant. At precisely the same time that the notion of civilization was acquiring critical social-scientific status, particularly in Germanic contexts, it was also rapidly becoming a normative, indeed a legal, concept in international relations and diplomacy. In the disciplinary set-up of the time this *inter*-societal aspect of 'the discourse of civilization' was overlooked by sociologists (and psychologists). Gong is much more aware of the general discourse than were the 'culture critics' of the early twentieth century. It should be noted, however, that the uses of 'civility' and 'civilization' can be traced in terms of definite *English* usage to the second half of the eighteenth century.[3] In any case, traditional inattention to international law on the part of sociologists can now be alleviated by consideration of Gong's important work on 'the standard of "civilization." '

The Standard of 'Civilization'

Gong (1984) has noted that there was quite a significant prehistory to the systematic employment of the standard of civilization but that it was during the early years of the twentieth century that it became central to international relations. While the standard was often imposed coercively upon non-European countries by major European powers, the leaders of a number of non-European countries also aspired to meet it. They, and here one thinks of Japan in particular, came to regard some kind of conformity to it as an entry ticket to Eurocentric 'international society'. To take two other examples, in the early weeks of 1918 Lenin proclaimed that the newly created Soviet Union would not be taken seriously as a member of civilized international society if it did not adopt the Gregorian calendar (Zerubavel, 1981: 99); while in 1912, on the day that the Republic of China was formally announced, its leader, Sun Yat-sen proclaimed that his provisional government would 'try [its] best to carry out the duties of a civilized nation so as to obtain the rights of a civilized nation' (quoted in Gong, 1984: 158). I could provide a number of other examples, but the main point is simple. Elias's ideas on the civilizing process take insufficient account of the respects in which 'civility' became a regulative principle in inter-state relations and indeed, that 'the civilizing process' operated as an *external*, politicocultural constraint on nation states. Elias uses the concept of civilizing process mainly in reference to a pattern of objectively discernible trends in the direction of self – as opposed to outer constraint – thus largely ignoring the ways in which the process of civiliz*ation* came to take on a global 'life of its own.'

The standard of 'civilization' reached its zenith during the 1920s as an essentially regulative principle concerning inter-state relations. Two things need to be said immediately about its demise. First, the standard appears to have been modified into the principle of national self-determination (not in itself the same as national democratization) which was strongly, but problematically, advocated by Woodrow Wilson at the Paris Conference following World War I and then generalized to what became known as the Third World after World War II. Second, the emergence of the relatively autonomous legal principles of humanity, human rights and so on can be traced to the period when the standard of civilization was in its most explicit phase in the early years of this century. The latter point is particularly relevant to such themes in Elias's work as his frequently expressed concern for 'humanity' and the accusation that his was but a version of a discredited Comte-like sociology of and for humanity.

It is necessary to say something about Elias's general orientation to long-term encompassing change. Elias has often been accused of undue optimism, indeed utopianism and naivety (in spite of pessimism about superpower confrontation). Ironically Elias's *bête noire*, Talcott Parsons, has often been similarly characterized. Unfortunately a number of Elias's students and *aficionados* have added fuel to the fire by contrasting, often in *ad hominem* ways, Parsons's alleged privileges at Harvard with Elias's struggles to achieve academic recognition. The irony as far as the latter is concerned is that while Parsons certainly did not, unlike Elias, experience at first, agonizing hand the inhumanity of German Fascism he did spend much of his formative intellectual period in opposing Fascism from the eastern shore of America (Nielsen, 1991); while Parsons's early academic career was in fact something of a struggle (Camic, 1991). In any case it is worth recording that Parsons and Elias have often been attacked for the same 'sins.' They have both been charged with a naive unilinear evolutionism, while Parsons's voluntarism and institutionalized individualism have been subjected to critiques which bear a strong resemblance to attacks on Elias's insistence on the universal tendency towards increasing self-restraint. Both were subjected to attacks on their 'multidimensionality' – their resistance to single-factor accounts of human society – at least until 'multidimensionality' became an axiom of much contemporary theory through the writings of Luhmann, Alexander, Giddens and others. Both Parsons and Elias were convinced that the interpretation and/or explanation of social life was impossible without an understanding of death and the sociocultural significance of the body. One could go on to talk about other points of positive and negative convergence; not the least would be the similarities between their four-dimensional (dare one say four-*functional*?) conception of 'survival units' (Elias, 1987).

I have remarked upon a basic problem of contemporary theory in the West, namely the tendency to 'postpone,' in Arnason's (1987a: 450) word, serious comparison with other contemporary civilizations. (Arnason, 1990, it might be noted, is one of the few to have comprehensively recognized the problematics of the series nationalism–globalization–modernity.) In this connection an additional comparison, indeed a contrast, between Elias and Parsons is necessary. For Parsons did attempt to deal simultaneously during the last ten years or so of his life with continuity in Western theory *and* what he called 'the system of modern societies' (Parsons, 1971). The results of this endeavor to combine societal evolution and modernization in the West with a relatively synchronic analysis of the global system were complex and uncertain, as Parsons himself conceded.[4] He argued that

Western societies had, differentially, acquired greater 'adaptive capacity' than 'all others,' emphasizing, on the other hand, that adaptive capacity is 'not necessarily the paramount object of human value' (Parsons, 1971: 3). He also entered two other caveats. First he maintained that his assessment of the superiority of Western adaptive capacity did not 'preclude the possibility that a "postmodern" phase of development may somehow emerge from a different social and cultural origin and with different characteristics' (Parsons, 1971: 3). Parsons also spoke, very significantly in the general context of the present book, of the importance of cultural penetration. Acknowledging that Western cultures already had non-Western ingredients, he stressed the notion of 'cultural inclusion' and held out the prospect of an evolving 'system of societies,' as opposed to a West-led system.

Clearly Parsons did not have a well developed sense of the relative autonomy of constraints in the global field as an expanding whole, but he did recognize some of the major issues in this area. His remark on a postmodern possibility is particularly intriguing in the light of present debates.

Let us, however, return to the standard of 'civilization.' The standard of civilization arose during the nineteenth century when Asia and Africa 'were brought within the compass of the expanding European-centered international system' (Bull, 1984: vii). From the European point of view a major issue was that of the conditions under which European states 'would or would not admit non-European political communities to membership of the international society they formed among themselves' (1984: vii). That issue was resolved in principle by the establishment of the standard of civilization. Asian or African 'communities' had to meet that standard if they were to be accepted into 'international society' (1984: vii). Yet the idea of civilization certainly acquired a bad name. Even in the nineteenth century people from such ancient cultures as China and Persia expressed their deep indignation about European arrogance and presumptuousness when the standard was presented to them, particularly when application of it was seen to involve a privileged legal status for Europeans in the form of the right of 'extraterritorial jurisdiction.' By the post-World War II period the standard of civilization was, as least in international law, completely dead and, as Bull (1984: viii) remarks, 'now appears to us part and parcel of an unjust system of domination and exploitation against which the peoples of Asia and Africa have rightly revolted.' Indeed it has by now become a forbidden term in certain circles, a good example of which is the rule that authors of papers presented at meetings of, or published in journals sponsored by, the British Sociological Association may not use it without heavy qualification. It is, however, of interest in the present context to note that the BSA makes a special exemption for the use of 'civilization' and terms of family resemblance. When the term 'civilizing process' is used within the tradition established by Norbert Elias the BSA considers it permissible for its participants to enter what we may call the discourse of civilization. One of my points is to show that things are not so simple.

Bull argues, in summary of Gong, that the view that the standard of civilization laid down by Europeans in the late nineteenth and early twentieth centuries was a central component of 'an unjust system of domination and exploitation' is without doubt true, but that 'the truth is more complex than that' (1984: viii). For a start, the requirement that

> governments aspiring to membership of international society should be able to meet standards of performance. . .similar to those which European states expected of each other rested not upon ideas of superior right but on a need for reciprocity in dealing between European and non-European powers, which the latter were either not able to or willing to meet. (Bull, 1984: viii)

While we may well have reservations about Bull's dismissal of the idea of the European presumption of superiority his point about reciprocity is important, for without adherence to such norms as protection of the rights of citizens, capacity to adhere to rules of international law and diplomatic relations, avoidance of slavery and so on, reciprocity was not attainable. So even though there was much unjust treatment and racism, it is difficult to deny Bull's main point:

> [T]he demand of Asian and African peoples for equality of rights in international law was one that the latter did not put forward until they had first absorbed ideas of equal rights of states to sovereignty, of peoples to self-determination, and of persons of different races to individual rights, which before their contact with Europe played little or no part in their experience. (1984: ix)

Gong adopts a politicocultural approach to international relations. Moreover he belongs to that school of international relations specialists who subscribe to the notion of international society. As defined by Bull and Watson (1984a: 1) an international society is 'a group of states (or, more generally, a group of independent political communities) which not merely form a system . . . but also have established by dialogue and consent common rules and institutions for the conduct of their relations, and recognize their common interests in maintaining these arrangements.' Gong's discussion of the standard of civilization is geared considerably to the problematic of the making of contemporary 'international society.' Thus although much of his book addresses the question of the admission of non-European political communities (including the Ottoman Empire, Abyssinia, China, Japan and Siam) to Eurocentric 'society,' he also insists that that standard of civilization was largely an outcome of *encounters between civilizations*. Even though a basically European standard came to prevail, that standard 'was central to the changes *within* the European international society and within those non-European countries which sought to enter it' (Gong, 1984: 238; emphasis added). Moreover, these changes were 'aspects of the greater global transformation which paralleled the expansion of the previously European international society into a

global "civilized" society' (1984: 238). Clearly, although he does not
specifically say so, Gong is allowing for the increasing 'presence' of non-
Western 'communities' on the global scene, stressing that, for all its warts,
the standard of civilization helped to facilitate this.

Gong is critical of the argument of Alexandrowicz (1967, 1973) for being
unsophisticated in its conceptions of 'the Family of Nations.' Gong argues
against the natural-law tendencies of many writers on international law
after Vitoria and Grotius, on the grounds that it was not the rise of positive
legal doctrines which brought about either the increasing specificity of
international law or the exclusion of non-European countries from the
Family of Nations. The classic, natural-law perspective was simply an
idealized 'conceptual creation of international theorists rather than the
product of universally-sustained international relations' (Gong, 1984: 239).
This argument, in effect against both natural *and* positive interpretation of
the history of international law, is important. Gong points out that to argue
that 'international law discriminated against non-European countries
simply beause it originated in Europe is a non sequitur' (1984: 45). On the
other hand, to consider how 'the social and intellectual assumptions
inherent in European society influenced' the emergence of the standard of
civilization 'is something else' (1984: 45). I would add, however, that the
natural-law tradition has played a significant part in developing ideas about
a shared global-human condition, ideas which are currently very relative to
and operative in the global field as a whole.

Civility, Inter-ethnic Relations and Modernity

Let us now turn, more briefly, to Cuddihy, whose major contribution to
the relevant theme is primarily addressed to what he has called 'the Jewish
struggle with modernity' and deals particularly with the writings of Freud,
Marx and Lévi-Strauss. Cuddihy is, however, not interested only in that
specific case. As we will see, he regards it as part of a much larger issue.
His book, *The Ordeal of Civility*, was criticized in some quarters when it
first appeared in 1974 on the grounds that it leaned in an anti-Jewish
direction, although it must be emphasized that that was not by any means
the dominant view. One reviewer (quoted on the cover of the second
edition) wrote: 'The book's greatest value lies in its heuristic *chutzpah*, its
"rude" stirring of the sediment of conventional thinking.' While I think
that Cuddihy's book is valuable for more substantive reasons than that, this
reviewer's opinion does address the issue of Cuddihy's 'rudeness' very
effectively. Cuddihy argues that it was 'the failure of civility [which] came
to define "the Jewish problem" as this problem reconstituted itself in the
era of social modernity' (Cuddihy, 1987: 3). He goes on to argue that 'this
ordeal, this problem of the ritually unconsummated social courtship of
Gentile and Jew. . .is formative for the labors of the secular intelligentsia
of the nineteenth and twentieth centuries' (1987: 3–4). According to
Cuddihy (1984: 4) the problem derives from what he calls 'a disabling

inability of Judaism to legitimate culturally the differentiation of culture and society,' a point which is well captured in the following paragraph:

> Thus, Jewish emancipation, assimilation, and modernization constitute a single, total phenomenon. The secularizing Jewish intellectual, as the avant-garde of his decolonized people, suffered in his own person the trauma of this culture shock. Unable to turn back, unable completely to acculturate, caught between 'his own' whom he had left behind and the Gentile 'host culture' where he felt ill at ease and alienated, intellectual Jews and Jewish intellectuals experienced cultural shame and awkwardness, guilt and the 'guilt of shame'. (Cuddihy, 1987: 4)

I shall not address here the details of Cuddihy's interpretation of Freud, Marx and Lévi-Strauss, except to say that for him Marxist, Freudian and closely related ideologies are both hermeneutical and practical. They seek to reinterpret and to change. Speaking specifically of Marx and Freud he argues that in each case the problem began with 'the public delict of Jewish behavior – the scene it was making in the public places of the Diaspora' and led to the advocacy of change (collective, revolutionary change for Marx and incremental, individual change for Freud).

Cuddihy (1987: 9) describes his as 'a study in subculture-boundedness.' His most general concern is with orientations to modernity, the argument being that 'with perhaps unpardonable oversimplification' the modern intelligentsia have, since at least the beginning of the nineteenth century, been opposing modernity (in the service of nostalgia). Modernity and thus, at least loosely, modernization was, according to Cuddihy, best captured by Parsons, specifically in the latter's 'differentiation model' of modernity and modernization: 'Parsons . . . displayed . . . an all but sovereign indifference to the high cost of [the] "passing of traditional society".' As Cuddihy further writes, 'members of the Protestant core-culture like Parsons, theorize from within the eye of the hurricane of modernization, where all is calm and intelligible. But for the underclass below, as for the ethnic outside, modernization is a trauma' (1987: 9). Cuddihy's central concept of civility is presented as 'the very medium of Western social interaction'; and it presupposes the differentiated structures of a modernizing 'civil society.' Civility is not merely regulative of social behavior; it is an order of ' "appearance" constitutive of that behavior' (Cuddihy, 1987: 14). Civility, argues Cuddihy, minimally requires differentiation between private affect and public demeanor. At the same time, Cuddihy is not a defender of 'the Protestant eye of the hurricane' (Cuddihy, 1978). However, he also tends to overlook the global significance of Parsons's notion of inclusion, which, like Gong's employment of the standard of civilization, emphasizes that inclusion does not refer simply to inclusion with respect to existing societal values.[5] Inclusion in ideal-typical terms goes hand in hand with value-generalization, *an expansion* or *a revision* of previous values.

The most important part of Cuddihy's analysis for present purposes is his attempt to generalize beyond his discussions of particular Jewish intellectuals to brief comparisons of the Jews and the Irish, as peoples rather than nations, who were latecomers to modernity; and of the experiences of Jewish emancipation and the new nations which – in some cases very ambivalently – sought global acceptance after World War II.[6] It is of course in the latter respect that Cuddihy's interest converges most clearly with that of Gong. Neither Gong nor Cuddihy refer to each other. There is one rather vague reference to Elias by Cuddihy; none, as far as I know, by Elias to Cuddihy. And neither Gong nor Elias refers to each other. Taken together, Gong and Cuddihy provide different but complementary additions to and revisions of Elias's work on the civilizing process and on inter-state relations. Gong supplies much on the internationally and interculturally negotiated dimensions of 'civilization' and the ways in which the standard of 'civilization' was at one crucial historical moment a definite external constraint, not just on 'uncivilized' and 'semi-civilized' but *also* on 'civilized' societies. On the other hand, Cuddihy provides much on the 'subcultural' aspects of civility and its negotiation.

At the same time it can be seen that Parsons's interrelated concepts of *differentiation, normative upgrading, inclusion* and *value-generalization* are both enriched and consolidated by such considerations. Gong's work tells us a lot about inclusion, normative upgrading, and value-generalization at the global level; Cuddihy's book informs us particularly about 'subcultural' inclusion, but it also has something to say about differentiation and, to some extent, inclusion in inter-societal terms.

Conclusion

Towards the end of his paper on Elias's theory of 'globalization,' Mennell (1990: 369) contends that even though Elias's writing about 'the globalization' of human society was centered on the possibility of nuclear war, there is much in his 'underlying theoretical strategy' which can be of assistance in our efforts to study the world as a whole. After observing that Elias began his work on European civilizing processes by noting 'that the notion of civilization represented the self-satisfaction of Europeans in a colonialist age,' Mennell asks: 'What are the implications now for a world-wide civilizing process, considered as changes in ways of demanding and showing respect, when Europe and Europe-over-the-ocean no longer occupy the hegemonic position?' (Wisely Mennell adds the question 'Or do they?')

The general point of this chapter has been that these are precisely the kinds of question which have been and continue to be tackled by theorists of globalization. Although not cast specifically in the language of globalization, Gong's work, as well as that of Bull and others, has been directly concerned with the ramifications of European 'self-satisfaction.' Gong has traced in some detail the ways in which the European standard of 'civilization' was developed, extended, modified and upgraded. From a different perspective, and with specific reference to some of the work which immediately preceded the current interest in globalization (Lagos,

1963; Nettl and Robertson, 1968), Cuddihy has directly addressed the issue of civility in terms of the dynamics of inclusion and exclusion (which certainly has some overlap with Elias's strong interest in the insider–outsider phenomenon) in a way that is clearly complementary to Parsons's work on long-term, increasingly large-scale change.

Consideration of the work of Elias, Gong, Cuddihy and Parsons in connection with the civilization process, civility and the standard of 'civilization' assists in the development of a theoretically and empirically rich perspective on globalization.

Notes

1. In addition to those specified in the text special mention should be made of Arnason, who has in various papers discussed the relationship between Elias's work and some of the themes of the present chapter. In particular, see Arnason (1989a) for critical discussion of Elias's 'disproportionate emphasis on power' and his over-concentration on the West.
2. In addition to the reference in the previous note, see Arnason (1987a) for discussion of Elias's neglect of culture. More generally, see Meyer (1989).
3. For discussion of the different senses of 'civilization' as process, the outcome of a process and as a condition, see Gong (1984: 45–53). See also Arnason (1988b).
4. Of course, this issue has been touched on previously. For a much more comprehensive discussion, see Robertson (1991c).
5. However, it should be emphasized that in *No Offense* (Cuddihy, 1978) the author is specifically concerned with the USA. Cuddihy's position with respect to the *global* situation might well in fact be in line with Gong and Parsons.
6. For comparisons of the Jewish-Israeli experience and that of the Irish from a more 'national' point of view, see the comments scattered through O'Brien (1986). For the idea of Islam's opposition to the *existing* terms of globalization, see Turner (1991).

8

GLOBALIZATION THEORY AND CIVILIZATION ANALYSIS

There have been a number of critiques and assessments of my work on globalization.[1] Probably the earliest of these was that of Vytautas Kavolis in his paper entitled 'History of consciousness and civilizational analysis' (1987),[2] to which I was invited to reply. Clearly, Kavolis's critique was made in reference to work which has subsequently been developed and modified. Nonetheless his essay touched upon some important issues and the invitation to respond provided me with an opportunity to make some of my earlier ideas about globalization even more explicit. Specifically, that opportunity enabled me to deal with what I consider to be some misconceptions of what Kavolis himself called 'globalization theory.'

In this chapter I thus respond to Kavolis's constructive comments on the globalization theory with which I have become associated and situate that perspective in the context of Kavolis's cogent and illuminating comparison of the 'history of consciousness' and civilization-analytic perspectives (Kavolis, 1987). In the former respect my strategy will consist in correcting what I regard as inadequate interpretations of globalization theory on Kavolis's part, and in indicating its development and implications. With respect to the relationship between globalization theory and Kavolis's comparison of the history of consciousness and the civilizational-analytic perspectives, my main concern will be with emphasizing the closeness of globalization theory to civilizational analysis. Indeed, I will claim that globalization theory is an elaboration of civilizational analysis. Unfortunately, I cannot deal here with the contrast between globalization theory and what Kavolis has called the history of consciousness perspective as such.

Reading Globalization Theory

Kavolis's major reservation about globalization theory appears to be that it drifts in the direction of being a version of an objectionable 'universal social science.' While it has the advantage, from his point of view, of *not* conceiving of the world unethically and, indeed, *having* a concern with values, it 'postulates a Durkheimian inevitability of moving, sooner or later, toward a universal value hierarchy in which the idea of humanity as a whole subsumes . . . locally differentiated responses.' In contrast, Kavolis's own leading commitment is, apparently, to the idea that civilizations are distinctive and that, moreover, the distinctiveness of each civilization ought to be protected – indeed, celebrated – by the analyst: 'If we do not pay primary attention to [civilizational distinctiveness] we slip from "civilization studies" into some version of a "universal social science."' I believe that this is dangerously close to being a *non sequitur*, since there can surely be such a thing as a 'universalistic' account of particularism. In other words, does the idea of having a general theory which applies to the world as a whole automatically lead to the diminution of civilizational (or, for that matter, societal) distinctiveness? I believe the temptation to respond in the affirmative to that question issues from equating theoretical generality with empirical homogeneity. But, more important in the immediate context, I want to argue that globalization theory partly rests on a pre-theoretical commitment to global heterogeneity and that, in any case, the theory itself leads, via its empirical investigations, to an emphasis on civilizational and societal variety. The pre-theoretical commitment arises from the view that a vastly homogenized world would have little vitality (other, perhaps, than in the form of the perception of extra-human heterogeneity), while the theory itself argues that the globalization process itself – the rendering of the world as a single place – constrains civilizations and societies (including assertive national-ethnic solidarities) to be increasingly explicit about what might be called their *global callings* (their unique geocultural or geomoral contributions to world history). In a nutshell, globalization involves the universalization of particularism, not just the particularization of universalism.

While the latter process does involve the thematization of the issue of universal (i.e. global) 'truth,' the former involves the global valorization of particular identities. In that connection it is crucial to recognize that the contemporary concern with civilizational and societal (as well as ethnic) uniqueness – as expressed via such motifs as identity, tradition and indigenization – largely rests on *globally diffused* ideas. Identity, tradition and the demand for indigenization only make sense *con*textually. Moreover, uniqueness cannot be regarded simply as a thing-in-itself. It largely depends both upon the thematization and diffusion of 'universal' ideas concerning the appropriateness of being unique *in a context*, which is an *empirical* matter, and the employment of criteria on the part of scholarly observers, which is an *analytical* issue. If either or both of these constitute(s) a form of 'universal social science,' so be it. But I do not say that defiantly. I say it, first, because I do not see how Kavolis's attempt to compare civilizations in terms of their 'specific range of theory–practice relationships' (an approach which I find very attractive, particularly in the light of Sahlins's recent work)[3] is much less than an exercise in 'universal social science'; and, second, because he appears to believe (although he isn't very clear about this) that globalization theory leans dangerously in the direction of the 'semiotic universalism' of the postmodernists. In the latter respect I would claim that globalization theory contains the seed of an account as to why there are current intellectual fashions of deconstruction, on the one hand, and postmodernist views concerning the 'confluence of everything with everything else,' on the other. In brief, globalization – as a form of 'compression' of the contemporary world *and* the basis of a new hermeneutic for world history – relativizes and 'equalizes' all socio-cultural formations. This has tempted many of our more fashionable colleagues into a celebration of Nietzschean arbitrariness; when, in fact, an understanding of the empirical grounding of 'the transvaluation of values' should lead precisely in the general direction that Kavolis favors – registration of the increasing salience of civilizational and societal distinctiveness. But that cannot now be done without our becoming, in a special sense, 'universalists.' Universalism is needed to grasp particularism itself; while, more empirically – as the case of Japan, over many centuries, shows – in certain circumstances particularism can be a path to a kind of universalism.

It may well be that with the respect to the two essays which Kavolis cites (Robertson and Chirico, 1985; Robertson and Lechner, 1985) the reader could justifiably claim that globalization theory 'underplays. . .the continuing vitality of the five living civilizations – the East Asian, the Southeast Asian Buddhist, the Indian, the Islamic, and the Western' (although I think even that would be a harsh judgement). However, Kavolis concedes that 'no one knows how much necessity' is involved in that alleged underplaying – and I have to assure him that there is no theoretical necessity whatsoever. I have been emphatic on a number of occasions in saying that in an increasingly globalized world – characterized by historically exceptional degress of civilizational, societal and other modes of interdependence and widespread consciousness thereof – there is an exacerbation of civilizational, societal and ethnic self-consciousness. Moreover, my emphasis on this has not been simply a matter of rhetorical claim. On the contrary, the insistence on heterogeneity and variety in an increasingly globalized world is integral to globalization theory. Yet the latter resists the attempt by some 'civilizationists' to cultivate at all analytical costs the 'purity,' indeed the 'essentialism,' of civilizational and societal traditions. It does not decline to produce (at least a sketch of) a theory of the world as a whole for fear that generalizing across the world flattens humanity into a homogeneous and potentially harmonious whole.

Kavolis also suggests that globalization theory conceives of 'individuals and societies as standing in an immediate relationship to global humanity.' This, I believe, is a misleading rather than an inaccurate observation. It is misleading, first, because – not without some ambiguity – I have tended in my most recent writing [i.e. up to 1987] to speak conceptually of the global circumstance as *the global-human condition* and to *include* individuals, societies, relations between societies and (in the generic sense) mankind as ' the major contemporary 'components' or dimensions of that condition. Indeed, I have *defined* the global-human circumstance in those terms. To state pejoratively that I conceive of individuals and societies as standing in an immediate relationship to global humanity is off the mark in so far as the latter has already been defined as partly *consisting in* individuals and societies. In that Kavolis worries about the conception of an 'immediate relationship' he should surely give reasons as to why global humanity should not be conceptualized so as to include those components. In so doing I hope that he would fully recognize that I have – again with occasional ambiguity – specified conceptually that I do not equate mankind with humanity. In my terminology mankind/womankind has to do with the 'communal-species' aspect of the global-human condition, which refers to the overall condition or circumstance of the world as a whole. It is important to note that even though I have, from time to time, used the term 'world system,' I have elected to use the slightly cumbersome term 'global-human' [and more recently 'global field'] as a way of rejecting the functionalistic and deterministic – as well as the narrow, economistic – thrust of self-proclaimed world-systems theorists. What world-systems theorists almost exclusively focus upon – along implausibly narrow and mechanistic lines – is the relations-between-societies aspect of the global-human condition. In the ideal-typical form of my conception of the global-human condition it is possible for there to be an equal emphasis upon societal uniqueness, on the one hand, and the commonality of mankind, on the other.

A more clearly empirical problem arises in connection with Kavolis's objection to the idea of individuals and societies being in a direct relationship to 'global humanity.' This is Kavolis's term and I am not quite sure of his usage. All I can say is that I have, indeed, argued that *globality* – defined in the immediate context as consciousness of the (problem of) the world as a single place – appears increasingly to permeate the affairs of all societies and multitudes of people across the world. This is not simply a matter of an increasing awareness of the challenge of other cultures but also of what is very misleadingly called the 'global village.' In other words, it is not merely the rapid increase in 'knowledge' of global variety, ways of coping with the attendant threat of relativization of individual and collective identities, and clearly increasing concern with and controversy about 'international education' (sometimes called 'global education') that is at issue. What we also have to acknowledge is that there is clear evidence of an even more direct concern with the theme of globality. Debates are occurring in a number of societies on the extent to which societies should be or become 'global,' and the degree to which they should modify their cultures and traditions so as to make the global 'system' work more adequately (most clearly to be seen at the present time in the econocultural confrontation between Japan and the USA). In more microscopic terms we have witnessed the growth of explicit 'anti-globalism' and rejection of 'one worldism' in a number of North American communities. (I don't have the clear evidence, but I am sure parallel tendencies are to be found in other societies.) In one way or another, civilizations and, more tangibly, societies (even individuals) are being constrained to frame their particular modes, negative or positive, of global involvement.

Whether concern with what I call globality (and the problem thereof) constitutes evidence against Kavolis's apparent claim that individuals and societies do *not* stand in a direct relationship to global humanity I cannot estimate. I suggest that the enhanced concern with globality is in and of itself of considerable significance, and that it constitutes little threat to the idea of civilizational distinctiveness. It can, I believe, be shown that each distinctive civilization possesses as part of its symbolic heritage a conception of the world as a whole. Under conditions of acute concern with the latter – when interest in the world as a whole has been globally thematized – civilizational images of global order come even more sharply into view. I would argue, moreover, that a central *Problemstellung* of contemporary civilizational analysis (as well as of so-called area studies) should be the comparison of civilizations with respect precisely to their histories of conceptions of the world as whole and of civilizational and societal modes of global participation. In that regard it may be said again that globalization theory turns world-systems theory nearly on its head – by focusing, first, on *cultural* aspects of the world 'system' and, second, by systematic study of *internal* civilizational and societal attributes which shape orientations to the world as a whole and forms of participation of civilizations and societies in the global-human circumstance.

It is possible that in using the term 'global humanity' Kavolis has in mind what I mean when I use the term mankind, or humankind – in reference to what I have called the communal-species aspect of the global-human condition. If so, it would then also be misleading to say that I think of individuals and societies as having an immediate relationship to global humanity, although I would nonetheless insist that in the contemporary world there is a perceptible shift in that direction.[4] From one angle we may surely consider the thematization of the idea of human rights – in fact, the global institutionalization of the idea of the latter – as a move along such a trajectory. More generally, invocation of 'the best interests of humanity at large' has become a common theme of international discourse. From a different angle concern with human life *per se* has arisen in connection with at least three major species-threatening phenomena – ecological disaster, nuclear annihilation and AIDS (each of which is a truly global-human problem). From yet another angle, questions concerning the beginning and end of individual human lives have been globally diffused in terms of controversies about abortion and about the prolongation of life by medical technology. However, nothing that I have said should be construed, in spite of these specifications of shifts in the direction of immediate relationships between individuals or societies and global humanity, as suggesting that the world should now be seen as a homogenized collectivity. All I am saying is that the mankind aspect of the global-human condition has been concretely thematized in modern times on a more or less global basis. Nevertheless – and this is a crucial point – there are movements and schools of thought which do actually subscribe to the idea

of the world as a human *Gemeinschaft*; one of the most conspicuous
being that strand of the loosely confederated world peace movement
which thinks of the world as evolving into a kind of loosely patterned
'village.'

Finally, as far as direct replies to Kavolis are concerned, I turn to the
charge that even though I allow for 'a range of clearly differentiated
responses to the sense of world-wide humanity having become the common
framework for both social action and interpretation of experience,' I
envisage the idea of humanity as a whole subsuming those responses. It is
said that my scheme is 'completely neutral to the particularity of the
cultural tradition' within which the responses occur. (Kavolis argues that
'each of them, in accordance with the presuppositions of a universalistic
social science, could occur anywhere.') It is also charged that while 'the
logic of globalization theory' allows for four major sets of responses it
actually *requires* one of them – what Kavolis designates as 'a Durkheimian
religion-of-humanity attempt to resolve global cultural conflict and remake
the world.' Here again I have difficulty in following his line of reasoning.
Specifically, I simply fail to see in what way a strong consciousness of the
world as a whole must rest upon or logically entail such an orientation;
although I would say that given a direct concern with the world as a whole
it seems almost inevitable in an empirical sense that an orientation of that
kind would arise. What I emphatically dispute is that one can *equate* that
orientation with a consciousness of increasing interedependence across the
entire world, the penetration of local life by globally diffused ideas, and so
on.

As I tried at some length to show towards the end of Chapter 4, if one
grants that it is plausible to think of societies, individuals, relations
between societies (the international system of societies) and mankind as
the most tangible 'touchstones' of the contemporary global-human circumstance, it is reasonable to suggest that each one of these may be, so to say,
chosen as being empirically definitive of the world as a whole – as an image
of actual or potential world order. To repeat some examples, it is surely the
case that some groups, movements, societies, or whatever, consider the
world primarily as being constituted mainly by international relations;
other sociocultural entities or individuals see it primarily as a series of
relatively closed communities of individuals; others see it in the form of a
set of state-run societies; yet others see it – as I have emphasized here – as a
single community. Each of these images can be combined with one or more
of the others – but it is unnecessary to go into full analytical detail in the
present context. The basic point is that there is, surely, an interesting
variety of images of world order (and disorder) and that a number of them
have long civilizational histories. But having such an image does not
necessarily involve what Kavolis calls a religion-of-humanity conception,
although that is certainly one possible image, empirically speaking.

Kavolis makes a good point, I believe, when he raises the question of
whether the responses of which I have been speaking are culturally neutral,

although I reject the idea that one can tell that they are neutral simply by reading Robertson and Lechner (1985). (The latter formed the basis of part of Chapter 4.) In that paper all that Lechner and I were trying to do was to raise some general alternatives to the Wallersteinian, world-system conception of world order (and the possibility of global socialism). At that stage I had only begun to embark on my attempt to be more empirically specific about which kinds of 'response' are more likely than others to arise in particular sociocultural settings. My main point, then, is that nothing in globalization theory involves a commitment to a particular response and that there is nothing in its logic or in the minds of its adherents which would lead to responses having to be considered as socioculturally rootless, as occurring anywhere in time or space. Indeed, I agree fully with Kavolis when he says that relating the type of response (in the sense that he and I are using that term) 'most likely to be made by a particular people to globalization to either the enduring qualities of their civilizations or to the trajectories of their national history' is the most pressing issue 'in any theory of contemporary culture.'

Civilizations in Context

I suspect that one of the reasons for Kavolis's tendency to distinguish so emphatically between globalization theory and civilizational analysis is that (thus far) the former has said relatively little about the concept of civilization *per se*. Before coming directly to this apparent – but misleading – lacuna it is necessary, however, to talk briefly about the general thrust of globalization theory, noting again that I distance myself as a proponent of the latter from world-systems and related economic-historical perspectives on the world as a whole. It has also to be stressed that in speaking of globalization, in its most general sense as the process whereby the world becomes a single place, I do not mean that globalization involves in and of itself the crystallization of a cohesive system. Yet I do maintain that globalization involves the development of something like a global culture – not as normatively binding, but in the sense of a general mode of discourse about the world as a whole *and* its variety.

My own conception of globalization theory has, as I have said, its deep roots in work which I did with Nettl in the mid-1960s (Nettl and Robertson, 1966, 1968). Our collaboration arose out of a shared opposition to conventional theories of societal modernization – in particular, their West-centeredness and their lack of positive interest in civilizational and societal distinctiveness. Utilizing, to some degree, developing ideas about the stratification of 'the international system,' we offered a perspective on societal modernization which rendered it as a very open-ended process and, in particular, as a process of change that involved societies in balancing their perceptions of their traditional identities and sociocultural characteristics against the global constraint to change in globally suggested directions. The cases of Peter the Great of Russia's attempt to copy and Meiji Japan's 'successful' borrowing from the West were used as crucial historical benchmarks. Subsequently, and partly in response to the growing presence of world-systems theory during the 1970s, I became involved in a series of attempts to deal simultaneously with the relationships between internal-societal attributes and the globalization process (i.e. the making of the world into a single place); with particular attention to globally diffused ideas concerning what seemed to be the major dimensions of the global-human condition – namely, societies, individuals, the system of inter-societal relations, and mankind. While 'civilizational analysis' has not been explicitly prominent in this work until recently, it has nonetheless consti-tuted a very significant and continuous part of my thinking – in ways which I will now briefly indicate via some comments on Kavolis's characterization of that perspective.

Each of the major representatives of civilizational analysis selected by Kavolis appears to have pivoted his work on a particular feature of Western (usually European) civilization. This may be less clear in connec-tion with Eisenstadt's writings than with those of Max Weber, Elias, Dumont and Nelson – but, generally speaking, the East–West cleavage is evident (although only implicitly in the work of Elias). The point I seek to make is that, by and large, a feature or set of features of the modern West has been adopted as a basic hermeneutic for these analysts, even though Dumont has provided a kind of critique of the West from an Eastern (more accurately South Asian) standpoint, Eisenstadt has been attempting to produce something like a general theory of civilizational patterning and change, and Nelson tried to soften the West-centeredness of Weber's writings. Moreover, of these important contributors to civilizational analysis only Dumont (1979, 1980) has endeavored to contextualize civilizations, in the sense of addressing directly the problem of *the coexistence* of different civilizational forms and the actual or potential contributions of different civilizations (and societies) to an overall human circumstance.

What *I* have been attempting is to move beyond the Western-centeredness of classic civilizational analysis, an endeavor which, I am sure, Kavolis supports in principle. Where Kavolis and I seem to diverge is over the question of what the new basis and focus of civilizational analysis should be. In Kavolis's view globalization theory appears to share some of the limitations of Eisenstadt's alleged quest for a universal, general theory of civilizations – a program driven only, according to Kavolis, by an analytical desire for cross-civilizational generalization which omits both cultural critique and celebration of civilizational distinctiveness. But in what way can an interest in the latter be *grounded*? How can one provide a solid *raison d'être* for such a focus, other than that the systematic display, in diachronic and synchronic terms, of global heterogeneity is intrinsically intriguing?

My own view on this pressing matter is that we must now seek an *empirical* basis for a form of civilizational analysis which will transcend and subsume the older West-centered mode of discourse. That grounding of the new civilizational analysis must, I insist, center on what I call the problem of globality. What Nelson called intercivilizational encounters have now come to constitute an almost globally institutionalized and thematized phemomenon. Such encounters set civilizations within the context of the world as a single place (not a community, or even a society) and it is in those terms that we may now 'bring civilizations back in' to the social sciences and humanities. In other words, my own strategy – if not always explicit – has been to map the context in which civilizations (and sub-civilizations) assert themselves and, in turn, the general basis upon which they can and should be analyzed. That, I suggest, gives a much more solid basis for our endeavors than other extant approaches. At the same time it complements – indeed, provides a rationale for – the kind of approach advocated by Kavolis (centered on the relationship between civilizational theory and civilizational practice). It also helps us to delineate civilizations and sub-civilizations better than before, since in terms of my approach we 'allow' civilizations to *identify themselves* both historically and contemporaneously, in relation to their extra-civilizational contexts. Along these lines the genuine study of world, or global, history can be combined with civilizational analysis.

Notes

1. See, for example, Shad (1988); Swatos (1989); King (1991); Roof (1991); Simpson (1991); Turner (1991); Wolff (1991); Beyer (forthcoming); Garrett (forthcoming); Tiryakian (forthcoming). Needless to say, some of these I find to be much more insightful than others.
2. All of my quotations from and my paraphrasings of Kavolis derive from Kavolis (1987). I have, however, also kept Kavolis (1986) carefully in mind. The present chapter was originally written at the invitation of Vytautas Kavolis, one of the editors of *Comparative Civilizations Review*, and published in that journal (17 (Fall), 1987). It is reproduced here with only minor changes of an editorial nature. In addition to the two articles by Kavolis which I originally mentioned the reader is also advised to consult Kavolis (1988).
3. See, in particular, Sahlins (1985).
4. I cannot here explore a very complex but, I believe, significant aspect of this question – namely, the degree to which there is an experiential-symbolic substratum that is common to human life as a whole. This 'Jungian' theme must, surely, become a part of the research agenda of globalization theory.

9

GLOBALITY, MODERNITY AND THE ISSUE OF POSTMODERNITY

Most of this chapter was originally published as a lengthy book review of Anthony Giddens's *The Consequences of Modernity* (1990). The general issue of the relationship between the theorization of globalization, on the one hand, and controversies concerning modernity-and-postmodernity (Turner, 1990c), on the other, promises to become increasingly salient. Hence the inclusion in this volume of my own reflections on Giddens's attempt to approach the problematic of globalization via his consideration of modernity. His view that what some theorize as postmodernity can be seen as an extension of, as basically inherent in, the 'project' of modernity is not unpersuasive. However, Giddens's argument is, in my judgement, vitiated by his attributing to modernity an impact which is unwarranted. In fact he tends to reify the notion of modernity (just as the idea of capitalism has been continuously reified). In my commentary on *The Consequences of Modernity* I try to show that direct, as opposed to indirect, attention to globalization makes a significant difference to matters that have arisen in the modernity-and-postmodernity debate.

In his 'extended essay' Giddens calls for 'an institutional analysis of modernity with cultural and epistemological overtones' (1990: 1); in reversal, as he sees it, of the current tendency to place primary emphasis on cultural and epistemological matters. Giddens claims that contemporary debates about modernity-and-postmodernity have failed to confront directly the weaknesses of 'established sociological positions,' largely because of the absence of direct concern with modern social *institutions* (1990: 3). He argues that the announcement of postmodernity is very misleading in so far as its proponents, as well as many who have purported to characterize modernity, have failed to grasp the nature of modernity itself. He characterizes modernity primarily in terms of its mixture of constraining and enabling tendencies (cf. Poster, 1990), as well as its globalizing proclivities. Postmodernity in its 'poststructuralist' representation is rejected as a viable interpretation of the current era. In its place Giddens proposes 'radicalized modernity.'

Central to the task of grasping the nature of modernity, says Giddens, is the discontinuity associated with that form of life. Compared with previous periods and circumstances, the changes of the last three or four hundred years 'have been so dramatic and so comprehensive in their impact that we get only limited assistance from our knowledge of prior periods of transition in trying to interpret them' (1990: 5). This I doubt, for reasons having to do with the long-historical significance of globalization, of which I have already spoken. Social evolutionism is held largely responsible for the lack of the 'discontinuist' interpretation of modernity which Giddens himself offers. On the other hand, the deconstruction of social evolution-ism does not lead to a chaotic vision in terms of which 'an infinite number of purely idiosyncratic "histories" can be written' (1990: 5–6). Generaliza-tions *can*, says Giddens, be formulated about 'definite episodes of historical transition' (1990: 6). Giddens also argues towards the end of his discussion that we need to create models of 'utopian realism,' to 'envisage alternative futures whose propagation might help them to be realized' (1990: 154), a project which has of course been proposed by a considerable number of social scientists – not to speak of philosophers of history, theologians, and so on.

The 'discontinuities' Giddens emphasizes are in one sense obvious: the great rapidity and pace of change in modern life; the global scope of change; and the uniqueness of modern institutions, such as the nation state, the commodification of products and labor, and the great reliance on inanimate sources of physical power. Similarly his perception of modernity as being double-edged in the sense of containing both great enabling opportunities and more sombre aspects is not at all original, as Giddens freely acknowledges. Where the claim to originality does arise is in Giddens's attempt to develop precisely an 'institutional' analysis of the double-edgedness of modern life, at the center of which is his discussion of the themes of security v. danger and trust v. risk. That discussion is prefaced by a summary of the weaknesses of the classical sociologists, in the course of which Giddens emphasizes the 'multidimensionality' of the institutional order of modernity (against an alleged but undocumented classical tendency to provide single-factor accounts of the rise of modernity); the limitations of the concept of 'society' (allegedly brought to its peak by Durkheim and allegedly perpetuated in Parsons's concern with societal order); and the lack of recognition of the 'double hermeneutic,' in terms of which *'sociological knowledge spirals in and out of the universe of social life, reconstructing both itself and that universe as an integral part of that process'* (1990: 15–16, italics in original).

The strategy in terms of which Giddens creates the space for his own arguments should by now be rather clear. Claims as to insufficient multidimensionality in classical sociology have become commonplace in recent years, particularly but not only in the works of Alexander and Luhmann, both of whom have been greatly, but in different ways, influenced by Parsons. The deficiency of the concept of society has in fact become one of the most frequently stated themes of modern theory, perhaps most persistently in the writings of Wallerstein; while Parsons, who did talk quite a lot about societal order, also insisted increasingly upon its multidimensionality and, of particular relevance to an assessment of *The*

Consequences of Modernity, was deeply interested in the problem of *global* order. Finally, the general idea of sociological knowledge spiralling in and out of social life is by now so widely accepted as to have become almost a sociological cliché. Moreover, the omission of Simmel from the direct discussion of the weaknesses of classical theory is both curious and at the same time convenient for Giddens, since it is not easy to charge Simmel with any of the three main alleged faults of classical theory. (However, Giddens does invoke Simmel in his discussion of money as a symbolic token.) Simmel was critical of one-sided characterizations of modern life, he was suspicious of and relativized conventional notions of society, and he was certainly more than simply aware of the reflexive nature of social life and of sociology. Simmel engaged directly with the issue of modernity, in such a way as to make his thoughts particularly relevant to present discussions of the idea of postmodernity. He may not have provided an 'institutional' analysis of modernity (or postmodernity) but he certainly did not proceed simply along cultural and epistemological lines.

The guiding thread of Giddens's book is the proposition that what has been announced as postmodernity does not actually constitute a break with, but that it is a 'radicalized' or 'high' version of, modernity. That does not mean, however, that he sees alleged postmodernity as having the same characteristics as those which he associates with radicalized modernity. Conceiving of what others have called the postmodern condition in the light of the idea of radicalized modernity alters the major diagnostic tendencies of those who have announced postmodernity. For example, Giddens claims that in the perspective of postmodernity the self is seen as 'dissolved or dismembered by the fragmentation of experience,' while in the frame of radicalized modernity the self is regarded as 'more than the site of intersecting forces' – for 'active processes of reflexive self-identity are made possible by modernity' (1990: 150). In particular, the standpoint of radicalized modernity is concerned with the identification of 'the institutional developments which create a sense of fragmentation and dispersal,' as opposed to the understanding of 'current transitions in epistemological terms or as dissolving epistemology altogether' (1990: 150).

The idea that postmodernity is 'simply' an extension of modernity and the more specific claim that there could be no general characterization, let alone a theory, of postmodernity without undoing most of the arguments of those who have proclaimed the end of grand narratives, of totality and of foundations, have been prominent in recent years. Yet Giddens fails to register any acknowledgment of this. Some writers have recently tried to produce a direct sociology of postmodernity, whereas Giddens takes the tack of doubting the existence of a condition of postmodernity, but approaching the central themes of those who have proclaimed its presence via a consideration of the institutions of modernity. He thus seeks, although he doesn't actually use the term, to 'ground' the postmodern flourish. The discourse of postmodernity is seen as symptomatic of a shift within modernity. It is at this point that Giddens comes, rather late, to the theme of globalization.

An argument I have been making all along is that one of the major consequences of globalization is the relativization of 'narratives' – that much but not all of what the advocates of a postmodern rupture have been emphasizing can be accounted for in reference to the phenomenon of globality. If one of the major features of globalization is the *compression* of the world, one of its main consequences is an exacerbation of collisions between civilizational, societal and communal narratives (as can be seen in a number of chapters of this book). The sociological problem from the standpoint of some theorists of globalization has been to comprehend the terms in which such encounters occur and also the moves toward and conflicts concerning what I call 'definitions' of the global situation. Thus in one sense the cultural and the epistemological interests of 'the post-modernists' can, indeed must, be maintained; but, contrary to the general thrust of the postmodernist way of thinking, much of globalization theory is interested in accounting for heterogeneity, without reducing it to a new homogeneity. Giddens makes no acknowledgment of this work. He himself claims to see, 'apart from the work of Marshall McLuhan and a few other individual authors' (1990: 65), discussion of globalization in only two bodies of literature: world-systems theory, particularly associated with Wallerstein (who never has acknowledged the usefulness of that term), and 'theorists of international relations.' The first is limited, as many others have said, by its concentration on the economic factor (although Waller-stein's own work has involved, as we have seen, increasing attention to cultural and, to a lesser extent, epistemological issues). The second, in so far as it addresses the issue of the move to 'one world,' does so largely, says Giddens, in terms of the increasing interdependency of the global inter-state system. Here again he neglects the more subtle and less restricted contributions to the analysis of inter-state and transnational relations, as well as international law and intercultural relations.

What does Giddens offer as a model of the global system? He defines globalization as 'the intensification of worldwide social relations which link distinct localities in such a way that local happenings are shaped by events occurring miles away and vice versa' (1990: 64) and he says that it has four dimensions: the nation-state system; the world capitalist economy; the world military order; and the international division of labor. It is important to realize that this four-dimensional image actually results from a rough transplantation to the global scene of 'the four basic institutional features of modernity' announced earlier in his book. Specifically, societal surveil-lance becomes the nation-state system; societal capitalism becomes the world capitalist economy; societal military power becomes the world military order; and societal industrialism becomes the international divi-sion of labor. Only the first of these does not involve a straightforward transfer of a dimension from *societal* modernity to the global circumstance. Thus one is readily able to see what Giddens means by 'the consequences of modernity.' Globality, or what Giddens calls globalization, is simply *an enlargement* of modernity, from society to the world. It is modernity on a global scale. As Giddens puts it, 'modernity is inherently globalizing' (1990: 63, 177), a proposition which inevitably leads to the question as to whether modernity is a Western project. His answer to that seems to be in the affirmative but, on the other hand, even though 'one of the fundamental consequences of modernity . . . is globalization', Giddens insists that globalization is 'more than a diffusion of Western institutions across the world, in which other cultures are crushed' (1990: 175). The decline in 'the grip of the West . . . is not a result of the diminishing impact of the institutions which first arose there but, on the contrary, a result of their global spread' (1990: 52). While certainly not without merit, that idea leaves entirely unexamined what exactly '*non*-Western' might now mean in a thoroughly modernized world. Giddens's neglect of culture is particularly disturbing at this juncture. At the same time, the problem of the conflation of 'modernity' and globality (also a reifiable term) becomes very apparent.

Giddens argues that it would be better to say that we are now in a situation of 'modernity coming to understand itself' (1990: 48) rather than that modernity is being overcome. While finding this view quite congenial, I do not believe that Giddens has gone anywhere near far enough along that line of thinking. He makes much of the idea that modernity is inherently reflexive and, in a certain sense, sociological, but he fails to explore the circumstances of classical sociology having had specific sets of interests rather than others. If modernity is inherently reflexive why then do we find that classical sociologists of the period 1890–1920 said exceedingly little about the space–time compression that was occurring with great rapidity as they wrote? Why did Durkheim and Weber say scarcely anything about such developments as, *inter alia*, the near completion of the global spread of the Gregorian calendar, the time-zoning of the world and the establishment of world time, the significance of the wireless, and the invention of the airplane? Why did they not speak of significant developments in international law? In sum, why did they not directly address the rapid moves that were occurring in their own time in the making of the world into a single place, if not a system? Of course there *were* elements of general recognition, as can be seen elsewhere in this book. One could certainly say that Weber in a general way recognized that what Giddens calls the institutional features of modernity were spreading across the world and that in a more sophisticated respect, Durkheim was interested, as he himself put it, in an emergent form of 'international life' and the increasing necessity for 'cosmopolitanism.' Nonetheless, these global or international themes were not very explicit in their published work. Rather they concentrated on the problem of individual-and-society and more diffusely of Western modernity. With the benefit of hindsight we can now say that in this they were both 'right' and 'wrong.' They were right in the sense that theirs was a period which was remarkable for its consolidation of the political force of the territorially integrated, nationally organized society. Yet they underplayed the fact that the modern national society was in significant part *produced by* the contingencies of the compression of the world, on the one hand, and the nearly global diffusion of ideas concerning the form that the national society should take, on the other. Compared with such people as Comte, Saint-Simon and Marx they appear to have been *relatively* uninterested in what we now call globalization.

We must recognize that globalization was one of the circumstances which produced the particular interests of sociology in its most crucial phase of institutionalization, but that the interest *in* globalization was rather slender. Giddens's concern with the institutional features of modernity and globalization often follows the strategy of those classical sociologists whom he criticizes, in spite of considerable discussion of time–space distanciation, during the course of which he gets into some difficulties. Not the least of these is his attempt to reformulate 'the problem of order' in a non-Parsonian way. Claiming, against all the clear-cut evidence in Parsons's work in the 1960s and 1970s, that Parsons defined the problem of order as simply a question of integration, Giddens maintains that that problem should be seen as 'the conditions under which time and space are organized so as to connect presence and absence' (a view which is not at all inconsistent with Parsons's theory). He then goes on to say that while 'modern societies (nation-states), in some respects at any rate, have a clearly defined boundedness . . . virtually no premodern societies were as clearly bounded as modern nation-states' (1990: 14). This undoubtedly accurate observation runs, however, against the thesis of modernity's rupture with all previous forms of life. For if globalization is a consequence or ramification of modernity how could modernity also constitute a kind of closure on *prior* globalizing tendencies?

Closely related to this problem is the perspective Giddens brings to bear upon time-and-space distanciation; disembedding, defined as 'the "lifting out" of social relations from local contexts of interaction and their restructuring across indefinite spans of time-space' (1990: 21); and reflexivity. Giddens is undoubtedly right in drawing attention to the ways in which time and space have become globally separated, recombined and standardized, in such a way as to make it possible to appropriate a 'unitary past . . . which is worldwide [and] forms a genuinely world-historical framework of action and experience' (1990: 21). (Although, as I have argued, this 'unitary post' has to be seen sociologically and historically in the light of the expanding 'space' of participants in the global field and with due recognition of the actual form of contemporary globalization.) However, this development is only loosely connected by Giddens to 'the institutional dimensions of modernity' (1990: 59) or 'the dimensions of globalization' (1990: 71). How those axial features of modernity and globalization relate specifically to the separation and recombination of space and time 'so crucial to the extreme dynamism of modernity' (1990: 20), disembedding and reflexivity is not at all clear. The latter are not, as such, says Giddens, types of institution, but rather 'facilitating conditions' (1990: 63) for the historical transitions of modernity. 'They are involved in, as well as conditioned by, the institutional dimensions of modernity' (1990: 63). Giddens's ambiguity and tentativeness here is easy to understand. For he has to make distanciation, disembedding and reflexivity central to modernity, in order to protect the thesis that globalization is a consequence of modernity. Yet he obviously cannot say that those 'non-institutions' are entirely unique to modernity. His problem could have been avoided by dropping the untenable claim that modernity in and of itself leads to globalization – but then that claim is central to his overall argument.

Giddens maintains that the concept of disembedding (and re-embedding) is an improvement on the idea of differentiation or functional specialization. Certainly he is right in trying to correct the view that functional differentiation has been *the* centerpiece of the transition to modernity. (Luhmann goes so far as to suggest that differentiation takes us directly into a world society.) And he is right to argue that time–space distanciation is a crucial aspect of globalization, but to claim that the concept of disembedding can replace the idea of differentiation is to throw the baby out with the bath water. While Giddens certainly has something of interest to say about disembedding mechanisms in specific reference to 'symbolic tokens' and 'expert systems,' he neglects the fact that social *and cultural* differentiation and the tensions and conflicts often occasioned by such, including 'fundamentalistic' attempts to dedifferentiate sociocultural systems, have been pivotal circumstances of recent world history.

While I find Giddens's attempt to ground, although not 'foundationally,' much of the poststructuralist enthusiasm about a condition of postmodern-ity acceptable, although certainly not original, I consider his attempt to diminish cultural considerations to be a great weakness. Giddens has, in spite of his claim to be providing an institutional analysis of modernity, actually produced an analysis which is more social-psychological, phenomenological, diffusely impressionistic, and eventually utopian than 'institutional.' Although I have some reservations about the 'neofunctionalist' conception of multidimensionality, I conclude that Giddens fails to meet the standards of a genuinely multidimensional approach. There are numerous rhetorical gestures in favor of economic and political institutions (so much so that Giddens could at certain points pass as a sort of Marxist). Yet he fails not merely to display the complexities of contemporary institutions, he almost completely neglects the significance of culture, largely because he has only a utopian-futuristic – indeed a quasi-theological – conception thereof. In other words, Giddens's ideas about the future are a substitute for interest in cultural variation and, indeed, contest in the here-and-now. While he may claim that globalization does not involve the crushing of non-Western cultures he does not seem to realize that such a statement requires him to theorize the issue of 'other cultures.' His suggestion that there is no Other in a globalized world apparently absolves him from undertaking such a task. He fails to understand that it is only in a (minimally) globalized world that a problem of 'the Other' could have arisen. What he apparently doesn't see is that a view of the world as marked by unicity can coexist with a view of the world as a place of others (leaving on one side the question of extraterrestrial others) – indeed that such recognition is central to the conceptual mapping of the global circumstance.

While it is true that a lot of the debate about postmodernity has been conducted in cultural*istic* terms and that therefore there is a need for certain 'institutional' corrections, it is a fundamental weakness of Giddens's book that he does not take cultural matters seriously. Maybe that is because he thinks that the concept of culture is inevitably bound to the common societal culture (or dominant ideology) thesis. But of course the contemporary debate about culture is much more fluid and nuanced than that. The whole idea that one can sensibly interpret the contemporary world without addressing the issues that arise from current debates about the politics of culture, cultural capital, cultural difference, cultural homogeneity and heterogeneity, ethnicity, nationalism, race, gender, and so on, is implausible. What appears to be the functional equivalent in Giddens's work of a direct engagement with culture is his concern with *self*-identity and his advocacy of 'utopian realism.' While what he has to say about the connections between personal life and global issues is certainly not without interest (see Giddens, 1991), he thereby avoids the tough issues of contingency and variation in the 'high modern' age. In any case, his discussion of 'the politics of self-actualization' in a globalized world invokes exceedingly little empirical evidence, even though this book is replete with what are claimed to be empirical generalizations. Giddens's overall argument in this book boils down, in spite of some useful insights, to an updated and overly abstract version of the convergence thesis – homogenized 'modern man' injected with a special dose of phenomenological reflexivity.

10

GLOBALIZATION AND THE NOSTALGIC PARADIGM

Much of our current critical and political project appears to me as a kind of unrealized mourning in which all of life has become reorganized around something that 'died.' (Dean MacCannell, 1989: xi–xii)

For the nostalgic, the world is alien. (Bryan S. Turner, 1987: 149)

The problem of nostalgia has assumed quite an important place in recent discussions in critical social and cultural theory. Yet it has not been theorized as a global issue. Perhaps the major problem in this appraisal has been insensitivity to the distinction between *nostalgic theory* and *the theory of nostalgia*. The first has to do with theory (and research) which is constrained by nostalgia. The second, on the other hand, is concerned with the comprehension of nostalgia. It is that second orientation which frames the discussion in this chapter. We lack a sociological, as opposed to a psychological, theory of nostalgia. In this chapter I take some steps towards rectification of this problem. More specifically, I continue the exploration of 'the nostalgic paradigm,' with particular reference to globalization. I am interested in the extent to which globalization encourages nostalgic theory and, more generally, casts light on the production of theory. Theorization of nostalgia is the 'flip side' of the theorization of globalization.

Stauth and Turner (1988a: 29) argue that sociology 'is dominated by a common episteme which provides the leading motif for the separate and jarring discourses of various sociological approaches.' There is, they say, wide variation in 'the terminologies' of the latter but those 'are actually dominated by a uniform problem, which is the problem of nostalgic memory' (1988a: 29). This is a heavy claim, which is so strong that even its proponents do not, I take it, mean to say that all of contemporary sociology and social theory or all contemporary practitioners in those intellectual areas are equally implicated in the reproduction of the nostalgic attitude. Nonetheless I believe that with allowance for some rhetorical exaggeration Stauth and Turner are persuasive. That being so and in so far as one tends to think that there must be something wrong with an academic discipline which is strongly tied to the nostalgic attitude, it follows that we should not merely render it more explicit – that is, describe it – we should also 'provide a critique of nostalgia in order to set sociology on a different course' (1988a: 29). Here I take up that challenge, by offering an interpretation of the circumstances that have promoted nostalgia on both social-theoretical and 'real-life,' empirical fronts, with particular reference to globalization.

While much of the discussion here is critical of the extent to which nostalgia permeates social theory it is not dogmatically directed towards the elimination of the nostalgic attitude *per se*. Such an effort would be both futile and 'unnatural,' for clearly there are respects in which nostalgia is 'normal.' Indeed, it might be useful to think of nostalgia along roughly the same lines as Freud considered narcissism, that is to distinguish between a primary, 'normal' type of nostalgia and a secondary, 'abnormal' form. Such a distinction is not, however, central to the present discussion, even though it diffusely informs it.

The Global Setting of Wilful Nostalgia

The thematization of the problem of nostalgia which Stauth and Turner have adamantly announced is, in their own terms, situated in an extended discussion of the relatively unexplored influence of Nietzsche in the history of social theory, an exercise which at the same time involves an advocacy of a Nietzschean outlook as far as the future of sociology is concerned. My own task here is to consider the issue of nostalgia both more directly and from a rather different angle. Bryan Turner has also, with Robert Holton, deployed the writings of Talcott Parsons in an apparently separate critique of sociological nostalgia (Holton and Turner, 1986: 209–34). Cuddihy (1978) has written along parallel lines. I have written in a similar vein of Parsons's sociology as being distinctively anti-nostalgic (Robertson, 1983a). In developing their argument that Parsons was 'against nostalgia, for the modern world, and unambiguously post-classical,' Holton and Turner maintain that his sociology also constitutes a decisive step beyond both the communitarian position in moral philosophy – as conspicuously represented by Alasdair MacIntyre's *After Virtue* (1981) – and the modernistic, perspectival stance of Nietzsche, to which MacIntyre is thoroughly opposed (Holton and Turner, 1986: 215). It is not my task here to discuss the extent to which Turner's virtually simultaneous advocacy of Nietzschean and Parsonian positions is sustainable. Rather I attempt to ground the nostalgic critique of modernity, as well as argue for the elimination of nostalgia from social theory *per se*. Specifically, I will try to expand on the argument of Stauth and Turner by addressing the issue of the foundations of what Tom Nairn (1988: 347) has called the 'modern, wilful kind' of nostalgia. In so doing I will be particularly concerned with the global dynamics and global significance of that phenomenon.

In his penetrating analysis of the British monarchy (more diffusely, of British – indeed, 'Ukanian' – identity as a whole) Nairn (1988: 347) argues that the kind of nostalgia which was to be found in, say, the late eighteenth century 'hadn't been more than a century or so behind the times.' Using Viscount Bolingbroke as an exemplar of late eighteenth-century English nostalgia, Nairn says that 'the actual wreckage of the world he had lost was all about him, some of its rooms inhabited, apparently still recuperable.' In contrast, with the late nineteenth-century interest in the invention of tradition (Hobsbawm and Ranger, 1983) there arose a kind of nostalgia which had scant, if any, concern with what Christopher Lasch (1988: 178) has called a 'conversational relationship with the past.' Instead this was a period, lasting from about 1870 to the early or mid-1920s, when there was considerable concern about issues surrounding national identity and national integration across the world; except for black Africa, which was an arena for the projection of the identities of the imperialist powers. But in Africa, as well as in parts of Asia and Oceana, these issues appeared not just as concrete extensions of Western identities – as in the idea of 'the white man's burden' – but also, with the arrival of early functionalist anthropology, as forms of identity and integration *conferral*. In other words, while Western imperialism of the late nineteenth and early twentieth centuries involved the political and symbolic incorporation of African and other territories into the national identities of the imperialist nations, it also involved the attribution to primal societies of cohesive functionality. That exercise actually combined a modernist notion of function with a nostalgic injection of a Western conception of *Gemein-schaft* (Ardener, 1985). This Western view of 'native *Gemeinschaft*' has not infrequently been opposed by a 'subliminal' promotion of 'indigenous *Gemeinschaft*.' And it has not been until recently that anthropologists (Comaroff and Comaroff, 1991) and historians (Walls, 1991) have begun to make the argument that the 'discovery' and 'invention' of tradition has to be situated within complex sets of *relations* between penetrating and penetrated societies in global context.

Sociology as we now know it crystallized precisely during the period of which I have spoken. The period during which modern *wilful* nostalgia developed in earnest was also the period when so-called classical sociology was formulated, in Western and, to some extent, Central Europe, along 'grand narrative' lines. In view of that circumstance, I present three main arguments.

First and most generally, I maintain that there was a close link between those two developments. They amplified each other in the main centers from which emanated the major traditions of social theory (notably Britain, France, Germany and, to some extent, the USA). Wilful nostalgia among national elites fed into the work of leading sociologists, and vice versa. It is of great importance to note that from the 1870s there was considerable and increasing concern among the elites of a large number of societies with the establishment of grandiose national symbols, monuments, ceremonials, and so on (Hobsbawm and Ranger, 1983). From Washington, DC across Europe to Tokyo the late nineteenth century witnessed the kind of wilful, politically driven nostalgia of which Nairn has spoken elaborately in reference to Britain, and fleetingly to Japan (Nairn, 1988: 271).

We should be careful not to overemphasize the quickening concern with grandiose symbolizations and ritualizations of national identity in the last twenty years of the nineteenth century. For by the middle of this time the search for the past had become a patriotic effort in nearly every West and Central European nation. Whereas West European elites had been engaged for centuries in discovering distant ancestors worthy of celebration and emulation – both local and in the lands of the Bible and of ancient Greece – the mid-nineteenth century witnessed a great intensification of that search. By that time, says Silberman (1989: 3) 'antiquarianism had ceased to be the pastime of adventurous individuals and had become a national quest.' Much of that quest was facilitated by 'the fledgling science of archeology,' which by 1850 or so had led to a situation in which 'imperial prestige . . . could be measured in sheer tonnage – at least in Germany, England, and France' (1989: 3–4). In public museums were to be found 'national cabinets of curiosities' (Silberman, 1989: 4) where such objects as the Elgin Marbles and the Rosetta Stone were displayed. In England this kind of enthusiasm reached a particular peak with the Crystal Palace exhibition of 1851. By the end of the century Sumerians, Hittites, Mycenaeans and Minoans had been added to the archeological focus on the Romans, the Egyptians, the Greeks and the Assyrians. More generally 'world' exhibitions of national accomplishments had become quite common.

Nevertheless, in spite of this necessary acknowledgment of the nineteenth century concern with local and primordial origins, it does appear that during the last two decades of that century there was a definite boom in the intensity and scope of interest in symbolic and ritualistic celebrations of nation and, where relevant, empire. As Stephen Kern (1983: 277) has written in his important study of the emergent global culture of that period, 'the self-images of nations in the full spectrum of time – past, present, and future – changed after 1880.' However, as we saw in Chapter 3, there were significant differences across nations concerning the sense of the past. While nostalgic concern was widespread – most explicitly among the major European powers such as Britain, France, Germany, Russia, Italy and Austria–Hungary – there was significant variation both in intensity and in the type of concern with the past.

While Kern, Nairn and the contributors to the influential volume edited by Hobsbawm and Ranger are probably correct in emphasizing the last quarter of the nineteenth century as the most crucial phase in the rise of modern wilful nostalgia, it has to be said that strains leading to explicit concern with national identity and tradition became manifest somewhat earlier than that in some Asian societies, of which China and Japan were (and remain) particularly important. In both China and Japan Western intrusions during the 1850s created an intense 'response to the West' (Schwartz, 1964: 9). As we have seen in the case of Japan, this led to a striking invention of national myths in the early Meiji period (Gluck, 1985), but in China it led to increasing ambivalence and instability. In China there was particular concern with tradition and its relationship to 'civilization' (Gong, 1984). That does not, of course, mean that a concept such as tradition was readily available to East Asians, for it was only in the late nineteenth century that the nineteenth-century Western category of 'tradition' was actually translated into Chinese (Schwartz, 1964: 50). (It is worth noting that the term 'nostalgia' – *hsiang-ch'ou* – has been a conspicuous topic in Chinese literature since at least the time of Confucius in the sixth century BC, although in registering this I am certainly not equating traditionalism with nostalgia.) The response of China and Japan to Western intrusion in the mid-nineteenth century presaged what was to become virtually a worldwide phenomenon – the formulation of ideologies of delayed modernization which combined, in various patterns, a nostalgic concern with a real or imagined past with a futuristic or 'progressive' rejection of tradition (Cuddihy, 1987: 173–4).

Second, I argue that in the period in question some of the leading motifs of Western social theory – notably the predicaments expressed in the thematization of the *Gemeinschaft–Gesellschaft* and related distinctions, and the search for integration-promoting national identities – diffused to other parts of the world (such as Latin America, Turkey, China and Japan) in such a way as to provide the beginning of a global discourse concerning the outlines of a modern society, what it should 'look like' and how it should operate. The early impact of Western classical sociology in that regard is probably, as I have suggested, the most overlooked of all aspects of the history and historiography of social theory. It may be that during its classical period (1890–1920) sociology made its greatest impact on international affairs as such; although, as I have also claimed, it was itself greatly affected – indeed, restricted – by the national and international circumstances of the time. What is of particular interest in the present context is the differential impact of the thinking of the sociologists of the classical period, particularly Herbert Spencer, on the national newcomers to 'international society,' of whom Japan was in some respects the most important. Japan had, of course, for long been 'successful' in manipulating its own history and of expressing its substantive identity, its 'essence,' in forms drawn from other cultures, most importantly China (Pollack, 1986). But the new Meiji elites were particularly explicit about and adept at reconstructing Japanese identity and tradition. R.J. Smith (1983: 9) quotes an unnamed Japanese who remarked to a German physician in 1876 that Japan 'has no history. Our history begins today.' That proclivity eventuated in the production by the end of the Meiji period of a highly serviceable nostalgia about such matters as the imperial system, Shinto as a native-national religion, the samurai ethic and the Confucian ethos as a way of consolidating Japan's 'national essence' and strengthening it, as an entirely 'unique' society, against the outside world (R.J. Smith, 1983; Buruma, 1989: 44; Gluck, 1985). The late nineteenth-century encounter with Asia also facilitated a nostalgic yearning on the part of Westerners for a more 'homely' *Western* past (not dissimilar to an Enlightenment hankering after Oriental 'harmony'). In Japan they saw a lost world of *the West*, a theme which is intriguingly explored in Yokoyama's (1987) discussion of images of Japan in Victorian Britain.

Japan's 'newcomer' status and the ability of its leaders to produce ideological ways of transcending the *Gemeinschaft–Gesellschaft* predicament gave it some advantages over the European latecomers, of whom the most important was obviously Germany; but from the latter it actually learned quite a lot about national-identity formation. At the same time, Japan also managed to reverse much of its historical relationship with China. In fact Japan's apparent success in responding to the West became a problematic model *for China*, one important aspect of which was that a very large portion of the Western ideas which reached China after 1900 came via Chinese students' experiences in Japanese universities and from Chinese translations of Japanese translations from European languages (Schwarz, 1964; Wang, 1966). (An interesting aspect of this 'conveyor belt' role of Japan concerns the failure of communistic Marxism to develop on a large scale in Japan in comparison with its success in China.) In the later period of World War II Germany and Japan were, of course, to become the leading Axis powers, both committed in their own ways, as 'deprived' nations, to 'the transcendence of the modern' or, more precisely, the calculated, synthetic transcendence of the uniquely *modern* myth of the tension between *Gemeinschaft* and *Gesellschaft*.

One can now say that 'no other major social structural distinction (certainly not that between the classes) has received such massive reinforcement as the ideological separation of the modern from the nonmodern world' (MacCannell, 1989: 8). One might well object that in at least one society sociological attention *has* been focused more on distinctions between 'the classes.' I refer, of course to Britain, where class has undoubtedly been the dominant motif of sociological analysis. Yet it is fairly easy to see that much of class analysis in Britain is, in fact, guided by the *Gemeinschaft–Gesellschaft* problematic. Specifically, enthusiasm for 'the way of life' of the 'working class' can be read as another way of expressing regret for the passing of *Gemeinschaft*. Returning to MacCannell's argument, we can see that the 'ideological distinction' has in various ways been globally institutionalized. Not merely is it codified and enacted as a central aspect of international and 'non-governmental' culture, it has been built into the fabric of intra-societal life, most notably in the curriculum of educational institutions in every corner of the world. It is, in sum, part and parcel of the modern way of thinking. That this may now be changing, in part through 'postmodern play,' does not alter the fact that the twentieth century has been a century during which geotemporal distinctions between clusters of nations became central to a globally shared mode of thought.

As MacCannell (1989: 8) has also written, 'the best indication of the final victory of modernity over other sociocultural arrangements is not the disappearance of the nonmodern world, but its artificial preservation and reconstruction in modern society.' This interpretation now has to be considered in the light of the growing debate about modernity-and-postmodernity, with particular reference to the significance of the word 'artificial.' Nonetheless MacCannell makes an important point. He argues further that 'the separation of nonmodern cultural traits from their original contexts and their distribution as modern playthings are evident in the various social movements toward naturalism, so much a feature of modern societies: cults of folk music and medicine, adornment and behavior, peasant dress' (1989: 8). The museumization of the premodern is a major feature of (post)modernity.

MacCannell's discussion of the postmodern impulse of the 1980s is an excellent version of the assessment that the idea of postmodernity is simply an (exaggerated) extension of the idea of modernity, though he sometimes falls too easily into the trap of maintaining without qualification that modernity really existed and that postmodernity is only an intellectual idea. In any case, MacCannell has stated as well as anybody the idea that the division of the world into the premodern and the modern is a feature of modernity. The various institutions and practices devoted to that division 'establish in consciousness the definition and boundary of modernity by rendering concretely and immediate that which modernity is not' (Mac-Cannell, 1989: 9). Let us briefly consider now a specific case: the nostalgic paradigm in German social theory.

Newly unified in the 1870s but lacking a readily serviceable national myth and a relatively unbroken past of the kind enjoyed by England (or Britain), France and Russia, 'it was impossible for [Germany's] citizens to believe . . . that their country has always been and always would be' (Kern, 1983: 278). The highly influential sets of sociological ideas produced in Germany at that time were remarkably pessimistic about the future and modernity in general (Liebersohn, 1988; also Ringer, 1969). In a number of respects the publication in 1887 of Ferdinand Toennies's *Gemeinschaft und Gesellschaft* (Toennies, 1957) set the tone for this, even though Toennies himself denied that he was condemning *Gesellschaft* and claimed that he rejected romantic longings for a medieval past. In the larger frame of German thought Oswald Spengler's *The Decline of the West* (1965), written during World War I and first published in 1918, constituted the apogee of the pessimism of the time.[1] It seems that among well known German social theorists only Georg Simmel had a definite, reflexive concern with the bases of nostalgia. Simmel, while not concerned directly with globalization, clearly indicated the nostalgic side of modernity when he said that while modernity seems to involve only a concern with the present a sense of personal identity in the modern world can be achieved, in Jedlowski's words (1990: 147), 'almost *only* on the basis of personal memory.' (It is also worth recording that Simmel's descriptions and interpretations of modern life were used by Spengler to illustrate his argument concerning 'the decline of the West': Hughes, 1952.) It doesn't take much to see that what Simmel said in connection with personal memory in relation to societal modernity can also be applied to the connection between societal memory and globality. In other words, *relative to* globality, at least in recent phases of globalization, the idea of society has become a vehicle of 'memory' (Smith, 1990: 177–80).

The *Kulturpessimismus* of Max Weber, the most influential of German sociologists, 'projected an indefinite glacial epoch for the whole of mankind' (Merquior, 1980: 187); while the later attempt by critical theorists – 'after Auschwitz' – to resume the old Enlightenment project has, on the other hand, been largely dominated in Germany by such ideas as 'modern myth' and 'total community.' As John Rajchman (1988: 184) has argued with specific reference to Jürgen Habermas, 'something of a retrospective "invention" ' is involved in the theorization of such motifs. In fact, Rajchman goes so far as to maintain that 'the great German *Angst* or lack of "self-reassurance" ' is best seen as 'the product of the "discourse on modernity" ' – suggesting that the will to nostalgia is, indeed, a distinctive issue of modernity (although it is as much a product of the early-modern phase of *globality* and the contemporary ramifications of the latter). Even more directly, Buruma (1989: 43), perhaps unfairly, accuses Habermas of contradictorily promoting both 'enlightened nationalism' and 'uncritical emotionalism'. That old, German contradiction centers, Buruma says, upon the idea of Germany as a politicolegal entity, on the one hand and, on the other, as 'a *Heimat*, devoid of politics, a land . . . anxiously searching for identity.' (This was, of course, argued before the recent reunification of Germany.)

Such sweeping characterizations are undoubtedly risky and lacking in nuance. A more refined perspective on German social theory's proclivity for nostalgia may be obtained from Jerry Muller's discussion of German conservatism in his *The Other God that Failed* (1987). The main pillar of Muller's analysis is his claim that the vast majority of German intellectuals, critical or conformist, were until the post-1945 period on the political Right. The Frankfurt School, the main predecessor of contemporary critical theory, is an apparent exception to this. But even in that case there is a strong element of adherence to the idea of a 'refined' world of 'good taste.'

One of the major features of modernity which has had a particularly powerful impact with respect to nostalgia is undoubtedly the homogenizing requirements of the modern nation state through much of the twentieth century in the face of ethnic and cultural diversity. In the wake of the French and American revolutions of the late eighteenth century there spread across the Western world the stipulation of people living as citizens of nationally constituted societies. More specifically, it was during the period 1750 to 1920 that nationalism triumphed as an ideal, involving the attempt to overcome local ethnocultural, as well as religious, diversity. The requirement was that nations should produce standardized citizens, whose loyalties to the nation would be unchallenged by extra-societal allegiances. Some would claim that the ideal of national identity is much older than that. For example, Simon Schama's rich discussion of Dutch identity in the seventeenth century is specifically concerned with 'the community of the nation, an entity not supposed to have existed before the French Revolution' (Schama, 1987: 6). Schama's suggestion is that 'the community of the nation' was an important sociocultural phenomenon, at least in the West, prior to the period beginning around the time of the French Revolution. However, even though I take Schama's argument seriously, I regard the kind of 'nationalism' which developed prior to the late eighteenth century as having only very incipient significance as far as globalization is concerned. Modern globalization did not begin to enter a relatively concrete phase until the appearance of explicit ideas concerning *the relationship between nationalism and internationalism* at the end of the eighteenth century (Kohn, 1971; Brubaker, 1990). In line with Schama (1987), McNeill (1986: 7) acknowledges that 'the idea that a government rightfully should rule only over citizens of a single ethos took root haltingly in western Europe, beginning in the late middle ages.' He also argues that that ideal has weakened considerably in Western Europe since the early 1920s, but that it has gained elsewhere, especially in the ex-colonial areas of Africa and Asia. Clearly, one would have to modify, but not drastically alter, that view in light of recent events in Central and Eastern Europe and the old Soviet Union.

As McNeill (1986: 34) has further remarked, 'something . . . happened in western Europe about 1750 to alter prevailing patterns of civilized society,' a central ingredient of his own account of the interruption of the historical norm of people living in polyethnic collectivities being the power exerted on European elites by what he calls 'the classical ideal.' 'As classical Latin and Greek became the staple of schooling, the pagan authors of Rome and Greece [offered] educated Europeans an ideal of life built around participation in a self-governing city-state' (McNeill, 1986: 36). The sculpture and vases of ancient Greece had fascinated aristocrats since the Renaissance but it was not until the middle of the eighteenth century that a more diffuse idealization of Greece took hold (Silberman, 1989: 4–5); and there can be little doubt that the classical ideal continued to have a strong impact upon European intellectual elites right into the period of classical sociology, and thus upon the development of twentieth-century social theory as a whole. Its impact on classical German theory is apparent in Max Weber's concern with the cultural homogenization of the German nation, in terms of which his orientation to the Polish and Jewish 'questions' can be readily understood, if not applauded (Abraham, 1992); while I have already remarked on its hold over some versions of critical theory, most explicitly in the work of Habermas. (On the other hand, Habermas clearly accepts the idea of a multiethnic society.) Some of Emile Durkheim's work was informed by Fustel de Coulanges's *The Ancient City* (1980), while the classical element in Durkheim's sociology has considerably affected the nostalgia-tinged work of Robert Bellah, most notably in his role as senior author of *Habits of the Heart* (Bellah et al., 1985), a work which is openly attuned to the 'Grecophilia' (Holmes, 1988: 36) of Alasdair

MacIntyre's *After Virtue* (1981) and *Whose Justice? Which Rationality?* (1987). However, while *The Ancient City* deals with problems of what might be called *inter*-communal problematics, *Habits of the Heart* deals with a single societal community.[2]

I cannot provide here comprehensive documentation of the impact of the classical ideal on social theory, as mediated to recent sociology via the symbiotic relationship between the rise of classical sociology and the global consolidation of the homogeneous national society in the period 1870–1925. However, it is important to note that nostalgia was built into the very origins of what McNeill has described as the classical ideal. Emphasizing that this ideal continuously involved failure to notice the foreigners and slaves who lived in ancient Athens (and Rome) in their periods of imperial glory, McNeill points out that nostalgia for 'a homogenous rural society' was a very significant aspect of the thinking of the major Athenian authors. They 'flourished while the transition from a homogenous rural society was underway; indeed their work was stimulated in large part by the strains and pains inherent in that transition' (McNeill, 1986: 23). Martha Nussbaum (1989: 41) has criticized MacIntyre's recent work from a somewhat different angle, pointing out that in his wish for a return to the ethical order of the ancient Greeks he fails to mention, among other things, that Aristotle's 'list of virtues is intended to be international, based upon experiences that all human beings share.' Thus Aristotle did not think that beliefs are only to be justified from within a single, local tradition. That is why he drew upon Persia, Sparta, Athens and Cyme in his quest for a model of the good life.

I contend, third, that globalization has been a primary root of the rise of wilful nostalgia. More specifically, it was the take-off period of rapidly accelerating globalization in the late nineteenth and early twentieth centuries that witnessed the flowering of the urge to *invent* traditions. Wilful nostalgia as a form of cultural politics – as well as the politics of culture – has been a major feature of globalization.

For certain purposes it is appropriate to think of politically motivated nostalgia on the part of actual or potential national elites as arising from a mixture of the perceived need for national integration and the threat of relativization of national identity by the compression of 'international society.' But, as I have been arguing in this book, the *universalization of particularism* is an intersecting diagnosis. The universalization of national (and other) particularisms is *an ingredient of* the compression which has come to be conceptualized as globalization. Put another way, the emphasis on national-societal identity is a component of *institutionalized societalism* (Lechner, 1989) – the institutionalization of globally diffused (and sometimes coercively imposed) expectations concerning the structure and functioning of societies, including the expectation of uniqueness of identity.

Sociology as an academic discipline entered its most crucial phase of early institutionalization during what I am calling the take-off period of modern globalization; and it did so in reference to the general theme of modernity and the more specific individual–society problem, rather than in explicit acknowledgment of globalization. The extent to which the classical sociologists were, in fact, concerned with the wider, global circumstance is an issue which I have already raised on a number of occasions. For the most part, sociologists were interested, often in very nostalgic ways, in the coming of diffuse modernity to Western societies and the problems of integration and meaning occasioned by the new kind of relatively standardized national society. Even Herbert Spencer, probably the most globally influential of the sociologists of the period in question, was not the cool embracer of 'rational modernity' that he is often made out to have been. For example, he advised the early Meiji elite in Japan to cling strongly to their religious traditions (Spencer, 1966: 417), while in talking about his own Britain Spencer undoubtedly assumed 'the actual nourishment that came from the more organic harmony of a medievalism that had not altogether disappeared' (Hartz, 1964: xv). The overt thrust of Spencer's ideas about progress and evolution provided both a theoretically viable conception of the relations between national societies (namely one of competitive, adaptive struggle) and a sense of a human destiny to which individual societies should contribute. But, like Weber, in the face of the international reception of his ideas he ignored *interactions* of societies, as well as of civilizations, as a critical variable. Spencer did, however, warn that patriotism is *sociologically* dangerous.

Nostalgia and the Sharpening Form of Globalization

Turner (1987) has briefly traced quite a lot of the history of the concept of nostalgia, emphasizing its close association with the idea of melancholy in classical and later thought, and its medical, literary and religious significance in the West. Following Fred Davis's discussion of nostalgia in symbolic-interactionist perspective (1974), Turner (1987: 149) points out that nostalgia in its literal meaning as homesickness 'was defined in medical analysis by Johannes Hofer in the seventeenth century as the symptoms (melancholy, weeping, anorexia and despair) of homesick [German-speaking] Swiss mercenaries, fighting in regions remote from their home-lands'; to which it might be added that nostalgia does not appear to have been used with any frequency in the English language (as indicating homesickness) until the eighteenth century (Onions, 1966: 615). Turner regards the quasi-medical notion of nostalgia as homesickness as 'somewhat debased,' since, in line with a richer tradition of discourse about melancholy, we ought to talk philosophically and sociologically about nostalgia as 'a fundamental condition of human estrangement' (Turner, 1987: 150). Although he is rather convincing in that regard, it should be emphasized that the notion of *homelessness* as a basic form of estrangement or alienation *has* been particularly evident in the very traditions of German philosophy where Turner seeks to locate nostalgia. Indeed,

Heidegger says somewhere that the rise of Japan was a specific stimulus for his attempt to reconstruct Western philosophy.

The most explicit and lengthy discussion of sociological homelessness (a less specific phenomenon than homesickness) as a psychological product of modernization and as itself a producer of 'nostalgia . . . for a condition of "being at home" in society, with oneself and, ultimately, in the universe' was indeed written largely within the Germanic phenomenological tradition of concern with the themes of alienation and estrangement. I refer, of course, to *The Homeless Mind*, by Peter Berger et al. (1973: 83). It also bears repeating that in at least one non-Western civilization the idea and condition of nostalgia have been traditionally pervasive. The Chinese term *hsiang-ch'ou* involves the combination of the words for homeland and sorrow, indicating a desire to return to a familiar place in one's earlier life. It also possesses a more pathological, connotation: that one experiences sorrow whenever one is tempted to think of one's original homeplace.[3]

Needless to say, I am not directly referring here to homelessness in the current widespread sense of being without a dwelling-place or a household. Nonetheless that sense of homelessness 'coexists with the persistent images of home as a place of comfort, safety and refuge' (Mack, 1991: 5). The fact that we are confronted frequently with images of and stories about homeless people, about domestic violence and poverty and about famines, refugees and those in exile across the globe undoubtedly helps to promote an 'ideology of home.' At the same time, we resort to ideas about 'rootlessness' with little or no consideration of that condition in premodern societies.

Mention of an ideology of home draws attention to the great weakness of sociological and other versions of phenomenology in omitting any consideration of global culture. Writing of Berger and Luckmann's *The Social Construction of Reality* (1966), John Meyer (1992: 11) says that their tendency 'to treat the cultural construction of identity and activity as going on in the same people and groups whose identities and activities are under study, and as going on in the same time frame' is a major deficiency. Meyer argues that what he calls the 'institutionalist' or 'neo-institutionalist' perspective emphasizes, in contrast, that processes of 'modern cultural construction' develop across large spaces and often across lengthy historical periods. Thus global culture 'shapes particular national identities and policies,' while 'broad sweeps of cultural rationalization precipitate isomorphic forms in particular organizations.' Moreover, 'selves reflect the constitution of individual identity in nation-states and other great institutions' (Meyer, 1992: 11). (Generally speaking the 'neo-institutionalist' perspective is (Thomas et al., 1987) compatible with the one I am presenting in its insistence upon the trans-societal significance of culture and its constraints on 'local' meaning.)[4]

Turner (1987) and Stauth and Turner (1988a: 47) suggest that there are four main presuppositions of the nostalgic paradigm: the idea of history as decline; the sense of a loss of wholeness; the feeling of the loss of expressivity and spontaneity; and the sense of loss of individual autonomy. The first and second of these are more frequently encountered than the third or fourth in general discussions of nostalgia; but it is important to note that in the contemporary period nostalgia for spontaneity and individual autonomy, once thought to be a hallmark of modernity, have become salient dimensions of nostalgia. Even some forms of individualistic rational-choice theory in contemporary social science should be classified as nostalgic, in the sense that they attempt to dedifferentiate modern life, to reduce it to one dimension. I want to press this scheme in a particular direction by relating the sociological and philosophical thematization of nostalgia in the period 1870–1925 to what Nairn (1988: 168) has described as 'a great tide of synthetic nostalgia' which reached its first peak at the end of the nineteenth century. In turn I want to discuss the kind of wilful nostalgia that we find in the late twentieth century, my argument being centered on my previous claim that we are currently in a new phase of accelerated, nostalgia-producing globalization. I suggest that we are witnessing, and participating in, a third major phase of modern globalization, which is clearly related to the rise of postmodernist ways of thinking. It will be recalled that I regard the take-off phase as beginning around 1870, and lasting into the mid-1920s. The second phase of twentieth-century globalization lasted until the mid- or late 1960s. The third phase involved the reconstruction and problematization of the four major reference points of globalization (societies, individuals, international relations and humankind) and the strengthening of the particular–universal 'dialectic.' These developments are generating a somewhat different and diffuse kind of wilful, synthetic nostalgia amounting to something like the global institutionalization of the nostalgic attitude. All the more reason, then, to eliminate nostalgia from social theory as analysis and thematize it as an object of sociological analysis. Let us by all means study it. But let us not allow it to structure or constrain our theory and our investigations.

The multidimensional image of nostalgia provided by Stauth and Turner is illuminating, but more can be done with respect to the issue of periodization. Moreover, the wilful political manipulation of nostalgia is a significant additional factor that has impinged on the development of social theory. Additionally, Turner's (1987) declaration that the world is alien to the nostalgic needs to be unpacked so as to double the meaning of 'the world' – the world as the mundane ingredient of modernity *and* the world as a concrete, singular field resulting from globalization. Before coming directly to these matters let me give a hint as to the kind of nostalgia which is particularly evident in the late twentieth century during a period when the phrase 'nostalgia isn't what it used to be' has become a commonplace (F. Davis, 1974). I do this via Frederic Jameson:

> The appetite for images of the past, in the form of what might be called simulacra, the increasing production of such images of all kinds, in particular in that peculiar postmodern genre, the *nostalgic film*, with its glossy evocation of the past as sheer consumerable fashion and image – all this seems to me

something of a return of the repressed, an unconscious sense of the loss of the past, which this appetite for images seeks desperately to overcome. (1988: 104)

Jameson argues that *culture* is a 'privileged area in which to witness' the current appetite for images of the past, although he also insists that that appetite can largely be explained by the dynamics of global capitalism. Indeed it is from the 'transdiscipline' of cultural studies as well, more generally, as from 'poststructuralism' (Poster, 1990), that some of the more interesting – and, in the best sense, subversive – challenges to the nostalgic paradigm in sociology have been issued. In the simplest terms, much of sociology *is* nostalgic, whereas much of cultural studies involves the *thematization* of nostalgia.

However, that is indeed an oversimplification. For although people on the more radical side of cultural studies have theorized the problem of nostalgia they have also tended to make it into something like an ideological litmus test. They have claimed to be against nostalgia in respect of such matters as the hankering after grand narratives, communalism and the liberal subject, but they have also vied with each other in arguments about who is less or more nostalgic (Poster, 1990). Indeed Jameson has himself been subject to the charge of nostalgia for adhering to a utopian vision of Marxist socialism. Jameson has argued that socialism should be reinvented as an effective cultural and social vision, to which John O'Neill (1988: 62) has responded that Jameson is guilty of 'a nostalgic neo-Durkheimian reaction to postmodernism.' On the other side, while sociology has tended to accept rather than to theorize nostalgia, there are or have been strong exceptions to that tendency, most notably in the concern of Talcott Parsons and Niklas Luhmann with the general problem of complexity, as well as in the interest in 'multidimensionality' expressed by Jeffrey Alexander and others.

It is clear that late twentieth-century nostalgia is intimately bound up with consumerism. Compared to wilful, synthetic nostalgia as an ingredient of late nineteenth- and early twentieth-century cultural politics, contemporary nostalgia is both more economic – in the sense of being a major product of global capitalism (which is itself bound by the global play between the universal and the particular) – and more 'democratically' cultural (or 'simulational'). This does not, of course mean that wilful, politically driven nostalgia has been overwhelmed. How could one say that at a time of flag-waving nostalgia about a mythical American past; Ukania-myth-making; the politically astute manipulation of the idea of Japanese uniqueness; the use of nostalgia in legitimizing ethnonationalism inside the areas of former Soviet domination; the cultivation of Chinese 'purity' and so on? (Not to speak of more definitely global types of nostalgia, to which I will refer again in a moment.) So my point is that politically driven nostalgia is now embedded in – although it has been partly responsible for – a more pervasive and diffuse, consumerist type of nostalgia. There is now a definite demand for and certainly a large supply of nostalgia. Prior to the late nineteenth century, before the onset of modern globalization, one tended to find a more directly existential type of nostalgia, arising more 'naturally' from estrangement or alienation. That does not mean that existential nostalgia was then replaced by wilful nostalgia (itself to be replaced by consumerist-simulational nostalgia). Rather, existential nostalgia was, for the most part nationalistically, incorporated into wilful nostalgia; which is now being incorporated – for the most part capitalistically – into consumerist, image-conveyed nostalgia, the latter being wrapped into the global institutionalization of the universalization of the particular and the particularization of the universal.

I have been arguing that the origins of what Nairn has called wilful nostalgia can best be understood and accounted for in reference to the take-off phase of recent globalization during the period 1870–1925 and that we are now in another phase – with the period 1925–68 as a kind of interregnum. This third, modern, phase is producing a more complex and globally institutionalized kind of nostalgia. Given the remarkable fluidity of 'world affairs' at the moment of writing, any analytical contribution to this issue itself undoubtedly becomes part of the process of contemporary global-reality construction. Perhaps this point can best be illustrated in terms of the debate which was sparked by Francis Fukuyama's (1989) argument concerning 'the end of history.' (Since then Fukuyama (1992) has published a somewhat different, book-length statement on the same problem, emphasizing 'the struggle for recognition' as a major factor in human and inter-societal affairs. This theme derives from Nietzsche and is to be found in Weber's work in specific reference to Germany.) Writing, at least in part, as deputy director of the US State Department's policy planning staff, and also as a devotee of Alexandre Kojève's (1947) interpretation of Hegel, Fukuyama spoke of the 'powerful nostalgia' which he had felt 'for the time when history existed' (Fukuyama, 1989: 18). The apparent end of the Cold War between the USSR and the USA and the supposed triumph of 'the Western idea' (Fukuyama, 1989: 3) left him sensing that it was *nostalgia* which would 'continue to fuel competition and conflict even in the post-historical world for some time to come' (Fukuyama, 1989: 18). According to Fukuyama, the 'very prospect of centuries of boredom . . . [would] serve to get history started once again.'

Fukuyama's, frequently misunderstood, statement and the extensive debate which it has engendered (Atlas, 1989; Fukuyama, 1992: xi–xxiii) amount to powerful support for the argument that nostalgia has become more evident in the global-human condition. In other words, nostalgia has increasingly assumed a global-cultural significance, quite regardless of its ontogenetic importance as a natural part of any individual's autobiography or lifestyle (F. Davis, 1974: 31–71). Although he has paid no attention to the experience of globality, Fred Davis's definition of 'collective nostalgia' is relevant here: 'Collective nostalgia . . . refers to that condition in which . . . symbolic objects are of a highly public, widely shared, and familiar character, those symbolic resources from the past that . . . can trigger wave upon wave of nostalgic feeling in millions of persons at the same time' (F. Davis, 1974: 122–3). In so far as Davis provides a sociological account of the conditions that are producing collective (or, from a somewhat different perspective, phylogenetic) nostalgia, he largely confines himself to what he calls the erosion of the sense of home as 'a specific geographic locale with its own distinctive atmosphere' (1974: 124). Thus 'homesickness *per se*' is largely produced by 'constant movement in sociographic space' and the rise of the 'nostalgia industry' (1974: 119). On the other hand, Davis suggests that we may now be in a stage of 'interpreted nostalgia,' involving the attempt to objectify it with 'analytically oriented questions' about its foundations, significance, and so on (1974: 24), which has been precisely the concern of this chapter.

While Davis is probably correct in drawing attention to the attenuation of the concreteness of 'home' and thus the problems involved in continuing to think of nostalgia as homesickness *per se*, as is well illustrated in the debate about Fukuyama's original article, it is also the case that the idea of home has recently become evident.

Again, I am not talking directly of the recent concern with the homeless as people without real, physical dwellings; although that concern is certainly related to the matters under discussion here. I refer particularly to the salience of 'home' in the growing environmental movement and its deployment by such movements as Greenpeace. The earth as home or as indicating the relationship between humankind and the natural environment (animate and inanimate) has become one of the most dessiminated symbolic motifs of our time, partly as a result of space travel. The world as *the place* in which we all live is increasingly being promoted on all kinds of fronts; for example, in attempts to legitimize the centrality of particular nations via thematization of environmental problems applicable to the world as a whole; in programs for legitimizing green, until recently extra-parliamentary, movements; in 'pre-contractual' justifications for the global scope of extra-national corporations; in municipal, prefectural and (in the American sense) state efforts to compete for a slice of the global-economic pie; in the efforts to restore geography to its 'rightful place' in the curriculum, and so on. By the same token, but in a certain sense on the other side of the coin, we witness the development of something like a global pro-family and pro-neighborhood movement, talk about Europe as a home; religious movements concerned with the unification of the entire world, and so on. So the notion of home is very much alive and well, even though it may not always refer to a small, specific locale. Nostalgia is simply not what it used to be – it is more than what it used to be. It has been doubly globalized. It has become both collective on a global scale and directed at globality itself.

Baudrillard (1983: 12–13) has observed that 'when the real is no longer what it used to be nostalgia assumes its full meaning. There is a proliferation of myths of origin and signs of reality; of second-hand truth, objectivity and authenticity.' One vital ingredient of the contemporary shift as far as 'reality' is concerned consists in the accelerated speed and more complex form of globalization. Twentieth-century globalization, particularly its current phase, has exacerbated the nostalgic tendency in a number of ways. The very fluidity of global change has invited, as we have seen, nostalgia for secure forms of 'world order,' as well as a kind of projective nostalgia for the world as a home.

We must, however, be careful not to exaggerate the amount of nostalgia in the contemporary world. The dangers of social-scientific diagnosis of nostalgia are apparent in some of the discussions of contemporary tourism, where there has been a tendency to characterize the contemporary proliferation of 'historical' tourist sites as straightforward nostalgia. While undoubtedly much nostalgia is involved in that, including nostalgia for industrial as well as rural settings, we have to bear in mind that much of contemporary tourism involves considerable reflexiveness. As John Urry (1990: 100) has argued, many of today's tourists are 'playful,' delight in multitude of choice, and, most importantly, know that 'tourism is a game, or rather a whole series of games with multiple texts and no single, authentic tourist experience.' This issue will be taken up in the next chapter.

Notes

1. It is more than passing interest to note that Arnold Toynbee, whose work, however controversial, has been an important stimulus to civilization analysis and world history, developed his basic ideas in negative reference to Spengler's *Decline of the West* (McNeill, 1989: 98–101). A key difference between Spengler and Toynbee was that Toynbee rejected Spengler's denial of *communication between* different civilizations. Toynbee insisted on seeing world history in terms of the *mixing* of ideas and/or people; Spengler considered such mixing to be a sign of *degeneration* (McNeill, 1989: 101). This inattention to 'mixing' and to inter-civilizational matters has been a common characteristic of much of German social theory to this day. On the other side of the coin, Hollander (1991: 37) has noted the great significance and the wide range of senses of the German word for 'home,' *Heim*: 'from the widened boundaries of *Heimat* to the extremely constricted notion of secrecy, let alone mere privacy, in the extended form *Geheim*.'
2. Bellah's work has also been deeply affected by the covenantal myth (Bellah, 1974). Indeed, it is important to acknowledge that the ancient Jewish, and more directly the sixteenth-century, Puritan, myth concerning communal covenants with God has had a powerful effect on American sociology. It should be noted, on the other hand, that Talcott Parsons attacked Bellah for 'absolutism' in emphasizing so strongly the moral-communal aspect of Durkheim's sociology (Coleman, 1980; Parsons, 1977a). Parsons never romanticized either ancient Israel or Greece in spite of his great emphasis on their evolutionary significance as 'seed-bed societies' – although he did cling to some elements of the covenant theme in his own version of the idea of civil religion. See also the argument of Vidich and Hughey (1988: 245) that 'there is an irreconcilable tension between the religious foundations of community and the very purposes of post-Enlightenment scholarship' and that 'scholarship is in this sense the enemy of community.' Baudrillard (1988: 79) draws attention to another nostalgic aspect of contemporary American intellectual thought – 'the unhappy transference' involved in 'the nostalgic eye' which is cast towards European history and metaphysics. European intellectuals, on the other hand, tend to 'remain nostalgic utopians, agonizing over [their] ideals, but balking, ultimately, at their realization' (Baudrillard, 1988: 78).

3. I am grateful to Chang Wang-Ho for pointing this out to me, as well as for his continuing interest in the theme of globalization.

4. I have in Chapter 4 tended to classify Meyer as a 'world-systems revisionist' and that indeed has been one of his roles – to bring a cultural perspective, particularly a political-cultural perspective, to bear on Wallersteinian world-systems theory. On the other hand, his own modifications of world-systems theory must be considered as but an aspect of his relatively autonomous 'institutionalist' theory. For a significant application of the latter, see Thomas (1989). One of my major differences with the 'institutionalists,' whose position must be clearly distinguished from Giddens's form of 'institutional analysis,' inheres in my own multidimensional attempt to analyze the globalization process as such. In particular, I insist on the politically *contested* nature of global, or world, culture, as well as the increasingly structured form of globalization.

11

'THE SEARCH FOR FUNDAMENTALS' IN GLOBAL PERSPECTIVE

'Fundamentalism' on a Global Scale

The suggestion that people are widely 'in search of fundamentals' raises issues which can be situated at the center of contemporary social science, as well as those areas of the humanities which have in recent years coalesced into the 'transdiscipline' of cultural studies.[1] To consider the question whether or not, and if so to what degree, 'people' are widely engaged individually and/or collectively in 'a search' for 'fundamentals' raises both a 'positivistic' question and an interpretive, indeed a critical, one. We can investigate via a positivistic definition of 'fundamentals' the degree to which there is, and the causes of, extensive concern with 'ultimate values.' Or we can, at the other extreme, explore – indeed 'deconstruct' – the discourse of fundamentals, including 'fundamentalism.' Moreover, in the terms of the more radical versions of cultural studies (briefly discussed in Chapter 2) we can consider the basis of the interest in the problematic of 'the search for fundamentals' from the perspective of a presuppositional commitment to 'liberation,' 'emancipation,' 'empowerment,' 'resistance,' or whatever.

The present discussion attempts to tackle, but at the same time to question, the meaningfulness of the intellectually popular theme 'people in search of fundamentals' from a standpoint which in one sense fuses but in another, more important, sense transcends the conventional social-scientific and the cultural studies ways of looking at 'things.' The contemporary cultural studies approaches, at least in their strong versions, teach us that the basis of our interest in a particular theme, the way in which we specify a *Problemstellung*, requires disclosure. They question the idea of the self-evidential nature of a problematic and ask us to probe deeper into both our reasons for posing a problem and the methods deemed appropriate for a particular line of inquiry. Moreover, cultural studies challenges 'traditional' procedures of disciplinary inquiry, declaring these to be conventions which are permeated by all sorts of substantive assumptions and preferences. It pushes us in the present case to explicate the discourse in terms of which the issue of fundamentals (and fundamentalism) is thematized. In the present discussion such discourse is deliberately situated within certain ideas about the contemporary global field and, contrary to much of the ostensible thrust of strong programs in current cultural studies, it does not reduce the entire issue of fundamentals and fundamentalism to discourse (or textuality) or to relatively specific ideas concerning the power/knowledge conjunction, the mode of production, or the mode of information (Poster, 1990). Rather the general disciplinary perspective of social science, of sociology in particular, is brought into conjunctural play with the emphasis on discourse and its 'ultimate' grounding in strong cultural studies programs.

I have noted that intellectual discussion of the global circumstance is currently in a state of great flux, which is not surprising in view of its relative newness as a topic of explicit theorization and research. It is in fact a field of disciplinary, interdisciplinary, metadisciplinary and paradisciplinary contestation – in my view the field upon which much of the fate of the entire notion of disciplinarity and of academic differentiation, as well as intellectual integration, will be increasingly contested during the next few decades. This applies particularly to the social sciences and the humanities, where people from traditional disciplines such as sociology, economics, anthropology, political science (including international relations), history, psychology, philosophy, theology and religious studies, and critical-literary studies are already engaged in struggles – and only occasionally collaboration – with respect to the global field. It also applies, if not so clearly, to the natural and physical sciences.[2] To summarize a complex situation, it seems to me that the growing focus on globality makes for particularly problematic relations between cultural studies (including the relatively new field of communication studies) and a revitalized, culturally sensitive sociology. Philosophy, history and anthropology I see as mediating and vacillating disciplines as far as the 'real' issues are concerned. Cultural studies in its 'strong' form seems to have aspirations quite similar to those of the original Comtean (and to some degree Saint-Simonian) program, in the specific sense that it claims to be *the* basic intellectual-political perspective.[3] At the same time contemporary sociology is rapidly recovering from many decades both of disciplinary 'professionalism,' and of ideological narrowness. A number of its practitioners are returning to the high ground of the history, structure and future of humanity, but leaving far behind Comte's assumption that global unicity facilitates and necessitates a 'positivistic' science of (wo)mankind.[4]

The present discussion of 'the search for fundamentals' proceeds in terms of ideas drawn from two of the current major contenders for privileged analytic and interpretive access to the global situation, with a tilt in favor of a genuinely global perspective that enables us to focus on both the discourse and the broadly institutional basis of present concern with the apparent paradox of globality, on the one hand, and locality, on the other. The global–local theme is nearly always discussed as if it were an antinomy, as if these were two sides of a coin. I will try to show that this is a form of 'false consciousness.' I will also try to show that the issue of 'the search for fundamentals' cannot be entirely divorced from the theme of fundamental-*ism*. I suspect that there are social scientists who regard the first phrase as a

kind of respectful acknowledgment, a courteous description, of 'peoples''
'real' practices, whereas in using the term 'fundamentalism' they are
referring to the 'extremists.' This is precisely where the cultural studies
perspective is helpful. It enables us to see that the declaration that people
are in search of fundamentals puts 'the people' in a very safe place – all of
them concerned with doing their own 'local' and/or 'essential' thing. In any
case, there is a lot of unavoidable elision involved in the ensuing
discussion. 'The search for fundamentals' slides into 'fundamentalism.' By
the same token, but less obviously, anti-foundationalism and anti-
totalization fold into 'fundamentalism,' for they are also, in the fashionable
cultural studies term, forms of 'representation' which give 'fundamental
identity' to their promulgators.

While rather strong claims are made in this chapter about the links
between globalization and 'the search for fundamentals,' it is not thereby
implied that discussion of globalization and globality completely accounts
for issues which can be raised under the rubric of 'the search for fundamentals.' In this discussion I shift back and forth between analytic and interpretive problems, on the one hand, and 'real world' matters, on the other.

Globality and 'Local Truth'

In so far as there is a widespread 'search for fundamentals,' it is most
appropriately seen, in the first instance, as an aspect of globalization.
Defining globalization in its basic sense as involving the compression of
the world, one must insist that it is the globality of 'the search for
fundamentals' which is its most interesting feature. More specifically, 'the
search' proceeds in various parts of the world and within various societies
in terms of *globally diffused ideas* concerning tradition, identity, home,
indigeneity, locality, community and so on. Even the notion of nostalgia
has been reflexively upgraded, so that increasingly it is an experience that
is calculatedly sought. To that extent many forms of 'fundamentalism' – in
the widest reach of the term – constitute ways of finding a place within the
world as a whole (occasionally withdrawal from the world), ways that
frequently involve attempts to enhance the *power* of the groups concerned.
Indeed it would appear that much of what is not infrequently referred to
under the rubric of 'postmaterial values' (Inglehart, 1977, 1990) actually
involves a quest for or an assertion of power. In the contemporary period,
at least, the representation of 'authenticity' can well be a formidable claim
to power, or at least to empowerment. Paglia (1991: 2) has put the matter
succinctly: 'identity is power.' There are, however, limitations in this view
with which I will deal briefly below. In any case, the idea of the *right* to
identity – 'the struggle for recognition' (Fukuyama, 1992) – is widespread
at the present time. And that claim may well involve, at least for strategic
purposes, the right to 'symbolic expression,' involving the display of
material resources. For example, the Inkatha movement in South Africa
claims the 'identity right' to display weapons.

In order for there to be a generalized 'search' there must be established criteria for recognizing and undertaking it. In that sense the search for fundamentals must be regarded as basically a modern-or-postmodern phenomenon. It involves a significant degree of *reflexivity* (e.g. 'the invention of tradition') and *choice* (increasingly global *bricolage*). The modalities of reflexivity and the structuring of choice (with its strong connotations of the 'rationality' of processes of optimization, if not maximization, of preferences) are constrained by, increasingly contained within, a global discourse concerning 'fundamentals.' One of the key issues in the discussion of fundamentals has to do with the analytical significance of choice in the contemporary world. Traditionally sociology has operated in terms of an antinomy between the idea of choice, usually seen in utilitarian terms and nowadays the central feature of rational-choice theory, and matters having to do with 'ultimate values.' That perception of an antinomy owes much, of course, to Max Weber's distinction between instrumental (or formal) and substantive (or value) rationality, consolidated in social theory by Parsons's critique of 'fundamentalistic' utilitarianism and his strong emphasis on religiocultural factors in his general action theory, and then added to and modified by Habermas in his critical theory. On the other hand, in the contemporary world we can clearly see that there has occurred, or at least is unevenly occurring, an 'economization' of 'basic' values in the sense that individuals and groups exhibit something like preference schedules in their adherence or conversion to 'fundamental values' (Robertson, 1992b).

The issues at stake in the present discussion are bound up with important shifts in the current practice of sociology, anthropology, history, philosophy and ascendant cultural studies. In varying degrees, each of these disciplines has experienced an anti-foundational, 'going native' shift, which often involves an 'essentialization' of 'the Other' (Abaza and Stauth, 1990). Abaza and Stauth (1990: 211) state that 'an increasing claim is being made for the "indigenisation" of social sciences,' in the face of alleged Westernization and the importation of social science. This involves an argument in favor of

the purity of cultural traits. . . . Those, however, who claim authenticity by 'indigenisation' might not yet be aware of the fact that local knowledge, upon which they want to construct an alternative, *has long since been part of global structures*; or of the fact that *they play a part in a global cultural game which itself calls for the 'essentialization' of local truth*. (1990: 211; emphasis added)

Abaza and Stauth are concerned with the examination of the ways in which religious 'fundamentalism' in non-Western societies has been interpreted, more specifically in Islamic regions. They argue against interpretations which stress the nativistic-localist character of religious fundamentalisms, while challenging a development on the opposite side of the coin (Abaza and Stauth, 1990: 218). For along with essentializing on the part of Western observers there has occurred a 'going native by natives' in the name of indigenization. My own argument hinges to a large extent on the perception of a twofold process of 'going native' and the resultant need to comprehend the general basis of that process. So dealing with the question of 'the search for fundamentals' involves penetration of the basis of social scientific diagnosis of these. As should be clear by now, indigenization programs are entrapped in, are indeed largely a product of modernity and, particularly, of globality. Speaking specifically, of predominantly Islamic societies, Abaza and Stauth (1990: 223) argue that the 'cultural valuations employed by the new fundamentalist movements cannot be explained by an analysis of the tradition of Islamic religion and history.' Instead they have to be regarded as 'an effect of inter-cultural exchange which is fundamentally based on a Western understanding of Islam as the culture of the Other.' But 'the search for authenticity within the creation of modernity is. . .not only an Islamic phenomenon.' It is, they say, a 'topic of its own right.' It is thus part of the task of the present discussion to generalize beyond Islamic cases.

One of the weaknesses of classical sociology of the period 1890–1920 was, as we have seen, its relative lack of sustained attention to relationships and encounters between civilizations and between societies. I am not so much thinking here of international relations and diplomacy, although those are certainly not irrelevant, but of more diffuse interactions and, particularly, of the ways in which images of the Other and the interpenetration of self-images and images of the Other have come to constitute aspects of contemporary global culture. We have seen, for example, that during the late nineteenth century a shifting set of images of Japan and Japanese tradition was articulated in English and Scottish journals; these varied from a projection of positive nostalgic images of English life on to Japan (and then back on to England itself) to negative images of a basically uncivilized Japanese society (Yokoyama, 1987). At the same time Japan began to invent its own tradition and formulate a national identity in basically Western *terms* (Gluck, 1985). In particular, its national identity was developed largely in the terms formulated by Toennies's *Gemeinschaft–Gesellschaft* imagery, so that Meiji elites sought consciously to have a 'familial nation,' or a 'national household.' A major result of this interpenetration of national identity formation was a characterization, in both East and West, of Japan and other Asian societies as being more 'traditional' and 'spiritual,' certainly less 'materialistic' and 'rational,' than Western societies. Notions of tradition and identity were for the most part alien to Asian societies. The idea of tradition did not, as we have seen, become part of Chinese discourse until the second half of the nineteenth century (Schwartz, 1964: 50). The same could be said in varying degrees about such terms as 'religion' and 'culture.'

Such 'dialectics' are by no means confined to relationships between societies or between civilizations. They can, for example, also be applied to gender relations. Recent formulations of female identity, particularly in the USA, have, as we have also seen, largely been made in terms of 'the siren calls of nostalgic and utopian communitarianisms' (Fox-Genovese, 1991: 54), which themselves derive in large part from opposition to a perception of male individual autonomy. 'Most feminist theorists who criticize male individualism . . . end by embracing the sentimental view of community' (1991: 52). Alternatively, the idea of nurturance plays an important part in current discourse on women. As Ginsberg (1991: 676) argues, nurturance is seen by feminists as a basis of female power and a critique of the wider societal context. But it is also 'constraining of women's identity and behavior.' So while identity can interlock with power, it is in fact double-edged, in that getting locked into the discourse of 'essentialism' (a kind of 'fundamentalism') may entail being held in subliminal thrall by that to which feminists are opposed (Butler, 1990).

This brief mention of contemporary feminism (which was also considered in Chapter 6) is not a digression from my main theme. For, as we have seen, essentialistic quests are encouraged by what Abaza and Stauth (1990: 225) call 'global mass cultural relations.' Choices in favor of fundamentalism – which, for example, Davidman (1991) and Kaufman (1991) describe in their books on American Jewish women turning to Orthodoxy – have to be seen as framed by an increasingly global discourse about 'the search for fundamentals.' This does not mean that the choices are not 'real,' but that they do have to be seen *as* choices within increasingly global modes of discourse and structurings of preferences. Moreover they have also to be seen in the light of the global diffusion of diagnostic terms concerning the human condition during the twentieth century: terms such as alienation, homelessness, anomie and anomia, rootlessness and so on, as well as motifs such as 'the loss of community' and 'the decline of the family.' Whatever the 'objective' insights which may have been generated by these and other sociological terms and ideas, it turns out that one of the major contributions of sociology to the world it claims to study is to encourage and facilitate the naming of a quest for fundamentals. In a general sense this tendency constitutes the nostalgic paradigm. To look at the matter from a different perspective, the term 'fundamentalism' was hardly used outside the USA as recently as the late 1970s and then only on a limited scale. In the wake of the Iranian revolution of 1978–9 there began a tendency in the early 1980s to speak of globe-wide fundamentalism (cf. Robertson, 1981; Robertson and Chirico, 1985; Lechner, 1985). Eventually this term was adopted by people and movements around the globe, even if there was no easily translatable word available in the language in question. At the same time, the indigenous or autochthonous movements which adopted this characterization accepted, at least implicitly, some of the diagnoses that had accompanied the rise of the notion of fundamentalism, in particular the idea that fundamentalisms are fueled by basically religious or spiritual orientations (Abaza and Stauth, 1990; Stauth, 1991).

None of this is to deny that the notion of fundamentalism is a useful sociological concept, so long as it is used carefully in a generic way. Thus Lechner's (1990a: 79) definition of 'generic fundamentalism' is very useful for analytical purposes: 'A value-oriented, antimodern, dedifferentiating form of collective action – a sociocultural movement aimed at reorganizing all spheres of life in terms of a particular set of absolute values.' But although his definition includes the phrase 'anti-modern' it is central to Lechner's analyses of fundamentalism that the latter is not *simply* anti-modern. It is both antimodern and distinctively modern. Not merely is it a product of modernity, in varying degrees given its opportunity for action via distinctive features of modernity itself, it is also modern in its employment of modern methods of mobilization. Indeed, not only are modern methods of mobilization frequently employed across the globe by 'fundamentalist' movements, their leaders seem to be increasingly involved in the invocation of diagnoses which have been disseminated concerning *the roots* of fundamentalism. In other words, leaders of fundamentalist movements, particularly the more intellectualist, attempt to attract poten-tial converts by appealing to distinctively *modern* diagnoses of the discontents of modernity.

Lechner (1990a: 94) argues that 'modernity has no mercy.' Speaking specifically of American Protestant fundamentalism, Lechner points out that it cannot succeed in its own terms. And while there are undoubtedly very distinctive features of fundamentalism in America, Lechner's analysis holds true, if in varying degrees, for most forms of contemporary fundamentalism. Lechner (1990a: 95) contends that 'where the particular institutional and cultural features of the American case are not present, and where the discontents of modernity are felt more keenly and defined more sharply, new and stronger fundamentalist movements are likely to emerge.' I suggest that by adding the variable of globality to modernity we can begin to see that fundamentalism is also a product of globality and that even though it may take ostensibly anti-global forms it tends to partake of the distinctive features of globality. Modernity has no mercy, nor has globality, a point which Wallerstein (1991b) makes from a different perspective. In this regard I can summarize briefly my own position on the modernity–globality–postmodernity issue. I certainly do not subscribe to Giddens's (1990) view that modernity has led directly to globalization (or globality) and that postmodernity is *simply* 'high modernity.' Rather, without denying that certain aspects of modernity have greatly amplified the globalization process, I insist that globalization of the contemporary type was set in motion long before whatever we might mean by modernity. Moreover, even though the idea that we should regard postmodernity as 'merely' radicalized modernity is not without merit, I insist that globaliza-tion – or globality – is a relatively independent source of ideas about the conception of postmodernity.

Octavio Paz (quoted in Berman, 1983: 125) has argued, in a well-known dictum, that all cultures are 'condemned to modernity,' a dictum which, as Tomlinson (1991: 140) points out, echoes Sartre's even better known claim that human beings are condemned to freedom. Tomlinson (1991: 140–1) argues that because 'all cultures are integrated at a structural level in the orders of the nation-state system and the global capitalist market,' they are all condemned to modernity. At the same time 'the terms of culture' are irrevocably altered. Integration in structural terms 'entails a one-way journey from "tradition" to "modernity,"' but because 'this journey is made by human agents and involves the emergence of new senses of possibility . . . it too can be understood in "existential" terms' (1991: 141). Tomlinson is specifically concerned with the theme of 'cultural imperialism.' He is persuasively skeptical about the usefulness and accuracy of that idea and in reference to the Sartre–Paz perspective argues that global, or globalized, modernity constrains cultural elites and leaders in popular culture to make cultural choices – including, presumably, constrained choices – as to identity and tradition.

One of the more interesting features of the current 'search for fundamentals' can be illustrated by the ways in which the movement for worldwide indigenization of a variety of social practices has been globally orchestrated, in the sense that that trend has been encouraged by international organizations or by cross-national alliances between movements concerned with indigenization. For example, at the present time there is a strong move across the world towards indigenous, communal medicine, much of it encouraged by the World Health Organization. In various parts of the world – Africa, Latin America, Asia and in various Islamic countries – while the drive towards the indigenization of health care has taken the form of demands for local autonomy, there also appears to be a desire for local medicine to make a definite contribution to 'world health.' Moreover the worldwide encouragement of local medicine frequently involves a syncretic combination of putatively local practices with universalistic ones, or the adaptation of 'alien' practices to local circumstances. Sometimes, indeed, local medicine is invented. As Keane (1990: 26) has written, 'much of the current borrowing, synthesizing, and syncretizing from several medical traditions is a particular form of adaptation to the whole world and a response to the relativizing effects of globalization.'

Or let us take the example of contemporary movements promoting the rights and identities of 'native peoples.' Many such movements are in fact cross- or international, in that they form strategic alliance across existing nations, even across continents and hemispheres. During the past twenty years or so there has developed a 'new solidarity' among native peoples (Chartrand, 1991) involving contact and increasing cooperation between Australian Aborigines and Canadian Akwesasne Indians, and between a wide variety of Indian communities across and beyond the western hemisphere. Much of this effort is directed as 'world opinion.' It both capitalizes on and feeds into the current concern with identity around the world. There is now a widely based World Council of Indigenous Peoples, while the United Nations Center for Human Rights has been involved in drafting a declaration of rights for indigenous peoples. There are estimated to be about five thousand 'nations,' in comparison to fewer than two hundred states (Chartrand, 1991). These movements partake of globality (and, of course, modernity) in that they involve recognition that the promotion of the local is only possible on an increasingly global basis, thus casting into doubt the wisdom and the accuracy of the 'think globally, act locally' maxim. *Acting* (and thinking) globally is increasingly necessary in order to make the very notion of locality viable. Locality is, to put it simply, globally institutionalized; although here again there are complications, which I shall shortly address.

We are able again to see that globalization itself produces variety and diversity, that in various respects diversity is a basic *aspect* of globalization. Whereas until quite recently comparative social science was relatively surprised to discover commonalities, with diversity being taken for granted, globalization has 'brought about the complete reversal of the cognitive situation' (Sztompka, 1990: 55). Sztompka insists that 'what really becomes baffling and problematic is the preservation of enclaves of uniqueness amid growing homogeneity and uniformity. . . . The emphasis shifts to the alternative types of comparative inquiry: seeking uniqueness among the uniformities, rather than uniformity among variety' (1990: 55). While I think that Sztompka expresses an interesting point about the shift in emphasis needed in current comparative inquiry under conditions of globalization, he does not press hard enough in the direction of tackling what he sees as a 'baffling and problematic' phenomenon. Specifically, he fails to recognize that globalization involves the simultaneity of the universal and the particular.

One of the fastest-growing areas of academic specialization – particularly within anthropology, psychology and linguistics – is that of 'intercultural communication.' Clearly this development is closely intertwined with the general process of global space–time compression. It is in one sense a positive reaction to the greatly increased compression of the world. In another more important sense it is itself a significant manifestation of globalization. The practitioners of this discipline are attempting to develop an applied science of communicative relations between 'unique' populational units. In order to claim academic, professional and advisory legitimacy they must display the universality of their insights, methodology, research results and advisory successes. But at the same time they have a vested professional interest in accentuating difference, at least in the middle run; for if there occurs an attenuation of the perception of difference their *raison d'être* is in doubt. In any case, the remarkably rapid expansion of the 'science' of intercultural communication should give pause to those who talk in deconstructive, but also generalizing, terms about the Self and the Other. The growing field of intercultural communication is an analytically neglected *concrete* site of practical communication between cultures (which while promoting, in a sense institutionalizing, difference and variety may also claim to be in the business of promoting 'intercultural personalities.')

Another area, which overlaps with that of intercultural communication, is that of tourism. International tourism has, from one perspective, been described as a 'utopia of difference' (Van den Abbeele, 1980). From a different standpoint, MacCannell (1989: xiv) has characterized it as being trapped 'in a seductive pseudo-empowerment, a prison house of signs.' Summarizing his own leanings in this respect MacCannell (1989: xv), has spoken of 'a pseudo-reconstruction of "authentic otherness"' as the most adequate description not merely of late twentieth-century tourism but of general features of the contemporary phase of the globalization of culture (1989: xvii). MacCannell's important book on tourism tends to rest on the idea that the contemporary tourist is in search of the authentic – often, for example, searching for and paying homage at a large number of sacred places, rather than a single center – but that such a search is actually inauthentic because of *the social relations of tourism*. In contrast, Urry (1990: 9–11) suggests that there is in modern tourism a strong element of reflexive *in*authenticity. It is not, says Urry, that tourism is by its nature inauthentic in relation to its 'objects,' but rather that the contemporary (the postmodern?) tourist comes close to 'delight in the inauthenticity of the normal tourist experience' (1990: 11). ('Inauthenticity' may not be quite the best term, but Urry's point is well taken.) International tourism is one of the most conspicuous sites for the contemporary production of the local and the different, including the sacred, as well as the ongoing production of the universal. It is also worth mentioning that it is by some counts the largest industry in the world.

This inevitably raises again the much-discussed issue of global capitalism and the thesis of the commodification and homogenization of culture across the contemporary world. Global capitalism both promotes and is conditioned by cultural homogeneity *and* cultural heterogeneity. The production and consolidation of difference and variety is an essential ingredient of contemporary capitalism, which is, in any case, increasingly involved with a growing variety of *micro*-markets (national-cultural, racial and ethnic; genderal; social-stratificational; and so on). At the same time micromarketing takes place within the contexts of increasingly universal-global economic practices. It must be emphasized, however, that capitalism has to accommodate itself both to the *materiality* of the heliocentric global world, with its inherent space–time contingencies, and to the *culturality* of human life, including the 'making sense' – indeed the 'construction' – of the geosocial contingencies of in-group/out-group relations.

We must thus recognize directly 'real world' attempts to bring the global, in the sense of the macroscopic aspect of contemporary life, into conjunction with the local, in the sense of the microscopic side of life in the late twentieth century. The very formulation, apparently in Japan, of a term such as *glocalize* (from *dochakuka*, roughly meaning 'global localization') is perhaps the best example of this. Glocalize is a term which was developed in particular reference to marketing issues, as Japan became more concerned with and successful in the global economy; against the background, as we have seen, of much experience with the general problem of the relationship between the universal and the particular. By now it has become, according to the *Oxford Dictionary of New Words* (1991: 134), 'one of the main marketing buzzwords' of the 1990s. At the same time the issue of 'travelling parochialism' has, according to the *Economist* (1991), emerged as a significant aspect of life in the late twentieth century: '[A]s the architecture of the global village grows more elaborate, another structure is being built with less fanfare – the cocoon for the traveller who needs to go abroad but does not want to leave home.' Citing the cases of the American traveler who finds as 'a global right' CNN access to American locality and 'the triumph' in contemporary American television of 'the local over the national,' the *Economist*'s commentator maintains that the headline of a Scottish newspaper in 1912 upon the occasion of the sinking of the *Titanic* – 'Aberdeen Man Lost at Sea' – was indicative of modern media trends. The conclusion that 'with satellite television, you never know you left home' has a persuasive ring. But what this kind of observation seriously downplays is the increasingly complex relationship between 'the local' and 'the global.' It underestimates the extent to which 'locality' is chosen; it underplays the extent to which 'the local' media are, certainly in the USA, more and more concerned with 'global' issues ('local' reporters reporting from various parts of the world, according to 'local' interest); and it is not explicit about the shared, global homogeneity of 'going home.' All of this comes about through an inability, or unwillingness, to transcend the discourse of 'localism–globalism.'[5]

Globalization and the Search for Fundamentals

The approach to globalization which I have been advocating takes its departure from empirical generalizations concerning the rapidly increasing compression of the entire world into a single, global field and conceptual ideas about the ways in which the world as a whole should be 'mapped' in broadly sociological terms. The two strands of elaboration are, of course, closely linked. In the relatively early stage of my attempts to theorize the topic of globalization the issue of 'fundamentalism' was conspicuous. Indeed it was partly in order to account for the resurgence of religious fundamentalism in the late 1970s and early 1980s that I revitalized my long-standing interest in 'international' phenomena. Coming to terms with fundamentalism and related issues has been a prominent aspect of my work on globalization, even though over the last ten years or so I have revised my thinking about the relationship between globalization and fundamentalism (more generally 'the search for fundamentals'). Whereas my first formulations tended to see politicoreligious fundamentalism as resulting largely from compression of the *inter-societal system* (fundamentalism as an attempt to express society identity), my more recent attempts to grasp analytically the more general problem of the assertion of 'deep particularity' on the global scene have centered upon the global construction and dissemination of ideas concerning the value of particularism. The first perspective involves an emphasis on space–time compression leading to the felt necessity for societies (and regions and civilizations, as well as 'subnational' entities) to declare their identities for both internal and external purposes. It tends to involve a focus on fundamentalism as a *reaction* to, rather than as an aspect – or, indeed, a creation – of, globalization; although that was not the exclusive focus of my earlier perspective. The second approach involves a more definite stress on the idea that the expectation of identity declaration is built into the general process of globalization. This does not mean that the notion of fundamentalism as reaction or resistance is thereby relinquished, but that that possibility is now viewed in a more general frame.

There have been four major focal points of the dominant globalization process since the sixteenth century: *nationally constituted societies*; *the international system of societies*; *individuals*; and *humankind*. At the risk of repetition, my argument in this respect can be restated. It is largely in terms of the enhancement of each of these reference points, in the sense of their being tangibly crystallized, and the raising of problems about the relationships between them that the globalization process has proceeded in recent centuries. At the same time there have been changes in the ways in which each of these major components of the overall global circumstance has been operatively constructed. All of this means that we have to conceive of the concept of globalization as having primarily to do with *the form* in terms of which the world has moved towards unicity. So when we speak of globalization we must realize that we are referring above all to a relatively specific path that the world has taken in the direction of it becoming singular. The world could in theory, as I have argued, have become a single entity along different trajectories – without, for example, involving the salience of the national society which has *actually* been a vital ingredient of the overall globalization process.

Having addressed the issue of globalization from a number of angles in the preceding chapters, I need do no more here than attend to the more important of my arguments. First it must be emphasized that there has been only one form of relatively recent globalization. To be sure, there have been rival prospectuses to that dominant form – such as those envisaged by the Soviet-led communist movement from the early 1920s onward; the Roman Catholic Church; certain 'fractions' within Islamic societies; the Japanese government during the 1930s and the early 1940s; British imperialists; German Nazis; and so on. At various times in human history a number of the 'great' empires have, with varying degrees of explicitness, promoted images and obviously taken concrete steps towards a single world, envisaging that possibility either in terms of one empire or a set of empires. One must also emphasize that each of the 'world' religions has, again with varying degrees of explicitness, promoted images of 'one world.' Moreover, since the mid-eighteenth century numerous images have been promoted, many along utopian lines, of a unified humanity (some by social theorists); as well as apocalyptic images of the *end* of the entire world as such. Nevertheless, globalization has actually been framed by the 'components' of which I have spoken, components which have themselves been contested and which have changed in content.

Second the overall process of globalization involves shifts both in the distinctiveness with which each of its four main components have been culturally thematized and in the degree to which each of the four has been differentially accorded relative autonomy. In sum, over recent centuries – but particularly during the twentieth century – the four principal reference points of globality have become relatively independent foci of social practice (Robertson, 1991a). One of the most important aspects and results of this general process of differentiation has been the relativization of basic reference points for 'being human' (Robertson, 1985d; Lechner, 1990b). Moreover the fact that this process of differentiation has also involved a strong trend in the direction of world unicity has accelerated the rise of competing *interpretations of world history* and its direction(s) (Robertson, 1987b). Taken together these two developments – increasing relativization of standpoints and proliferation of orientations to the global situation – encourage the rise of the discourse of fundamentals, including both 'total-izing fundamentalisms,' and 'anti-totalizing fundamentalistic' tendencies.

There are other, often more diffuse, meanings of 'globalization' which are secondary to but for the most part compatible with the primary conceptual meaning that I have attributed to it. As the discussion of globalization has rapidly expanded in recent years – so as to become a common feature of journalism and intellectual discussion – it has tended to cluster around two major tendencies. On the one hand, globalization is used to refer diffusely to growing interdependence across the world on a number of different dimensions (of which the economic has, at least until quite recently, been the most emphasized). On the other hand, the term is frequently used in the sense of the globalization *of* institutions, collectiv-ities and practices – as in such phrases as 'the globalization of science,' 'the globalization of education,' and so on. Cutting across these two tendencies is that which stresses the 'lifting' or the 'disembedding' (Giddens, 1990) of structures and activities from 'local' contexts so as to become global. As I have suggested, there is no contradiction between these ways of defining globalization and the model which I have announced, so long as what I call the dominant form of globalization is accorded a central place in any attempt to make the issue of globalization into a genuine research program. Each of these seemingly alternative ways of approaching or defining globalization depends in varying degrees, but usually implicitly, upon something like my own conceptualization of the dominant form, or frame, of globalization. The advocates of each of these perspectives on globalization tend to acknowledge that globalization as increasing inter-dependence, including consciousness of such, and/or globalization of particular practices are subject to certain constraints of the general structure and formation of the global field.

This is an appropriate point to return to the global–local issue, made part of contemporary (global) consciousness largely by the injunction to 'think globally and act locally.' That phrase is of great sociological interest and of considerable relevance to the present discussion because it involves the strategic attempt to link the local to the global on the assumption that local problems can be effectively treated only by recognizing their embeddedness in a much larger context. At the same time it appears to suggest that only at the local level can 'social problems' be adequately dealt with. This way of thinking has its analytical perils, in that there is an inherent danger of presenting a view of the world as a whole which *excludes the local*. In contrasting the global and the local there is considerable risk that the local will be omitted from the global. But if we are talking about the increasing unicity of the world in one sense or another, how could it be that all the localities in the world are *not* parts of the world? Clearly there is something misleading in this current of modern, or postmodern, thought and it is one of the tasks of the serious student of the planetary circumstance to correct it. Part of this problem arises from the mistake of thinking simply of the local–global relationship along micro–macro or, which is not precisely the same thing, small–large lines. In my own conception the notion of the global refers to the world *in its entirety* and that is a primary basis of my formulating the process of globalization as involving the major, but not the only, dimensions of social existence. (The fact that I myself may occasionally have slipped into the conventional rhetoric of referring to the local–global along micro–macro lines should not obscure my dominant claim that this is a misleading conception.)

It is important to recognize that not merely do conceptions of societies, international relations, individuals and humankind become increasingly differentiated. They also undergo internal shifts. It should be noted that one of the most significant shifts with respect to national societies is in the direction of multiculturality and/or polyethnicity, earlier post-eighteenth-century conceptions having been largely directed by the principle of homogeneity. The current problematic of multiculturality/polyethnicity, along with increasingly complex conceptions of gender differentiation, exacerbates the search for fundamentals and also, which is very important, brings globality increasingly into the center of many societies' affairs. Societies themselves, as well as regional entities such as the European Community, increasingly become what Balibar (1991) has called 'world spaces.' At the same time, within 'the new Europe' there is considerable interest in cultural regions. It should be noted, however, that the discourse of regionality is increasingly 'universal,' in spite of EC attempts to exclude additional Asians and/or Muslims.

Universalism and Particularism Globalized

In my perspective globalization in what I call its primary sense is a relatively autonomous process. Its central *dynamic* involves the twofold process of the particularization of the universal and the universalization of the particular. The particularization of the universal, defined as the global concretization of the problem of universality, has become the occasion for the search for *global* fundamentals. In other words, the current phase of very rapid globalization facilitates the rise of movements concerned with the 'real meaning' of the world, movements (and individuals) searching for the meaning of the world as a whole. The universalization of the particular refers to the global universality of the search for the particular, for increasingly fine-grained modes of identity presentation (Robertson, 1991b). To put it as sharply as possible, I propose that 'fundamentalism' is a mode of thought and practice which has become almost globally institutionalized, in large part, as far as the twentieth century is concerned, in terms of the norm of national self-determination, announced after World War I by Woodrow Wilson, given new life after World War II with respect to what became known as the Third World, and then expanded on a global scale to all manner of 'entities' from the 1960s onwards. In so far as analysts see 'the search' entirely in terms of an atavistic response to globalization they are failing to deal with the participatory aspect of globalization. This does not mean that there are no atavistic, isolationist or anti-global responses to globalization. But we have to be very careful in delineating these. They are by no means self-evident. There is much to the argument that it is the particular which makes the universal work (Udovich, 1987). (It is also the case that cosmopolitanism depends on localism: Hannerz, 1990.)

This is of course not only an analytical problem. It is not just a matter of making sense of the prevalence of the 'search for fundamentals'; this has a history or a series of histories. In order to talk about 'fundamentalism' in our time we have to do genealogical work on that theme. As part of that work, we have to consider the relationship between the quest for community, for stable values and beliefs and so on, on the one hand, and nostalgia, on the other. This is not to say that all of 'the quest' is dynamized by a sense of loss, of homelessness (or homesickness) and so on; but rather that the contemporary way of doing the search for fundamentals is often framed and/or analyzed in implicitly nostalgic terms. In so far as the idea of a search for fundamentals becomes reflexively organized on a panlocal, ecumenical or concultural basis the whole idea of a return to 'real' fundamentals is rendered problematic. There are, as I have already hinted, interesting questions to be addressed about the simultaneity of the recent crystallization of postmodernist theories and rational-choice theories. Postmodernism depicts a world of 'small narratives'; while rational-choice theory, notably in its sociology-of-religion version (Stark and Bainbridge, 1985), promotes the idea of the 'rational' selection of 'ultimate' beliefs and values. While both claims are, on the face of it, problematic, the more interesting observation in the present context is that these two, super-ficially opposite, standpoints actually constitute two sides of the same coin. Whereas the postmodern perspective suggests a fluid, 'disorderly' global field of forms of life, identity presentation, and consumerism (Feather-stone, 1991b), the rational-choice program indicates the standardized ways in which preferences are exercised in increasingly complex situations of choice. Whereas the former parades heterogeneity and variety, the latter is rooted in assumptions about global homogeneity and the sameness of humankind. In sum, the first promotes particularity, the second promotes universality. But their simultaneity is inherently interesting and requires interpretation.

In addressing globalization I have paid particular attention to what I have called the take-off period of modern globalization, lasting from about 1870 through to the mid-1920s; and I have been struck by the extent to which in that period the general issue of the coordination of the particular and the universal received widespread practical and political attention. This was a time when there was great emphasis on the need to invent tradition and national identity (Hobsbawm and Ranger, 1983; Kern, 1983; Robertson, 1990b) within the context of an increasingly compressed, globalized world. Indeed much of the desire to invent tradition and identity derived from the contingencies of global compression and the concomitant spread of expectations concerning these. During the period lasting from about 1870 to 1925 basic geohuman contingencies were formally worked out in such terms as the time-zoning of the world and the establishment of the international dateline; the near-global adoption of the Gregorian calendar and the adjustable seven-day week; and the establishment of international telegraphic and signaling codes. At the same time, there arose movements which were specifically concerned with the relationship between the local and the panlocal, one of the most notable being the ecumenical movement which sought to bring the major 'world' religious traditions into a coordinated, concultural discourse. On the secular front, the international socialist movement had parallel aims, but it was even more ambitious in that it sought to overcome *strong* particularism in the name of internationalism. A more specific case is provided by the rise at the end of the nineteenth century of the International Youth Hostel movement, which attempted an international-coordination of particular-istic, 'back to nature' ventures. Other particular–universal developments of the time include the modern Olympic Games and Nobel prizes. The contemporary use of such terms as 'fundamentals' and 'fundamentalism' was also established, mainly in the USA, in the same period.

What is particularly significant about this period is that the material circumstance of the world (as a heliocentric globe) was, as it were, dealt with in relationship to the rapidly spreading consciousness of the global world as such, greatly facilitated by recently developed rapid means of travel and communication, such as the airplane and the wireless. One crucial aspect of these trends was that events and circumstances previously segregated in space and time increasingly came to be considered as simultaneous in terms of categories which were universalistically particular and particularistically universal. Spatial and temporal categories and measures were globally institutionalized so as to both accentuate consciousness of difference and to universalize difference.

Needless to say, such developments did not emerge *de novo* during the period in question. The steady growth in map-making and its globalization, the interpenetration of modes of 'travelers' tales,' the growth of postal services, the increase in the spread of travel, the early rise of tourism – all these, and still other, developments lay in the background to the rapid trends of the crucial take-off period of modern globalization. One particularly important development of a somewhat different kind concerned what has been called the politicization of archeology in the mid-nineteenth century (Silberman, 1989). As we have seen, in that earlier period the monuments of classical and biblical civilization in Egypt, Mesopotamia, Greece and other areas of the Near and Middle East became national quests, within the context of increasingly international and industrialized society (Silberman, 1989: 3–7). In turn these monuments have become the bases of the official national symbols of the peoples of the Middle East and the eastern Mediterranean. Now in those areas both local and non-local archeologists are shaping 'a new past for the peoples of that region' (Silberman, 1989: 248). All of this began, it should be remembered, in a period of great (often imperial) concern with the unification of humankind.

In sum I argue that the search for fundamentals – in so far as it exists on any significant scale – is to a considerable degree both a contingent feature of globalization and an aspect of global culture. In a sense 'fundamentalism within limits' makes globalization work. Yet I would not insist that all of the search for fundamentals should be regarded or analyzed in those terms. We do need, for example, to make distinctions between fundamentalism-*within*-globalization and fundamentalism-*against*-globalization, and between both pro- and anti-fundamentalistic globalism. Nevertheless my general point is that the concern with fundamentals is itself widely 'grounded.'

As far as the general practice of the social sciences, and indeed cultural studies, is concerned we would do well to heed the recent 'conversion' of Geertz. Having been so influential with respect to the 'thick' study of 'the local' (Geertz, 1983), Geertz now emerges as an advocate of a much more subtle and demanding practice. He speaks of the necessity 'to enlarge the possibility of intelligible discourse between people quite different from one another in interest, outlook, wealth, and power, and yet contained in a world where, tumbled as they are into endless connection, it is necessary to get out of each other's way' (Geertz, 1988: 147). We now live, says Geertz (1988: 148), in a world which is 'one of a gradual spectrum of mixed-up differences.' This is the world 'in which any would-be founders of discursivity must now, and quite probably for some time to come, operate. . . . The There's and the Here's, much less insulate, much less well-defined, much less spectacularly contrastive (but no less deeply so) have again changed their nature.' Geertz goes on to maintain that 'something new having emerged both in "the field" and in "the academy," something new must appear on the pages.' The theme of 'the search for fundamentals' goes to the heart of empirically sensitive late-century cultural and social theory. It brings together in problematic but comprehensible ways the simultaneous advocacy of 'totalizing' and 'anti-totalizing' positions.

Notes

1. This chapter had its origins in papers presented at two conferences organized by the Netherlands Commission for UNESCO. The phrase 'people in search of fundamentals' is a distinctively UNESCO type of expression, deriving from a distinctively UNESCO program. Tomlinson (1991: 70–5) has some interesting things to say about 'UNESCO discourse': 'The rhetoric of a universal humanism . . . underwrites the UNESCO commitment to defence of cultural difference . . .. Pluralism is a necessary part of UNESCO's existence as an institution for the conduct of the global conversation, so pluralism cannot be contested within its rhetoric' (Tomlinson, 1991: 71). In so far as UNESCO was founded during an important phase of relatively recent globalization my discussion is indeed geared to the global realities to which UNESCO has itself adapted (and which it has consolidated). At the same time this chapter can be read as an attempt to make UNESCO more sensitive to new realities.
2. See, for example, the double issue of *Mosaic* (1988), published by the (American) National Science Foundation and devoted to 'global change' within the context of the International Geosphere-Biosphere Program. The latter was broadly established in 1986 by the General Assembly of the International Council of Scientific Unions.
3. My conception of cultural studies shades into ostensibly *anti*-foundational intellectual-political programs advocated by self-proclaimed adherents to 'postmodern' theory and practice (cf. Lash, 1990; Featherstone, 1991a).
4. In my double invocation of Comte I am not suggesting for a moment that the cultural studies perspective is *substantively* Comtean. For Comte's view of woman, see above, p. 106.
5. For an interesting contribution to this theme, see Friedman (1990).

12

CONCLUDING REFLECTIONS

I have emphasized throughout much of this book that globalization, including the definition thereof is a basically contested process. I have, on the other hand, claimed that the form in which it has proceeded in relatively recent times has been rather well established and that it is identifiable in terms of relationships between the components of my fourfold scheme: national societies; individual selves; the international system of societies; and, in the generic sense, mankind. I have also periodically argued that this is essentially a dynamic and sequential model. While reiterating my view that what has been accomplished in the name of world-systems analysis and related schools of inquiry is considerable, I want again to insist on the relative autonomy of the development of this expanding 'mould' of globalization (at the same time maintaining that there is nothing everlasting about it). As a form with its own dynamics it began to take shape during the period of the decline of feudalism in Europe. During that period there was an acceleration in the early shaping of the nationally organized society; the mounting thematization of the (primarily male) individual; the enhancement of the system of inter-state relations; and the beginnings of modern ideas of humanity, particularly in philosophy and in early international law. (Lechner (1991) has shown that international law itself has developed largely in terms of the four components which I have been employing.)

I have maintained that as important as it may be to recognize the widespread interconnectedness of the world quite a few centuries ago, we must not allow such recognition to blind us to the realities of relatively recent centuries. For all that we may learn about the expanses of space occupied by chains of commercial interconnectedness in the relatively distant past (for example, J. Abu-Lughod, 1989), showing how in certain ways the world was long ago 'globalized' in a very loose sense of that word, we have to be very careful about mounting arguments simply on that basis. We happen to be in a period when the appeal to historical length, and depth, has become a major form of legitimizing a large variety of perspectives (as well as ideologies). In and of itself, as I argued in Chapter 10, this can to some degree be regarded as an aspect, or consequence, of the contemporary phase of intense globalization. While demonstrations of vast chains of connectedness are of great importance, we would do well to understand the grounds upon which these exercises are undertaken. In one sense such inquiries tend to confirm the proposition that globalization has to do with the 'organization' of the world as a whole, in all of its four major dimensions. In other words, there was *already* a world to be, in the Simmelian sense, *formed* prior to the actual establishment of that form. Yet the appeal to history and historical anthropology can divert us from an important task. Lest there be any misunderstanding, I wish to state that I consider historical inquiries into old or indeed ancient, even primal, 'worlds' to be of great importance – so long as they do not involve the attempt merely to show that the relatively recent moves to 'one world' are simply extensions, interrupted or otherwise, of long-established patterns of 'world-system' formation or deformation.

A crucial variable in such considerations is the scope and depth of consciousness of the world as a single place. When we speak of contemporary globalization we are very much concerned with matters of consciousness, partly because that notion carries reflexive connotations. Globalization does not simply refer to the objectiveness of increasing interconnectedness. It also refers to cultural and subjective matters. In very simple terms, we are thus talking about issues surrounding the idea of the world being 'for-itself.' The world is not literally 'for-itself' but the *problem* of being 'for-itself' has become increasingly significant, in particular because of the thematization of humankind in a number of respects. In that respect global consciousness has partly to do with the world as an 'imagined community' (B. Anderson, 1983).

This leads me to some specific points concerning my sequential phase model. The basic idea is that through each phase certain changes occur with respect to each component. Most basically, each component becomes a more definite aspect of the global field during each phase, although that process does not occur evenly. For example, it is almost certain that the humankind component tended to lag behind the other three as a constraining element until at least the early take-off phase of about a hundred years ago (Simpson, 1991). Then during that phase, in fact the phase when the standard of 'civilization' was at its high point, the humankind component became rapidly more significant, as expressed in conventions concerning the conduct of war and the establishment of the International Court of Justice (Gong, 1984). The fact that the four components were accorded more symmetrical emphasis during the take-off period is precisely why I have given that phase that name. Another important 'settlement' was reached, during what I have called the struggle-for-hegemony phase, with the establishment of the United Nations Organization. This involved a more explicit recognition of the categories of sovereign societies, individuals, the inter-state system and humankind. Since then, particularly during the current uncertainty phase, there have been significant shifts along each dimension. As far as the category of national society is concerned, there have been changes which involve the questioning of the theme of its homogeneity. In other words, the themes of multiculturality and polyethnicity have come strongly to the fore. At the same time, the theme of 'meganations' has arisen, specifically the relationships between nations and larger regional, supranational units. However, to date there is nothing to suggest that the nationally organized society, more specifically the state, is about to wither away. With respect to the component of individuals, we have seen that in the current phase of globalization there has been an accentuation of the 'formal' individual. 'Modern man' – and increasingly 'modern woman' – has become a globally meaningful notion. On the other hand, issues of gender, ethnicity and culture have become increasingly salient and fluid. As far as the system of inter-societal relations is concerned, there has been a sharp move, particularly in the recent past, away from bipolarity and the coming into being of a much more multipolar international circumstance. I will briefly attend to a particularly important aspect of the latter when I turn to what some empirical economists call the triadic division of the contemporary world (a Japan-centered East, a Germany-centered Europe, and a USA-centered western hemisphere). At this point it is necessary to emphasize the increasing significance of the United Nations and the problems it faces with respect to nuclear proliferation and a more representative Security Council as far as permanent members are concerned, including the crucial issue of the membership of Germany and Japan. Finally, in the recent past the component of humankind has become explicitly thematized in a number of ways. Although the principle of human rights is in one sense applied to individuals, its general significance has to do with the consolidation of the conception of humanity. In recent years the issue of the future of the human species has been increasingly thematized via controversies about the relationship between that species and its environment and the quality of life of the species as a whole. Increasingly, these kinds of issue have been made relevant to the lives of individuals, the affairs of societies and relations between societies.

Many developments and phenomena have brought us to the present sense of the world as a single place. Needless to say, there are millions of people who remain relatively unaffected by this circumstance, even though they are certainly linked to the world economy. Nonetheless, the expansion of the media of communication, not least the development of global TV, and of other new technologies of rapid communication and travel, has made people all over the world more conscious of other places and of the world as a whole. Notwithstanding their commercial and political manipulation, environmental concerns have enhanced this sense of shared fate. From a different angle, we can point to the ways in which the Cold War, with its shadow of nuclear disaster, also heightened that sense of the world as being one. That vast portions of the world remain uninformed and lacking in 'adequate' and 'accurate' knowledge of the world at large and of societies other than their own (indeed of their own societies) does not diminish the significance of these basic points.

Of course the issue of globalization does not in and of itself exhaust the range of important questions which must be asked about the contemporary world, but a focus on globalization is a major route to consideration of them. One such question arises in connection with the trends toward a *triadic* world identified by some observers of the global economy in the 1980s. In the triadic scenario, the world is being economically and politically divided into the three economically dominant areas I have already identified: East Asia, Europe and America. Each area has a dominant economic power: Japan, Germany and the USA. This general idea of the global triad was partly presented before the collapse of communism in Central and Eastern Europe and in what was the Soviet Union. However, the basic idea of this triadic division makes a lot of sense; the apparent demise of the Soviet empire constituting a complication of the scenario, rather than an undoing of it. The main axes of the protectionist sentiments of the early 1990s have indeed tended to confirm it. Nonetheless, that triadic scenario is greatly lacking from a sociological point of view, for it naively concentrates on trends in the global economy and neglects the significance of political and sociocultural issues. Thus clearly Islam, and not only its 'fundamentalist' forms, constitutes a massive – but certainly not homogeneous – presence in the contemporary world. In the triadic conception the Muslim countries, as well as a large proportion of what is still known as the Third World, are entirely secondary as far as major economic forces are concerned. But even within the regions of the triad one can speak of the trend towards large regions becoming what Balibar (1991) calls, in reference to Europe in the largest sense, *world spaces*. That term refers to the phenomenon of a whole continent or subcontinent becoming increasingly heterogeneous and complex in ethnic and racial terms, that circumstance arising largely because of economically motivated migration, the search for cheap labor and so on.

Europe itself, which along one geographical dimension stretches from Dublin to Baghdad, contains, according to Balibar, three major ethno-cultural constituencies: the EuroAmerican, the EuroSlavic, and the Euro-Islamic. This insertion of 'the world' into particular regions and societies within regions is extremely suggestive, indicating that at the minimum the notion of the triad, plus the vital case of Africa (and Latin America, in so far as it is not 'economically attached' to either the USA or Europe), needs to be expanded sociologically. There are complications, notably those arising in connection with China, Russia, and British reluctance concerning European political unity. My major point here is to emphasize the fact that in both North America and Europe, and, in a less clear-cut way, in Asia, extra-economic and economic factors are intertwined with the trend towards multiculturality and polyethnicity within nations and 'mega-nations.' More specifically, many, if not most, societies and regions are subject to cross-cutting and often 'contradictory' axes of ethnicity and race, axes which define the range and scope of the world spaces that such societies and regions increasingly become. This overall process is consolidated in many parts of the world by global capitalism's tendency, within the context of an extensive consumer culture (Featherstone, 1991a; Sklair,

1991), to engage in what is called by such names as glocal, multicultural or micro-marketing.

One should add that growing societal self-consciousness about multi-culturality and the like places the old sociological, but much disputed, problem of order in a new light. The question is no longer whether societies have problems of order along the lines indicated by Parsons in *The Structure of Social Action* (1937). 'Parsons's problem' has become politically thematized and thus is a matter for reflexive contestation. Touraine (for example, 1981) has made important contributions to this theme. He has argued that 'we should set out to discover the new actors and the new struggles for society taking shape under our very eyes' (1981: 2), and goes on to argue that 'it is only now that the social history of society is really beginning, a history that is no longer anything other than the entire accumulation of relations and conflicts, the stakes involved being the social control of a new culture, of society's ability to act upon itself.' This is a persuasive argument in so far as it draws attention away from the positions of both 'modernists' and 'postmodernists,' pointing instead to contests over trajectories of change. While I do not subscribe to many of the more detailed points of Touraine's general sociological position, I do think that he indicates some crucial trends in the contemporary world. Touraine (1981: 2) insists that 'we are entering a society which has neither laws nor foundations, which is no more than a complex of actions and social relations.' Among the roles of the sociologist, argues Touraine, is that of indicating 'what is at stake by going beyond the awareness of crisis, the doubt, and the resistance to change or rejection of it. The time of utopia is drawing to its end.' This reference to utopia is, I take it, to the strong tendency in most of Western theory (including the 'post-Marxist' strand in postmodern theory) to operate in terms of a basically Western project. Touraine is arguing for the *analysis of* the struggle for 'control of a new culture.' While I believe that he greatly overstates the absence of constraints, he does draw attention to the important theme of competing conceptions of order and to the centrality of culture in that respect. We have moved into a situation in which internal-societal and global concep-tions of order have become intertwined and overtly politicized. At the present time there are competing approaches to order on both, interrelated fronts. Societal and regional multiculturality is debated in reference to such themes as common cultures and identities; while the theme of world order is much in the political air, and likely to be much disputed in the decades ahead.

I have had occasion in the preceding chapters to mention the theme of 'international education,' sometimes called 'global education.' Analysts and interpreters of globalization are confronted with an ambiguous task in this respect. On the one hand, the increasing concern with 'other cultures' and with global trends is to be greatly welcomed. The 'internationalization' of the curriculum appears, on the face of it, to be a strong step in the direction of a concern with the global circumstance. On the other hand, we must realize that in considerable part that step is predicated on the proposition that countries which do not promote 'international education' will suffer in economic and political terms in an increasingly interdependent world. In other words, much of the drive to 'internationalize' the curriculum is based on, or is at least legitimized in terms of, national or regional politicoeconomic self-interest. (The local component is so strong that in the USA and elsewhere local governments compete against each other for international investment, which is a major example of the globalization of locality.) Without necessarily criticizing this motivation and/or form of legitimation, it has to be said that it usually leads to the neglect of the systematic study of the world as a whole, not least because the latter is often pejoratively associated with the basically Marxist thrust of world-systems theory. Moreover, it is interesting to note that curricula designed under the rubric of 'international' or 'global' studies rarely include sociology (or even cultural studies). Rather, they include economics, political science and international relations because those disciplines quite clearly relate to the 'tough realities' of the contemporary world. Anthropology and 'intercultural communication' get some attention because they appear to deal with the problem of 'other cultures,' while environmental issues are frequently discussed, for obvious reasons. Sociology is often left out because it appears of only minor relevance to pressing 'international issues.' The irony in all this is obvious. For it is sociology which, in spite of its strong 'national' tendencies, is playing a major, possibly *the* major, role in the theorization of globality and globalization on the disciplinary front. The consequence is that many programs in so-called international education and international studies fail to study the global field, or the global-human condition.

Clearly the wave of protectionist sentiment which has gained momentum in the early 1990s will modify the big drive in the direction I have just indicated. Moreover there are tensions between inward-looking multicultural education and outward-looking international education, although the two are obviously linked from a sociological point of view. The task of the sociological student of globalization must now include that of comprehending the bases and thrusts of movements in the field of education, not least because such movements are major sites of socialization into our greatly compressed world. Those movements are significant arenas for the study of what I referred to early in this book as processes of relativization in the global field as a whole. In any case, universities have become significant 'players' on the global scene. Traditionally, they have contributed much to transnational communication through cross-national 'communities' of scientists and other academics. But recently universities *per se* have begun to act in a much more dynamic way with respect to the global field, and to the world spaces within it.

I conclude with some observations on what Ferguson (1992) has called 'the mythology about globalization.' Among the 'myths' to which Ferguson claims globalization theorists, including the author of this book, subscribe are the 'disappearance of time and space,' 'global cultural homogeneity,' 'big is better,' 'the new world order,' 'economic determinism,' and 'saving planet earth.' It should be clear by now that as a theorist of globalization I have promoted none of these ideas. Ferguson writes as if being eager to talk about globalization means that one both enthusiastically embraces it and attributes to it a general homogenization and 'saving' of the world. But I have spoken, among other things, of the patterning of time and space, global heterogeneity, disputes over 'world order,' the great limitations of economism, and the 'fundamentalism' of some aspects of the 'save planet earth' movement. Contemporary globalization involves considerable increase in global, including 'local,' complexity and density. What we make of this is up to us; although, as I have frequently emphasized, the way in which we think about it is crucial. Ferguson, like many others, chooses – I think unrealistically, indeed 'fundamentalistically' – to conceive of globalization in a one-sided way. The point of my discussions has, in contrast, been to promote a fluid perspective, which indeed is centered on the global variety that Ferguson herself seems to prefer.

BIBLIOGRAPHY

Abaza, M. and Stauth, G. (1990) 'Occidental reason, orientalism, Islamic fundamentalism: a critique', in M. Albrow and E. King (eds), *Globalization, Knowledge and Society*. London: Sage.

Abercrombie, N., Hill, S. and Turner, B.S. (1980) *The Dominant Ideology Thesis*. London: Allen & Unwin.

Abercrombie, N., Hill, S. and Turner, B.S. (1990) *Dominant Ideologies*. London: Unwin Hyman.

Abraham, G.A. (1992) *Max Weber and the Jewish Question*. Urbana, IL: University of Illinois Press.

Abu-Lughod, J. (1989) *Before European Hegemony: The World System A.D. 1250–1350*. New York: Oxford University Press.

Abu-Lughod, L. (1991) 'Writing against culture', in R.G. Fox (ed.), *Recapturing Anthropology: Working in the Present*. Santa Fe, NM: School of America Research Press.

Albrow, M. (1990) 'Globalization, knowledge and society', in M. Albrow and E. King (eds), *Globalization, Knowledge and Society*. London: Sage.

Alexander, J.C. (1988) 'Introduction: Durkheimian sociology and cultural studies today', in J.C. Alexander (ed.), *Durkheimian Sociology: Cultural Studies*. Cambridge: Cambridge University Press.

Alexander, J.C. (1990) 'Analytical debates: understanding the relative autonomy of culture', in J.C. Alexander and S. Seidman (eds), *Culture and Society: Contemporary Debates*. Cambridge: Cambridge University Press.

Alexander, J.C. (1992) 'Some remarks on "agency" in recent sociological theory', *Perspectives* (Theory Section of ASA) 15 (1).

Alexandrowicz, C.H. (1967) *An Introduction to the History of the Law of Nations in the East Indies*. Oxford: Oxford University Press.

Alexandrowicz, C.H. (1973) *The European–African Confrontation*. Leiden: Sijthoff.

Alger, C. (1988) 'Perceiving, analyzing and coping with the local–global nexus', *International Social Science Journal*, 117 (August).

Anderson, B. (1983) *Imagined Communities*. London: Verso.

Anderson, P. (1976) *Considerations on Western Marxism*. London: NLB.

Anderson, P. (1984) *In the Tracks of Historical Materialism*. Chicago: University of Chicago Press.

Appadurai, A. (1990) 'Disjuncture and difference in the global cultural economy', *Public Culture*, 2 (2).

Archer, M.S. (1982) 'The myth of cultural integration', *British Journal of Sociology*, 36 (3).

Archer, M.S. (1988) *Culture and Agency: The Place of Culture in Social Theory*. Cambridge: Cambridge University Press.

Archer, M.S. (1990) 'Foreword', in M. Albrow and E. King (eds), *Globalization, Knowledge and Society*. London: Sage.

Ardener, E. (1985) 'Social anthropology and the decline of modernism', in J. Overing (ed.), *Reason and Morality*. London: Tavistock.

Arendt, H. (1957) 'Karl Jaspers: citizen of the world', in P.A. Schlipp (ed.), *The Philosophy of Karl Jaspers*. La Salle, IL: Open Court.

Arnason, J.P. (1987a) 'Figurational sociology as a counter-paradigm', *Theory, Culture & Society*, 4 (2–3).

Arnason, J.P. (1987b) 'The modern constellation and the Japanese enigma: Part I', *Thesis Eleven*, 17.

Arnason, J.P. (1988a) 'The modern constellation and the Japanese enigma: Part II', *Thesis Eleven*, 18/19.

Arnason, J.P. (1988b) 'Social theory and the concept of civilization', *Thesis Eleven*, 20.

Arnason, J.P. (1989a) 'Culture and imaginary significations', *Thesis Eleven*, 22.

Arnason, J.P. (1989b) 'Civilization, culture and power: reflections on Norbert Elias' genealogy of the West', *Thesis Eleven*, 24.

Arnason, J.P. (1990) 'Nationalism, globalization and modernity', *Theory, Culture & Society*, 7 (2–3).

Aron, R. (1966) *Peace and War: A Theory of International Relations*. London: Weidenfeld & Nicolson.

Atlas, J. (1989) 'What is Fukuyama saying?', *New York Times Magazine*, 22 October.

Baker, W. and Rappaport, A. (1989) 'The global teenager', *Whole Earth Review* (Winter).

Balibar, E. (1991) 'Es gibt keinen Staat in Europa: racism and politics in Europe today', *New Left Review*, 186 (March/April).

Barber, B.R. (1992) 'Jihad vs. McWorld', *The Atlantic*, 269 (3).

Baudrillard, J. (1983) *Simulations*. New York: Semiotext(e).

Baudrillard, J. (1988) *America*. London: Verso.

Baum, R.C. (1974) 'Beyond convergence: toward theoretical relevance in quantitative modernization research', *Sociological Inquiry*, 44 (4).

Baum, R.C. (1980) 'Authority and identity: the case for evolutionary invariance', in R. Robertson and B. Holzner (eds), *Identity and Authority: Explorations in the Theory of Society*. Oxford: Basil Blackwell.

Baykan, A. (1992) '*The Turkish Woman*: an adventure in feminist historiography'. Paper presented to the Third Biennial Symposium on New Feminist Scholarship, State University of New York at Buffalo.

Beck, U. (1992) 'From industrial society to risk society: questions of survival, social structure and ecological enlightenment', *Theory, Culture & Society*, 9 (1).

Bellah, R.N. (1957) *Tokugawa Religion*. New York: Free Press.

Bellah, R.N. (1964) 'Religious evolution', *American Sociological Review*, 29.

Bellah, R.N. (1965) 'Epilogue', in R.N. Bellah (ed.), *Religion and Progress in Modern Asia*. New York: Free Press.

Bellah, R.N. (1974) *The Broken Covenant*. New York: Seabury.

Bellah, R.N. (1985) *Tokugawa Religion: The Cultural Roots of Modern Japan*, 2nd edn. New York: Free Press.

Bellah, R.N., Madsen, R., Sullivan, W.M., Swidler, A. and Tipton, S.M. (1985) *Habits of the Heart: Individualism and Commitment in American Life*. Berkeley: University of California Press.

Bentham, J. (1948) *The Principles of Morals and Legislation*. New York: Lafner.

Bentham van den Bergh, Godfried van (1983) 'Two scorpions in a bottle: the unintended benefits of nuclear weapons', in W. Page (ed.), *The Future of Politics*. London: Frances Pinter.

Bentham van den Bergh, Godfried van (1990) *The Taming of Great Powers*. Aldershot: Gower.

Berger, P.L. (1974) *Pyramids of Sacrifice: Political Ethics and Social Change*. New York: Basic Books.

Berger, P.L. (1986) *The Capitalist Revolution*. New York: Basic Books.

Berger, P.L. and Luckmann, T. (1966) *The Social Construction of Reality*. New York: Basic Books.

Berger, P.L., Berger, B. and Kellner, H. (1973) *The Homeless Mind: Modernization and Consciousness*. New York: Random House.

Bergesen, A. (1980a) 'From utilitarianism to globology: the shift from the individual to the world as a whole as the primordial unit of analysis', in A. Bergesen (ed.), *Studies of the Modern World-System*. New York: Academic Press.

Bergesen, A. (ed.) (1980b) *Studies of the Modern World System*. New York: Academic Press.

Berlin, I. (1991) 'The ingathering storm of nationalism', *New Perspectives Quarterly*, 8 (4).

Berman, H.J. (1982) 'The law of international commercial transactions', in W.S. Surrey and D. Wallace (eds), *International Business Transactions*, Part III. Philadelphia: American Law Institute Bar Association Committee on Continuing Professional Education.

Berman, M. (1983) *All That is Solid Melts into Air: The Experience of Modernity*. London: Verso.

Beyer, P.F. (forthcoming) *The Roles of Religion in Global Society*.

Blacker, C. (1964) *The Japanese Enlightenment: A Study of the Writings of Fukuzawa Yukichi*. Cambridge: Cambridge University Press.

Bloch, M. (1983) *Marxism and Anthropology*. Oxford: Oxford University Press.

Bogner, A. (1987) 'Elias and the Frankfurt School', *Theory Culture & Society*, 4 (2–3).

Boli, J.B. (1980) 'Global integration and the universal increase of state dominance', in A. Bergesen (ed.), *Studies of the Modern World-System*. New York: Academic Press.

Bourdieu, P. (1984) *Distinction*. Cambridge, MA: Harvard University Press.

Bourricaud, F. (1981) *The Sociology of Talcott Parsons*. Chicago: University of Chicago Press.

Bourricaud, F. (1987) 'Modernity, "universal reference" and the process of modernization', in S.N. Eisenstadt (ed.), *Patterns of Modernity, Volume I: The West*. New York: New York University Press.

Bovenker, F., Miles, R. and Verbunt, G. (1990) 'Racism, migration and the state in Western Europe: a case for comparative analysis', *International Sociology*, 5 (4).

Bowen, W.M. (1984) *Globalism: America's Demise*. Shreveport, LA: Huntington House.

Boyne, R. (1990) 'Culture and the world-system', in M. Featherstone (ed.), *Global Culture*. London: Sage.

Bozeman, A.B. (1971) *The Future of Law in a Multi-cultural World*. Princeton, NJ: Princeton University Press.

Brubaker, W.R. (1990) 'Immigration, citizenship and the nation-state in France and Germany: a comparative historical analysis', *International Sociology*, 5 (4).

Bryant, C.G.A. and Jary, D. (1991) *Giddens's Theory of Structuration*. London: Routledge.

Bull, H. (1984) 'Foreword', in G.W. Gong, *The Standard of 'Civilization' in International Society*. Oxford: Clarendon Press.

Bull, H. and Watson, A. (eds) (1984a) *The Expansion of International Society*. Oxford: Clarendon Press.

Bull, H. and Watson, A. (1984b) 'Introduction', in H. Bull and A. Watson (eds), *The Expansion of International Society*. Oxford: Clarendon Press.

Burton, J. (1972) *World Society*. Cambridge: Cambridge University Press.

Buruma, I. (1989) 'From Hirohito to Heimat', *New York Review of Books*, 36 (16).

Butler, J. (1990) *Gender Trouble: Feminism and the Subversion of Identity*. New York: Routledge.

Camic, C. (ed.) (1991) *Talcott Parsons: The Early Essays*. Chicago: Chicago University Press.

Campbell, C. (1987) *The Romantic Ethic and the Spirit of Modern Consumerism*. Oxford: Basil Blackwell.

Castoriadis, C. (1987) *The Imaginary Institution of Society*. Cambridge: Cambridge University Press.

Cavell, S. (1991) '*The Idea of Home*: introduction', *Social Research* 58 (1).

Chakrabarty, D. (1992) 'The death of history? Historical consciousness and the culture of late capitalism', *Public Culture* 4 (2).

Chartrand, L. (1991) 'A new solidarity among native peoples', *World Press Review*, August.

Chase-Dunn, C. (ed.) (1983) *Socialist States in the World System*. Beverly Hills, CA: Sage.

Chase-Dunn, C. (1989) *Global Formation*. Oxford: Basil Blackwell.

Chirot, D. and Hall, T.D. (1982) 'World system theory', *Annual Review of Sociology*, 81.

Cohen, E. (1987) 'Thailand, Burma and Laos – an outline of the comparative social dynamics of three Theravada Buddhist societies in the modern era', in S.N. Eisenstadt (ed.), *Patterns of Modernity, Volume II: Beyond the West*. New York: New York University Press.

Cohen, I.J. (1989) *Structuration Theory: Anthony Giddens and the Constitution of Social Life*. New York: St Martin's Press.

Coleman, J.A. (1980) 'The renewed covenant: Robert N. Bellah's vision of religion and society', in G. Baum (ed.), *Sociology and Human Destiny*. New York: Seabury Press.

Collins, R. (1986) *Weberian Sociological Theory*. Cambridge: Cambridge University Press.

Comaroff, J. and Comaroff, J. (1991) *Of Revelation and Revolution*, Volume I. Chicago: University of Chicago Press.

Cuddihy, J.M. (1978) *No Offense: Civil Religion and Protestant Taste*. New York: Seabury.

Cuddihy, J.M. (1987) *The Ordeal of Civility: Freud, Marx, Lévi-Strauss and the Jewish Struggle with Modernity*, 2nd edn. Boston: Beacon Press.

Davidman, L. (1991) *Tradition in a Rootless World: Women Turn to Orthodox Judaism*. Berkeley: University of California Press.

Davis, F. (1974) *Yearning for Yesterday: A Sociology of Nostalgia*. New York: Free Press.

Davis, W. (1992) *Japanese Religion and Society*. Albany, NY: State University of New York Press.

Der Derian, J. (1989) 'The boundaries of knowledge and power in international relations', in J. Der Derian and M.J. Shapiro (eds), *International/Intertextual Relations: Postmodern Readings of World Politics*. Lexington, MA: Lexington Books.

Der Derian, J. and Shapiro, J. (eds) (1989) *International/Intertextual Relations: Postmodern Readings of World Politics*. Lexington, MA: Lexington Books.

Diamond, I. and Orenstein, G.F. (eds) (1990) *Reweaving the World: The Emergence of Ecofeminism*. San Francisco: Sierra Club Books.

Dumont, L. (1977) *From Mandeville to Marx*. Chicago: University of Chicago Press.

Dumont, L. (1979) 'The anthropological community and ideology', *Social Science Information*, 18.

Dumont, L. (1980) 'On value', in *Proceedings of the British Academy*. Oxford: Oxford University Press.

Dumont, L. (1983) *Essais sur l'individualisme*. Paris: Editions du Seuil.

Dumont, L. (1984) 'German idealism in a comparative perspective: hierarchy in the thought of Fichte', in E.V. Walter, V. Kavolis, E. Leites and C.M. Nelson (eds), *Civilization East and West*. Atlantic Highlands, NJ: Humanities Press.

Dunn, J. (1979) *Western Political Theory in the Face of the Future*. Cambridge: Cambridge University Press.

Dupre, L. (1983) *Marx's Social Critique of Culture*. New Haven, CT: Yale University Press.

Durkheim, E. (1961) *The Elementary Forms of the Religious Life*. New York: Collier Books.

Durkheim, E. (1962) *Socialism*. New York: Collier Books.

Durkheim, E. (1974) *Sociology and Philosophy*. New York: Free Press.

Durkheim, E. and Mauss, M. (1971) 'A note on the notion of civilization', *Social Research*, 58.

Economist (1991) 'Global village, travelling peasants', *The Economist*, 14 December.

Eisenstadt, S.N. (1982) The axial age: the emergence of transcendental visions and the rise of clerics', *Archives Européennes de Sociologie*.

Elias, N. (1978) *The Civilizing Process Volume I: The History of Manners*. New York: Pantheon Books.

Elias, N. (1982) *The Civilizing Process Volume II: State Formation and Civilization*. Oxford: Basil Blackwell.

Elias, N. (1987) 'The retreat of sociologists into the present', *Theory, Culture & Society*, 4 (2–3).

Emerson, R. (1964) *Self-Determination Revisited in the Era of Decolonization*. Harvard: Center for International Affairs, Harvard University.

Enloe, C. (1990) *Bananas Beaches and Bases: Making Feminist Sense of International Politics*. Berkeley: University of California Press.

Etzioni, A. (1965) *Political Unification: A Comparative Study of Leaders and Forces*. New York: Holt, Rinehart & Winston.

Featherstone, M. (1987) 'Norbert Elias and figurational sociology: some prefatory remarks', *Theory, Culture & Society*, 4 (2–3).

Featherstone, M. (1990) 'Global culture: an introduction', *Theory, Culture & Society*, 7 (2–3).

Featherstone, M. (1991a) *Consumer Culture and Postmodernism*. London: Sage.

Featherstone, M. (1991b) 'Consumer culture, postmodernism, and global disorder', in R. Robertson and W.R. Garrett (eds), *Religion and Global Order*. New York: Paragon.

Ferguson, M. (1992) 'The mythology about globalization', *European Journal of Communication*, 7.

Fox-Genovese, E. (1991) *Feminism without Illusions: A Critique of Individualism*. Chapel Hill, NC: University of North Carolina Press.

Frank, A.G. (1969) *Latin America: Underdevelopment or Revolution*. New York: Monthly Review Press.

Fraser, N. (1989) *Unruly Practices*. Minneapolis: University of Minnesota Press.

Fregosi, P. (1990) *Dreams of Empire: Napoleon and the First World War*. New York: Brick Lane Press.

Friedman, J. (1990) 'Being in the world: globalization and localization', *Theory, Culture & Society*, 7 (2–3).

Frisby, D. (1992) *Simmel and Since*. London: Routledge.

Fukuyama, F. (1989) 'The end of history?', *The National Interest*, 16 (Summer).

Fukuyama, F. (1992) *The End of History and the Last Man*. New York: Free Press.

Fustel de Coulanges, N.D. (1980) *The Ancient City*. Baltimore, MD: Johns Hopkins University Press.

Galtung, J. (1966) 'Rank and social integration: a multidimensional approach', in J. Berger (ed.), *Sociological Theories in Progress*. Boston: Houghton Mifflin.

Galtung, J. (1980) *The True Worlds: A Transnational Perspective*. New York: Free Press.

Galtung, J. (1985) 'Global conflict formations: present developments and future directions', in P. Wallersteen, J. Galtung and C. Portales (eds), *Global Militarization*. Boulder, CO: Westview Press.

Garrett, W.R. (forthcoming) 'Thinking religion in the global circumstance: a critique of Roland Robertson's globalization theory', *Journal for the Scientific Study of Religion*.

Geertz, C. (1963) *Old Societies and New States*. New York: Free Press.

Geertz, C. (1983) *Local Knowledge*. New York: Basic Books.

Geertz, C. (1984) 'Anti anti-relativism', *American Anthropologist*, 86 (2).

Geertz, G. (1986) 'The uses of diversity', *Michigan Quarterly*, 25 (1).

Geertz, C. (1988) *Works and Lives: The Anthropologist as Author*. Stanford, CA: Stanford University Press.

Gellner, E. (1983) *Nations and Nationalism*. Ithaca, NY: Cornell University Press.

Gerth, H.H. and Mills, C.W. (1948) *From Max Weber*. London: Routledge & Kegan Paul.

Giddens, A. (1987) *The Nation-State and Violence*. Berkeley: University of California Press.

Giddens, A. (1990) *The Consequences of Modernity*. Stanford: CA: Stanford University Press.

Giddens, A. (1991) *Modernity and Self-Identity: Self and Society in the Late Modern Age*. Stanford, CA: Stanford University Press.

Giddens, A. and Turner, J. (1987) 'Introduction', in A. Giddens and J. Turner (eds), *Social Theory Today*. Stanford, CA: Stanford University Press.

Ginsberg, F.D. (1991) 'Gender politics and the contradictions of nurturance: moral authority and constraints to action for female abortion activists', *Social Research*, 58 (3).

Gluck, C. (1985) *Japan's Modern Myths: Ideology in the Late Meiji Period*. Princeton, NJ: Princeton University Press.

Goetz, A.M. (1991) 'Feminism and the claim to know: contradictions in feminist approaches to women in development', in R. Grant and K. Newland (eds), *Gender and International Relations*. Bloomington: Indiana University Press.

Gold, T.P. (1986) *State and Society in the Taiwan Miracle*. New York: M.E. Sharpe.

Gong, G.W. (1984) *The Standard of 'Civilization' in International Society*. Oxford: Clarendon Press.

Goodenough, W.H. (1981) *Culture, Language, and Society*, 2nd edn. Menlo Park, CA: Benjamin Cummings.

Granovetter, M. (1985) 'Economic action and social structure: the problem of embeddedness', *American Journal of Sociology*, 91 (3).

Grant, R. (1991) 'The sources of gender bias in international relations theory', in R. Grant and K. Newland (eds), *Gender and International Relations*. Bloomington: University of Indiana Press.

Grant, R. and Newland, K. (1991) *Gender and International Relations*. Bloomington: Indiana University Press.

Grossberg, L., Nelson, C. and Treicher, P.A. (eds) (1992) *Cultural Studies*. New York: Routledge.

Habermas, J. (1974) 'On social identity', *Telos*, 7.

Habermas, J. (1981a) *Theorie des kommunikativen Handelns*, 2 vols. Frankfurt am Main: Suhrkamp.

Habermas, J. (1981b) 'Modernity versus postmodernity', *New German Critique*, 81.

Haferkamp, H. (1987a) 'From the intra-state to the inter-state civilizing process', *Theory, Culture & Society*, 4 (2–3).

Haferkamp, H. (1987b) 'Reply to Stephen Mennell', *Theory, Culture & Society*, 4 (2–3).

Hall, S. (1986) 'Gramsci's relevance for the study of race and ethnicity', *Journal of Communication Inquiry*, 10 (2).

Hannerz, U. (1990) 'Cosmopolitans and locals in world culture', in M. Featherstone (ed.), *Global Culture: Nationalism, Globalization and Modernity*. London: Sage.

Harasym, Sarah (1990) 'Editor's note', in G.C. Spivak, *The Post–Colonial Critic: Interviews, Strategies, Dialogues*. London: Routledge.

Hardacre, H. (1986) *Kutozumikyo and the New Religions of Japan*. Princeton, NJ: Princeton University Press.

Harootunian, H.D. (1989) 'Visible discourses/invisible ideologies', in M. Miyoshi and H.D. Harootunian (eds), *Postmodernism and Japan*. Durham, NC: Duke University Press.

Hartz, L. (1964) 'Introduction', in B. Schwartz *In Search of Wealth and Power*. Cambridge: Belknap Press of Harvard University Press.

Harvey, D. (1989) *The Condition of Postmodernity*. Oxford: Basil Blackwell.

Hertz, J.H. (1932) *The Battle for The Sabbath at Geneva*. London: Humphrey Milford Oxford University Press.

Hobhouse, L.T. (1906) *Morals in Evolution. A Study of Comparative Ethics*, Volume I. New York: Henry Holt.

Hobsbawm, E. (1990) *Nations and Nationalism since 1780: Programme, Myth, Reality*. Cambridge: Cambridge University Press.

Hobsbawm, E. (1991) 'Exile: a keynote address – introduction', *Social Research*, 58 (1).

Hobsbawm E. and Ranger, T. (eds) (1983) *The Invention of Tradition*. Cambridge: Cambridge University Press.

Hollander, J. (1991) 'It all depends', *Social Research*, 58 (1).

Holmes, S. (1988) 'The polis state', *New Republic*, 6 June.

Holton, R.J. and Turner, B.S. (1986) *Talcott Parsons on Economy and Society*. London: Routledge & Kegan Paul.

Holzner, B. and Robertson, R. (1980) 'Identity and authority: a problem analysis of processes of identification and authorization', in R. Robertson and B. Holzner (eds), *Identity and Authority*. Oxford: Basil Blackwell.

Hopkins, T.K. (1982) 'The study of the capitalist world economy', in T.K. Hopkins and I. Wallenstein (eds), *World-Systems Analysis: Theory and Methodology*. Beverley Hills: Sage.

Hopkins, T.K. and Wallerstein, I. (1967) 'The comparative study of national societies', *Social Science Information*, 6 (5).

Hori, I., et al. (eds) (1972) *Japanese Religion*. Tokyo: Kodansha International.

Horowitz, I.L. (1966) *The Three Worlds of Development: The Theory and Practice of International Stratification*. New York: Oxford University Press.

Hughes, H.S. (1952) *Oswald Spengler: A Critical Estimate*. New York: Scribner.

Inglehart, R. (1977) *The Silent Revolution: Changing Values and Political Styles among Western Publics*. Princeton, NJ: Princeton University Press.

Inglehart, R. (1990) *Culture Shift in Advanced Industrial Society*. Princeton, NJ: Princeton University Press.

Inkeles, A. (1981) 'Convergence and divergence in industrial societies', in M.O. Attit, B. Holzner and Z. Suda (eds), *Directions of Change*. Boulder, CO: Westview Press.

Inkeles, A. and Smith, D.H. (1974) *Becoming Modern: Individual Change in Six Developing Countries*. Cambridge, MA: Harvard University Press.

Inoue, N. (1991) *New Religions: Contemporary Papers in Japanese Religion*. Tokyo: Institute for Japanese Culture and Classics.

Ishida, T. (1983) *Japanese Political Culture*. New Brunswick, NJ: Transaction Books.

James, H. (1989) *A German Identity: 1770–1990*. New York: Routledge.

Jameson, F. (1984) 'Postmodernism, or the cultural logic of late capitalism', *New Left Review*, 146.

Jameson, F. (1986) 'Third-World literature in the era of multinational capitalism', *Social Text*, 15 (Fall).

Jameson, F. (1988) 'On *Habits of the Heart*', in C.H. Reynolds and R.V. Norman (eds), *Community in America: The Challenge of Habits of the Heart*. Berkeley: University of California Press.

Janeway, E. (1980) *Powers of the Weak*. New York: Knopf.

Jaspers, K. (1953) *The Origin and Goal of History*. New Haven, CT: Yale University Press.

Jaspers, K. (1957) 'Philosophical autobiography', in P.A. Schlipp (ed.), *The Philosophy of Karl Jaspers*. La Salle, IL: Open Court.

Jedlowski, P. (1990) 'Simmel on memory', in M. Kaern, B.S. Phillips and R.S. Cohen (eds), *Georg Simmel and Contemporary Sociology*. Dordrecht: Kluwer.

Kaufman, D.R. (1991) *Rachel's Daughters: Newly Orthodox Jewish Women*. New Brunswick, NJ: Rutgers University Press.

Kavolis, V. (1986) 'Civilizational paradigms in current sociology: Dumont vs Eisenstadt', *Current Perspectives in Social Theory*, 7.

Kavolis, V. (1987) 'History of consciousness and civilization analysis', *Comparative Civilizations Review*, 17 (Fall).

Kavolis, V. (1988) 'Contemporary moral cultures and the "return of the sacred"', *Sociological Analysis*, 49 (3).

Keane, C. (1990) 'Globality and constructions of world health', Department of Sociology, University of Pittsburgh (mimeo).

Keohane, R. and Nye, J. (eds) (1973) *Transnational Relations and World Politics*. Cambridge, MA: Harvard University Press.

Kern, S. (1983) *The Culture of Time and Space, 1880–1918*. Cambridge, MA: Harvard University Press.

Kerr, C., Dunlop, J.T., Harbison, F.H. and Myers, C.A. (1960) *Industrialism and Industrial Man*. London: Heinemann.

Kierney, H. (1989) *The British Isles*. Cambridge: Cambridge University Press.

King, A.D. (1990) 'Architecture, capital and the globalization of culture', *Theory, Culture & Society*, 7 (2–3).

King, A.D. (1991) 'Introduction: spaces of culture, spaces of knowledge', in A.D. King (ed.), *Culture, Globalization and the World-System: Contemporary Conditions for the Representation of Identity*. Binghamton: State University of New York; London: Macmillan.

Kitagawa, J.M. (1966) *Religion and Japanese History*. New York: Columbia University Press.

Kitawaga, J.M. (1987) 'Japanese religion: an overview', in M. Eliade (ed.), *The Encylopedia of Religion*, Volume VII. New York: Macmillan and Free Press.

Kohn, H. (1971) 'Nationalism and internationalism', in W.W. Wagar (ed.), *History and the Idea of Mankind*. Albuquerque: University of New Mexico Press.

Kojève, A. (1947) *Introduction à la lecture de Hegel*. Paris: Editions Gallimard.

Kroeber, A.L. and Parsons, T. (1958) 'The concepts of culture and of social system', *American Sociological Review*, 23 (October).

Kroker, A. (1985) 'Baudrillard's Marx', *Theory, Culture & Society*, 2 (3).

Kuhn, T. (1964) *The Structure of Scientific Revolutions*. Chicago: University of Chicago Press.

Lagos, G. (1963) *International Stratification and Underdeveloped Countries*. Chapel Hill: University of North Carolina Press.

Lasch, C. (1988) 'The communitarian critique of liberalism', in C.E. Reynolds and R.V. Norman (eds), *Community in America: The Challenge of Habits of the Heart*. Berkeley: University of California Press.

Lash, S. (1990) *Sociology of Postmodernism*. London: Routledge.

Lash, S. and Urry, J. (1987) *The End of Organized Capitalism*. Madison: University of Wisconsin Press.

Lechner, F.J. (1984) 'Ethnicity and revitalization in the modern world system', *Sociological Focus*, 17 (3).

Lechner, F.J. (1985) 'Fundamentalism and sociocultural revitalization in America: a sociological interpretation', *Sociological Analysis*, 46 (3).

Lechner, F.J. (1989) 'Cultural aspects of the modern world-system', in W.H. Swatos (ed.), *Religious Politics in Global and Comparative Perspective*. New York: Greenwood Press.

Lechner, F.J. (1990a) 'Fundamentalism revisited', in T. Robbins and D. Anthony (eds), *In Gods We Trust: New Patterns of Religious Pluralism in America*. New Brunswick, NJ: Transaction Books.

Lechner, F.J. (1990b) 'Fundamentalism and sociocultural revitalization: on the logic of dedifferentiation', in J.C. Alexander and P. Colomy (eds), *Differentiation Theory and Social Change*. New York: Columbia University Press.

Lechner, F.J. (1991) 'Religion, law, and global order', in R. Robertson and W.R. Garrett (eds), *Religion and Global Order*. New York: Paragon House.

Lesourne, J.F. (1986) *World Perspectives: A European Assessment*. New York: Gordon & Breach.

Liebersohn, H. (1988) *Fate and Utopia in German Sociology, 1870–1923*. Cambridge, MA: MIT Press.

Littlejohn, C. Scott (1985) 'Introduction: Lucien Lévy-Bruhl and the concept of cognitive relativity', in L. Lévy-Bruhl, *How Natives Think*. Princeton, NJ: Princeton University Press.

Lowenthal, D. (1985) *The Past is a Foreign Country*. Cambridge: Cambridge University Press.

Luhmann, N. (1976) 'Generalized media and the problem of contingency' in J.J. Loubser, R.C. Baum, A. Effrat and V.M. Lidz (eds), *Explorations in General Theory in Social Science*, Volume II. New York: Free Press.

Luhmann, N. (1982a) *The Differentiation of Society*. New York: Columbia University Press.

Luhmann, N. (1982b) 'The world society as a social system', *International Journal of General Systems*, 8.

Lyotard, J. (1984) *The Postmodern Condition: A Report on Knowledge*. Minneapolis: University of Minnesota Press.

Macbride Commission (1980) *Many Voices, One World*. Paris: UNESCO.

MacCannell, D. (1989) *The Tourist: A New Theory of the Leisure Class*, 2nd edn. New York: Schocken.

MacIntyre, A. (1981) *After Virtue: A Study in Moral Theory*. Notre Dame: South Bend, IN: University of Notre Dame Press.

MacIntyre, A. (1987) *Whose Justice? Which Rationality?* Notre Dame: South Bend, IN: University of Notre Dame Press.

Mack, Arien (1991) 'Editor's introduction' [to *Home: A Place in the World*], *Social Research*, 58(1).

Mann, M. (1986) *The Sources of Social Power: Volume I, A History of Power from the Beginning to AD 1760*. Cambridge: Cambridge University Press.

Markoff, J. (1977) 'The world as a social system', *Peasant Studies*, 4 (1).

Markoff, J. and Reagan, D. (1987) 'Religion, the state and political legitimacy in the world's constitutions', in T. Robbins and R. Robertson (eds), *Church–State Relations*. New Brunswick, NJ: Transaction Books.

Mazrui, A.A. (1980) *A World Federation of Cultures: An African Perspective*. New York: Free Press.

Mazrui, A.A. (1990) *Cultural Forces in World Politics*. London: James Currey.

McFarland, H.N. (1967) *The Rush Hour of the Gods*. New York: Macmillan.

McGrane, B. (1989) *Beyond Anthropology*. New York: Columbia University Press.

McLuhan, M. (1960) *Explorations in Communication*, ed. E.S. Carpenter. Boston: Beacon Press.

McNeill, W.H. (1986) *Polyethnicity and National Unity in World History*. Toronto: University of Toronto Press.

McNeill, W.H. (1989) *Arnold J. Toynbee: A Life*. Oxford: Oxford University Press.

Mennell, S. (1987) 'Comment on Haferkamp', *Theory, Culture & Society*, 4 (2–3).

Mennell, S. (1990) 'The globalization of human society as a very long-term social process: Elias's theory', in M. Featherstone (ed.), *Global Culture: Nationalism, Globalization and Modernity*. London: Sage.

Merle, M. (1987) *The Sociology of International Relations*. New York: Berg.

Merquior, J.G. (1979) *The Veil and the Mask*. London: Routledge & Kegan Paul.

Merquior, J.G. (1980) *Rousseau and Weber: Two Studies in the Theory of Legitimacy*. London: Routledge & Kegan Paul.

Merquior, J.G. (1991) 'The other West: on the historical position of Latin America', *International Sociology*, 6 (2).

Meyer, J.W. (1980) 'The world polity and the authority of the nation-state', in A. Bergesen (ed.), *Studies of the Modern World System*. New York: Academic Press.

Meyer, J.W. (1987) 'Self and life course: institutionalization and its effects', in G. Thomas, J.W. Meyer, F. Ramirez and J. Boli (eds), *Institutional Structure: Constituting State, Society and the Individual*. Newbury Park, CA: Sage.

Meyer, J.W. (1989) 'Conceptions of Christendom: notes on the distinctiveness of the West', in M.L. Kohn (ed.), *Cross-National Research in Sociology*. Newbury Park, CA: Sage.

Meyer, J.W. (1992) 'From constructionism to neo-institutionalism: reflections on Berger and Luckmann', *Perspectives* (Theory Section of ASA), 15 (2).

Meyer, J.W. and Hannan, M.T. (eds) (1979) *National Development and the World System: Educational, Economic and Political Change 1950–1970*. Chicago: University of Chicago Press.

Miller, J. (1973) *Marshall McLuhan*. New York: Viking Press.

Miyoshi, M. and Harootunian, H.D. (eds) (1989) *Postmodernism and Japan*. Durham, NC: Duke University Press.

Modelski, G. (1978) 'The long cycle of global politics and the nation-state', *Comparative Studies in Society and History*, 20 (2).

Modelski, G. (1983) 'Long cycles of world leadership', in W.R. Thompson (ed.), *Contending Approaches to World System Analysis*. Beverly Hills: Sage.

Moore, W.E. (1966) 'Global sociology: the world as a singular system', *American Journal of Sociology*, 71 (5).

Moravcsik, A. (1991) 'Arms and autarky in modern European history', *Daedalus*, 120 (4).

Mosaic (1988) 19 (3–4).

Muller, J.Z. (1987) *The Other God that Failed*. Princeton, NJ: Princeton University Press.

Murakami, S. (1980) *Japanese Religion in the Modern Century*. Tokyo: University of Tokyo Press.

Nairn, T. (1988) *The Enchanted Glass: Britain and its Monarchy*. London: Hutchinson Radius.

Nelson, B. (1969) *The Idea of Usury: From Tribal Brotherhood to Universal Otherhood*. Chicago: University of Chicago Press.

Nelson, B. (1981) 'Civilizational complexes and intercivilizational encounters', in T.H. Huff (ed.), *On the Roads to Modernity: Conscience, Science and Civilizations*. Totowa: Rowman & Littlefield.

Nettl, J.P. and Robertson, R. (1966) 'Industrialization, development or modernization', *British Journal of Sociology*, 17 (3).

Nettl, J.P. and Robertson, R. (1968) *International Systems and the Modernization of Societies: The Formation of National Goals and Attitudes*. New York: Basic Books.

Nielsen, J.K. (1991) 'The political orientation of Talcott Parsons: the Second World War and its aftermath', in R. Robertson and B.S. Turner (eds), *Talcott Parsons: Theorist of Modernity*. London: Sage.

Nussbaum, M. (1989) 'Recoiling from reason', *New York Review of Books*, 36 (19).

O'Brien, C.C. (1986) *The Siege: The Saga of Israel and Zionism*. New York: Simon and Schuster.

O'Neill, J. (1988) 'Religion and postmodernism: the Durkheimian bond in Bell and Jameson', *Theory, Culture & Society*, 5 (2–3).

Onions, C.T. (ed.) (1966) *The Oxford Dictionary of English Etymology*. Oxford: Oxford University Press.

Oxford Dictionary of New Words (1991) compiled by Sara Tulloch. Oxford: Oxford University Press.

Paglia, C. (1991) *Sexual Personae: Art and Decadence from Nefertiti to Emily Dickinson*. New York: Vintage.

Parsons, T. (1937) *The Structure of Social Action*. Glencoe, IL: Free Press.

Parsons, T. (1961) 'Culture and the social system: introduction', in T. Parsons, et al. (eds), *Theories of Society*. New York: Free Press.

Parsons, T. (1964) 'Communism and the West: the sociology of conflict', in A. Etzioni and E. Etzioni (eds), *Social Change: Sources, Patterns and Consequences*. New York: Basic Books.

Parsons, T. (1967) *Sociological Theory and Modern Society*. New York: Free Press.

Parsons, T. (1971) *The System of Modern Societies*. Englewood Cliffs, NJ: Prentice-Hall.

Parsons, T. (1973) 'Culture and social system revisited', in L. Schneider and C.M. Bonjean (eds), *The Idea of Culture in the Social Sciences*. Cambridge: Cambridge University Press.

Parsons, T. (1977a) 'Law as an intellectual stepchild', *Sociological Inquiry*, 47 (3–4).

Parsons, T. (1977b) *The Evolution of Societies*, ed. J. Toby. Englewood Cliffs, NJ: Prentice-Hall.

Parsons, T. (1978) *Action Theory and the Human Condition*. New York: Free Press.

Parsons, T. (1979) 'Religious and economic symbolism in the western world', *Sociological Inquiry*, 47: 11–58.

Peterson, R.A. (ed.) (1976), *The Production of Culture*. Beverly Hills: Sage.

Polanyi, K. (1957) *The Great Transformation*. Boston: Beacon Press.

Pollack, D. (1986) *The Fracture of Meaning: Japan's Synthesis of China from the Eighth through the Eighteenth Centuries*. Princeton, NJ: Princeton University Press.

Poster, M. (1990) *The Mode of Information: Poststructuralism and Social Context*. Cambridge: Polity Press.

Rajchman, J. (1988) 'Habermas's complaint', *New German Critique*, 4–5 (Fall).

Rasmussen, D. (ed.) (1990) *Universalism vs Communitarianism: Contemporary Debates in Ethics*. Cambridge, MA: MIT Press.

Riley, D. (1988) *'Am I that Name?' Feminism and the Category of 'Women' in History*. Minneapolis: University of Minnesota Press.

Ringer, F.K. (1969) *The Decline of the German Mandarins*. Hanover: University Press of New England.

Robertson, R. (1968) 'Strategic relations between national societies: a sociological analysis', *Journal of Conflict Resolution*, 12 (2).

Robertson, R. (1974) 'Towards identification of the major axes of sociological analysis', in J. Rex (ed.), *Approaches to Sociology*. London: Routledge.

Robertson, R. (1977) 'Individualism, societalism, worldliness, universalism: thematizing theoretical sociology of religion', *Sociological Analysis*, 38 (4).

Robertson, R. (1978) *Meaning and Change: Explorations in the Cultural Sociology of Modern Societies*. Oxford: Basil Blackwell.

Robertson, R. (1980) 'Aspects of identity and authority in sociological theory', in R. Robertson and B. Holzner (eds), *Identity and Authority*. Oxford: Basil Blackwell.

Robertson, R. (1981) 'Considerations from within the American context on the significance of church-state tension', *Sociological Analysis*, 42 (3).

Robertson, R. (1982) 'Parsons on the evolutionary significance of religion', *Sociological Analysis*, 43 (4).

Robertson, R. (1983a) 'Religion, global complexity and the human condition', in *Absolute Values and the Creation of the New World*, Volume I. New York: International Cultural Foundation.

Robertson, R. (1983b) 'Interpreting globality', in *World Realities and International Studies Today*. Glenside, PA: Pennsylvania Council on International Education.

Robertson, R. (1985a) 'Scholarship, partisanship, sponsorship and "the Moonie problem"', *Sociological Analysis*, 46 (4).

Robertson, R. (1985b) 'The development and modern implications of the classical socio-logical perspective on religion and revolution', in B. Lincoln (ed.), *Religion, Rebellion, Revolution*. London: Macmillan.

Robertson, R. (1985c) 'The sacred and the world system', in P. Hammond (ed.), *The Sacred in a Post-Secular Age*. Berkeley: University of California Press.

Robertson, R. (1985d) 'The relativization of societies: modern religion and globalization', in T. Robbins, W.C. Shepherd and J. McBride (eds), *Cults, Culture and the Law*. Chico, CA: Scholars Press.

Robertson, R. (1985e) 'Max Weber and German sociology of religion', in N. Smart, J. Clayton, P. Sherry and S.T. Katz (eds), *Nineteenth-Century Religious Thought in the West*, Vol. III. Cambridge: Cambridge University Press.

Robertson, R. (1986) 'Church–state relations and the world system', in T. Robbins and R. Robertson (eds), *Church–State Relations: Tensions and Transitions*. New Brunswick, NJ: Transaction Books.

Robertson, R. (1987a) 'Bringing modernization back in', *Contemporary Sociology*, 17 (6).

Robertson, R. (1987b) 'Globalization theory and civilizational analysis', *Comparative Civilizations Review*, 17 (Fall).

Robertson, R. (1987c) 'Globalization and societal modernization: a note on Japan and Japanese religion', *Sociological Analysis*, 47 (S): 35–42.

Robertson, R. (1988) 'Modernity and religion: towards the comparative genealogy of religion in global perspective', *Zen Buddhism Today*, 6 (November).

Robertson, R. (1989a) 'Globalization, politics, and religion', in J.A. Beckford and T. Luckmann (eds), *The Changing Face of Religion*. London: Sage.

Robertson, R. (1989b) 'A new perspective on religion and secularization in the global context', in J.K. Hadden and A. Shupe (eds), *Secularization and Fundamentalism Reconsidered*. New York: Paragon House.

Robertson, R. (1990a) 'Japan and the USA: the interpenetration of national identities and the debate about orientalism', in N. Abercrombie, S. Hill and B.S. Turner (eds), *Dominant Ideologies*. London: Unwin Hyman.

Robertson, R. (1990b) 'The globalization paradigm: thinking globally', in D.G. Bromley (ed.), *Religion and the Social Order: New Directions in Theory and Research*. Greenwich, CT: JAI Press.

Robertson, R. (1990c) 'After nostalgia? Wilful nostalgia and the phases of globalization', in B.S. Turner (ed.), *Theories of Modernity and Postmodernity*. London: Sage.

Robertson, R. (1990d) 'Mapping the global condition: globalization as the central concept', *Theory, Culture & Society*, 7 (2–3).

Robertson, R. (1991a) 'Social theory, cultural relativity and the problem of globality', in A.D. King (ed.), *Culture, Globalization and the World-System: Contemporary Conditions for the Representation of Identity*. Binghamton: State University of New York; London: Macmillan.

Robertson, R. (1991b) 'Globalization, modernization, and postmodernization: the ambiguous position of religion', in R. Robertson and W.R. Garrett (eds), *Religion and Global Order*. New York: Paragon House.

Robertson, R. (1991c) 'The central significance of "religion" in social theory: Parsons as an epical theorist', in R. Robertson and B.S. Turner (eds), *Talcott Parsons: Theorist of Modernity*. London: Sage.

Robertson, R. (1992a) 'Globality, global culture and images of world order', in H. Haferkamp and N.J. Smelser (eds), *Social Change and Modernity*. Berkeley: University of California Press.

Robertson, R. (1992b) 'The economization of religion? The promise and limitations of the economic approach', *Social Compass*, 39 (1).

Robertson, R. (1992c) 'Globality and modernity', *Theory Culture & Society*, 9 (2).

Robertson, R. and Chirico, J. (1985) 'Humanity, globalization and worldwide religious resurgence: a theoretical exploration, *Sociological Analysis*, 46 (3).

Robertson, R. and Lechner, F. (1984) 'On Swanson: an appreciation and an appraisal', *Sociological Analysis*, 45 (Fall).

Robertson, R. and Lechner, F. (1985) 'Modernization, globalization and the problem of culture in world-systems theory', *Theory Culture & Society*, 2 (3).

Robertson, R. and Tudor, A. (1968) 'The Third World and international stratification: theoretical considerations and research findings', *Sociology*, 2 (2).

Roof, W.C. (ed.) (1991) *World Order and Religion*. Albany, NY: State University of New York Press.

Rosencrance, R. (1986) *The Rise of the Trading State: Commerce and Conquest in the Modern World*. New York: Basic Books.

Ruddick, S. (1989) *Material Thinking: Towards a Politics of Peace*. Beacon Press.

Sahlins, M. (1976) *Culture and Practical Reason*. Chicago: University of Chicago Press.

Sahlins, M. (1985) *Islands of History*. Chicago: University of Chicago Press.

Sakai, N. (1989) 'Modernity and its critique: the problem of universalism and particularism', in M. Miyoshi and H.D. Harootunian (eds), *Postmodernism and Japan*. Durham, NC: Duke University Press.

Schama, S. (1987) *The Embarrassment of Riches: An Interpretation of Dutch Culture in the Golden Age*. London: Collins.

Schama, S. (1991) 'Homelands', *Social Research*, 58 (1).

Schwartz, B. (1964) *In Search of Wealth and Power: Yen Fu and the West*. Cambridge, MA: Belknap Press of the Harvard University Press.

Seidman, S. (1983) *Liberalism and the Origins of European Social Theory*. Berkeley: University of California Press.

Shad, J. (1988) 'Globalization and Islamic resurgence', *Comparative Civilizations Review*, 19 (Fall).

Shweder, R.A. (1984) 'Anthropology's romantic rebellion against the enlightenment, or there's more to thinking than reason and evidence', in R.A. Shweder and R.A. LeVine (eds), *Culture Theory*. Cambridge: Cambridge University Press.

Silberman, N.A. (1989) *Between Past and Present: Archeology, Ideology, and Nationalism in the Middle East*. New York: Anchor.

Simmel, G. (1950) *The Sociology of Georg Simmel*, ed. K. Wolf. New York: Free Press.

Simmel, G. (1968) *The Conflict in Modern Culture and Other Essays*. New York: Teachers College Press.

Simmel, G. (1978) *The Philosophy of Money*. London: Routledge & Kegan Paul.

Simmel, G. (1986) *Schopenhauer and Nietzsche*. Amherst: University of Massachusetts Press.

Simpson, J.H. (1991) 'Globalization and religion: themes and prospects', in R. Robertson and W.R. Garrett (eds), *Religion and Global Order*. New York: Paragon House.

Sklair, L. (1991) *Sociology of the Global System*. Baltimore, MD: Johns Hopkins University Press.

Smelser, N.J. (1959) *Social Change in the Industrial Revolution*. Chicago: University of Chicago Press.

Smith, A.D. (1979) *Nationalism in the Twentieth Century*. New York: New York University Press.

Smith, A.D. (1981) *The Ethnic Revival*. New York: Cambridge University Press.

Smith, A.D. (1983) *Theories of Nationalism*, 2nd edn. New York: Holmes & Meier.

Smith, A.D. (1990) 'Toward a global culture?', *Theory, Culture & Society*, 7 (2–3).

Smith, M.J. (1991) *Realist Thought from Weber to Kissinger*. Baton Rouge, LA: Louisiana State University Press.

Smith, R.J. (1983) *Japanese Society: Tradition, Self and the Social Order*. Cambridge: Cambridge University Press.

Smith, W.C. (1981) *Towards a World Theology: Faith and the Comparative History of Religion*. Philadelphia: Westminster Press.

Spencer, H. (1966) *A System of Synthetic Philosophy*. Osnabruck: Otto Zeller.

Spengler, Oswald (1965) *The Decline of the West*. New York: Modern Library.

Spivak, G.C. (1987) *In Other Worlds: Essays in Cultural Politics*. New York: Methuen.

Spivak, G.C. (1990) *The Post-Colonial Critic: Interviews, Strategies, Dialogues*. London: Routledge.

Stark, R. and Bainbridge, W.S. (1985) *The Future of Religion*. Berkeley: University of California Press.

Stark, W. (1958) *The Sociology of Knowledge*. London: Routledge & Kegan Paul.

Stauth, G. (1991) 'Revolution in spiritless times: an essay on Michel Foucault's enquiries into the Iranian revolution', *International Sociology*, 6 (3).

Stauth, G. and Turner, B.S. (1988a) *Nietzsche's Dance: Resentment, Reciprocity and Resistance in Social Life*. Oxford: Basil Blackwell.

Stauth, G. and Turner, B.S. (1988b) 'Nostalgia, postmodernism, and the critique of mass culture', *Theory, Culture & Society*, 5 (2–3).

Stocking, G.W., Jr (1968) *Race, Culture and Evolution*. New York: Free Press.

Swanson, G.E. (1968) 'To live in concord with a society: two empirical studies of primary relations', in A.J. Reiss (ed.), *Cooley and Sociological Analysis*. Ann Arbor: University of Michigan Press.

Swatos, W.H. (ed.) (1989) *Religious Politics in Global and Comparative Perspective*. New York: Greenwood Press.

Swidler, A. (1986) 'Culture in action: symbols and strategies', *American Sociological Review*, 51 (2).

Sztompka, P. (1990) 'Conceptual frameworks in comparative inquiry: divergent or convergent?', in M. Albrow and E. King (eds), *Globalization, Knowledge and Society*. London: Sage.

Thomas, G. (1989) *Revivalism and Cultural Change*. Chicago: Chicago University Press.

Thomas, G.M., Meyer, J.W., Ramirez, F. and Boli, J. (eds) (1987) *Institutional Structure: Constituting State, Society and the Individual*. Beverly Hills, CA: Sage.

Thompson, H. (1983) *The New Religions of Japan*. Rutland, VA: Tuttle.

Tiryakian, E.A. (forthcoming) 'From modernization to globalization', *Journal for the Scientific Study of Religion*.

Toennies, F. (1957) *Community and Society*. New York: Harper and Row.

Tomlinson, J. (1991) *Cultural Imperialism: A Critical Introduction*. Baltimore, MD: Johns Hopkins University Press.

Touraine, A. (1981) *The Voice and the Eye*. Cambridge: Cambridge University Press.

Touraine, A. (1992) 'Beyond social movements', *Theory, Culture & Society*, 9 (1).

Turner, B.S. (1987) 'A note on nostalgia', *Theory, Culture & Society*, 4 (1).

Turner, B.S. (1990a) 'Conclusion: peroration on ideology', in N. Abercrombie, S. Hill and B.S. Turner (eds), *Dominant Ideologies*. London: Unwin Hyman.

Turner, B.S. (1990b) 'The two faces of sociology: global or national?', in M. Featherstone (ed.), *Global Culture: Nationalism, Globalization and Modernity*. London: Sage.

Turner, B.S. (1990c) 'Periodization and politics in the postmodern,' in B.S. Turner (ed.), *Theories of Modernity and Postmodernity*. London: Sage.

Turner, B.S. (1991) 'Politics and culture in Islamic globalism', in R. Robertson and W.R. Garrett (eds), *Religion and Global Order*. New York: Paragon House.

Turner, B.S. (forthcoming) 'The concept of "the world" in sociology: a commentary on Roland Robertson's theory of globalization', *Journal for the Scientific Study of Religion*.

Udovich, A.L. (1987) 'The constitution of the traditional Islamic marketplace: Islamic law and the social context of exchange', in S.N. Eisenstadt (ed.), *Patterns of Modernity Volume II: Beyond the West*. New York: New York University Press.

Urry, J. (1990) *The Tourist Gaze: Leisure and Travel in Contemporary Societies*. London: Sage.

Urry, J. (1991) 'Time and space in Giddens' social theory', in C.G. Bryant and D. Jary (eds), *Giddens' Theory of Structuration*. London: Routledge.

Van den Abbeele, G. (1980) 'Sightseers: the tourist as theorist', *Diacritics*, 10 (December).

Vidich, A.J. and Hughey, M.W. (1988) 'Fraternalization and rationality in the global perspective', *International Journal of Politics, Culture and Society*, 2 (2).

Wagar, W.W. (ed.) (1971) *History and the Idea of Mankind*. Albuquerque: University of New Mexico Press.

Wallace, A.F.C. (1956) 'Revitalization movements', *American Anthropologist*, 58.

Wallerstein, I. (1974a) *The Modern World System*. New York: Academic Press.

Wallerstein, I. (1974b) 'The rise and future demise of the world capitalist system: concepts for comparative analysis', *Comparative Studies in Society and History*, 16.

Wallerstein, I. (1979) *The Capitalist World-Economy*. Cambridge: Cambridge University Press.

Wallerstein, I. (1980) *The Modern World-System II: Mercantilism and the Consolidation of the European World Economy*. New York: Academic Press.

Wallerstein, I. (1982a) 'Socialist states: mercantilist strategies and revolutionary objectives', in E. Friedman (ed.), *Ascent and Decline in the Modern World-System*. Beverly Hills: Sage.

Wallerstein, I. (1982b) 'Crisis as transition', in S. Amin, G. Arrighi, A.G. Frank and I. Wallerstein (eds), *Dynamics of Global Crisis*. New York and London: Monthly Review Press.

Wallerstein, I. (1983a) 'Crisis: the world-economy, the movements, and the ideologies', in A. Bergesen (ed.), *Crises in the World-System*. Beverly Hills: Sage.

Wallerstein, I. (1983b) 'An agenda for world-systems analysis', in W.R. Thompson (ed.), *Contending Approaches to World System Analysis*. Beverly Hills: Sage.

Wallerstein, I. (1984a) *The Politics of the World–Economy*. Cambridge: Cambridge University Press.

Wallerstein, I. (1984b) 'Het moderne wereldsysteem als beschaving', *Sociologisch Tijdschrift*, 11 (2). Paper presented at conference on Civilizations and Theories of Civilizing Processes, Bielefeld, June.

Wallerstein, I. (1987) 'World-systems analysis', in A. Giddens and J. Turner (eds), *Social Theory Today*. Stanford, CA: Stanford University Press.

Wallerstein, I. (1990) 'Culture as the ideological battleground of the modern world-system', in M. Featherstone (ed.), *Global Culture: Nationalism, Globalization and Modernity*. London: Sage.

Wallerstein, I. (1991a) *Unthinking Social Science: The Limits of Nineteenth-Century Paradigms*. Cambridge: Polity Press.

Wallerstein, I. (1991b) 'The national and the universal: can there be such a thing as world culture?', in A.D. King (ed.), *Culture, Globalization and the World-System*.

Wallerstein, I. (1991c) *Geopolitics and Geoculture*. Cambridge: Cambridge University Press.

Walls, A.F. (1991) 'World christianity, the missionary movement and "the ugly American"', in W.C. Roof (ed.), *World Order and Religion*. Albany, NY: State University of New York Press.

Wang, Y.C. (1966) *Chinese Intellectuals and the West: 1872–1949*. Chapel Hill: University of North Carolina Press.

Weber, M. (1958) *The Religion of India*. New York: Free Press.

Weber, M. (1978) *Economy and Society*. Berkeley: University of California Press.

Westney, D.E. (1987) *Imitation and Innovation: The Transfer of Western Organizational Patterns to Meiji Japan.* Cambridge, MA: Harvard University Press.

Williams, R. (1983) *The Year 2000.* New York: Pantheon.

Wolf, E.R. (1982) *Europe and the People without History.* Berkeley: University of California Press.

Wolferen, Karel von (1989) *The Enigma of Japanese Power.* New York: Knopf.

Wolff, J. (1991) 'The global and the specific: reconciling conflicting theories of culture', in A.D. King (ed.), *Culture, Globalization and the World-System.* London: Macmillan.

Woodward, W.P. (1972) *The Allied Occupation of Japan 1945–1952 and Japanese Religions.* Leiden: Brill.

Worsley, P. (1984) *The Three Worlds: Culture and Development.* London: Weidenfeld & Nicolson.

Wuthnow, R. (1978) 'Religious movements and the transition in world order', in J. Needleman and G. Baker (eds), *Understanding the New Religions.* New York: Seabury Press.

Wuthnow, R. (1980) 'World order and religious movements', in A. Bergesen (ed.), *Studies of the Modern World-System.* New York: Academic Press.

Wuthnow, R. (1983) 'Cultural crises', in A. Bergesen (ed.), *Crises in the World-System.* Beverly Hills: Sage.

Wuthnow, R. (1984) 'Introduction', in R. Wuthnow et al., *Cultural Analysis.* Boston: Routledge.

Wuthnow, R., Hunter, J.D., Bergesen, A. and Kurzweil, E. (1984) *Cultural Analysis.* Boston: Routledge & Kegan Paul.

Yokoyama, T. (1987) *Japan in the Victorian Mind: A Study of Stereotyped Images of a Nation, 1850–80.* London: Macmillan.

Zerubavel, E. (1981) *Hidden Rhythms: Schedules and Calendars in Social Life.* Chicago: University of Chicago Press.

Zolberg, A.R. (1981) 'Origins of the modern world system: a missing link', *World Politics*, 33 (2).

Zolberg, A.R. (1983) '"World" and "system": a misalliance', in W.R. Thompson (ed.), *Contending Approaches in World System Analysis.* Beverly Hills: Sage.

INDEX